Not For Resale

Springer
*Berlin
Heidelberg
New York
Barcelona
Hong Kong
London
Milan
Paris
Singapore
Tokyo*

Acknowledgements

We would like to thank all the people who have contributed to this work. Among the contributors, we are particularly grateful to:

- Marlène Arevalo and Laurence Boissieux, for testing the software and designing fashion show garment models shown in this book using the MIRALab cloth software.
- Jean-Claude Moussaly, Prithweesh De, and Nabil Sidi-Yacoub for their contribution to the CD-ROM illustrating this book.
- Endre Bangerter and Sunil Hadap for their contributions to the geometric-wrinkle technologies.
- Professor David Sankoff, from the University of Montreal, for his thorough review of parts of the manuscript and for his helpful criticism.
- Professor Prem Kalra, from the Indian Institute of Technology in New Dehli, for his contribution to some parts of the book and his valuable comments.

Not forgetting all the MIRALab people for their suggestions on the research work, ideas, software development and artistic design, a necessary combination for producing these valuable systems and results, particularly Dr. Laurent Moccozet.

The research work in this book has been sponsored mainly by the Swiss National Fund for Scientific Research (FNRS).

Table of Contents

1	Introduction	1
	1.1 A Brief Historical Background	3
	1.2 Problems	5
	1.2.1 Shape and Geometry	5
	1.2.2 Behavior	6
	1.2.3 Interaction with Environment	6
	1.2.4 From Cloth to Garment	7
	1.2.5 Rendering	7
	1.3 Garment Design and Simulation System: An Example	8
2	Simulation Models	11
	2.1 Introduction	11
	2.1.1 Dynamics	11
	2.1.2 Designing a Mechanical Simulation System	12
	2.2 Mechanical Properties of Fabric Materials	15
	2.2.1 Fabric Mechanical Parameters	15
	2.2.2 Experimental Analysis of Fabric Properties	19
	2.3 Implementing Mechanical Models	25
	2.3.1 Defining Behavior Laws	25
	2.3.2 Fundamental Laws of Mechanics	28
	2.3.3 Defining a Simulation Scheme	30
	2.4 Mechanical Simulation Systems	35
	2.4.1 A Good Simulation System	35
	2.4.2 Geometrical Models	40
	2.4.3 Continuum Mechanics Models	42
	2.4.4 Particle System Models	52
	2.4.5 A Fast Particle System for Irregular Meshes	60

  2.5 Numerical Integration 72
    2.5.1 Integration Techniques 73
    2.5.2 Choosing the Suitable Integration Method................................. 98

3 Collision Detection... 103
  3.1 The Collision Detection Problem 103
    3.1.1 Introduction 103
    3.1.2 Mastering Complexity 106
    3.1.3 An Overview of Different Techniques 108
    3.1.4 Robustness 126
  3.2 A Hierarchical Scheme for Polygonal Meshes 128
    3.2.1 Collision Detection on Hierarchical Meshes 128
    3.2.2 Optimizing for Self-Collision Detection 132
    3.2.3 Efficiency 142

4 Collision Response... 145
  4.1 Characterizing Collisions Geometrically 145
    4.1.1 Intersections and Proximities 146
    4.1.2 Collisions and Surface Orientation... 150
  4.2 Implementing Collision Response 155
    4.2.1 Collision Response on Polygonal Meshes................................ 156
    4.2.2 Collision Models 160
  4.3 Constraints & Seaming 174
    4.3.1 Elastics to Bring Objects Together.. 175
    4.3.2 Controlling the Elastic Effect 176
    4.3.3 Applications 182

5 Smoothing & Wrinkles.. 185
  5.1 Multilayer Models... 185
  5.2 A Simple Geometrical Interpolation Algorithm 187
    5.2.1 The Problem 187
    5.2.2 Constructing the Surface 188
    5.2.3 Results 193
    5.2.4 Texture as a Height Field 195
    5.2.5 Modulating Wrinkle Amplitude 196
    5.2.6 Multilayer Wrinkle Textures 199

| | | 5.2.7 | Rendering Wrinkles .... | 202 |
| | | 5.2.8 | Applications .... | 203 |

6 Rendering Garments 207
6.1 Rendering Techniques 207
6.1.1 Visualization Principles 207
6.1.2 Rendering Systems 220
6.2 Rendering Textiles 224
6.2.1 Anisotropic Lighting of Textiles 224
6.2.2 Volumetric Textile Models 226
6.2.3 Rendering Choices for Realistic Garments 227

7 The MIRACloth Software 231
7.1 Introduction 231
7.2 Approach 234
7.2.1 Design of Garment Patterns 234
7.2.2 Putting Patterns on Bodies 235
7.2.3 Seaming and Constructing Garments 237
7.2.4 Animation of Garments 239
7.2.5 Defining the Garment Materials and Textures 242
7.2.6 Cutting and Modifications 242
7.3 Software Description 243
7.3.1 Program Features 243
7.3.2 Interface Description 245
7.3.3 V.R. Manipulation Tools 248
7.4 MIRACloth at Work 249
7.4.1 Versatile Fabric Simulation 250
7.4.2 Computer Films and Fashion Shows 253
7.4.3 Model Design 256
7.4.4 Garment Prototyping 257

8 Potential Applications 261

Bibliography 263

1 Introduction

In this book, we investigate the problem of simulating clothes and clothing. A range of topics are addressed, from shape modeling of a piece of cloth to the realistic garments on virtual humans. Different situations demand different properties a cloth. Existing solutions, though useful for many applications, reveal that further improvements are required.

Cloth modeling has been a topic of research in the textile mechanics and engineering communities for a very long time. However, in the mid 1980s, researchers in computer graphics also became interested in modeling cloth in order to include it in the 3D computer-generated images and films. The evolution of cloth modeling and garment simulation in computer graphics indicates that it has grown from basic shape modeling to the modeling of its complex physics and behaviors. Chapter 2 provides a summary of the different methods developed in computer graphics over the last 15 to 20 years. In computer graphics, only the macroscopic properties of the cloth surface are considered. Physical accuracy is given less importance in comparison to the visual realism. However, a trend of employing a multi-disciplinary approach has started, and the community of textile engineering and computer graphics have begun to combine their expertise to come up with solutions that can satisfy that of both communities. While the textile engineering offers precise details of modeling cloth, at a microscopic level, the computer graphics provides the framework for animation and visualization. Since it is difficult to cover all the methods with adequate details in the book, additional details of the modeling of cloth and garment simulation have been included for the MIRACloth system as a case study. The current techniques in computer graphics enable the simulation of a piece of cloth, as well as a complete set of garments with the interaction with their environment.

The different schemes of collision detection are presented in Chapter 3. Collision detection and response is an integral part of cloth simulation. Collision determines the contact of the cloth with its environment, as in the case of a garment in contact with the body. Thus, collision detection is an extremely important aspect of cloth simulation, taking into account the cloth's interaction with other objects. Collision response determines the feedback to the collision, which may depend on friction and other physical phenomena. Collision detection is conceived as geometrical processing in order to find potential interpenetration of the regions or individual elements of the corresponding surfaces. The methods to optimize the processes for both collision with other objects and self-collision are also studied. An efficient algorithm for collision detection for polygonal mesh representing cloth surface, is detailed with special attention to the issues relating to self-collision which is the employing of a curvature criteria to help resolve the problem of "false adjacency". For collision response, a hybrid model is described where the geometrical basis (e.g., proximity) is used to determine the nature of the response. The notion of friction is added without affecting the efficiency of the mechanical simulation.

Seaming is another kind of constraint, which is required during mechanical simulation to construct a complete garment from the 2D patterns. The notion of "elastic" or "elastic lines" is used to join the points of the pattern boundaries collectively or individually. It is like putting some attraction forces between the boundaries to be joined or stitched.

For rendering clothes, many of the simulation models use classical rendering packages or modules. Not much research has been undertaken exclusively on the rendering of materials like cloth. We briefly present some conventional rendering methods, which are commonly used in cloth simulations. Some particular methods for rendering anisotropic reflections, the microscopic structures and weaving styles are also discussed. This book gives a limited coverage of the rendering within its present scope. However, we believe that the rendering of cloth requires special attention.

In order to further enhance the realism of cloth modeling, finer wrinkles are added. These wrinkles are not computed as the surface deformation based on physics, but instead these are created using the prescribed perturbation to the geometrical information – surface normal. In this way, we avoid the overheads on both the computation and the data.

A separate chapter is devoted to MIRACloth, a system developed at MIRALab, University of Geneva, for building and animating the garments on virtual actors. In fact, it is a general animation framework where different types of animation can be associated with the different objects – static, rigid, and deformable (key frame, mechanical simulation). The methodology for building garments relies on the traditional garment design in real-life. The 2D patterns are created through a polygon editor, which are then taken to the 3D simulator and placed around the body of a virtual actor. The process of seaming brings the patterns together. The garment can be animated with a moving virtual actor. Many applications are shown: the production of computer generated films, web based production suitable for E-commerce, and computer aided garments design.

Cloth modeling and simulation have attained some maturity in computer graphics research. However, there is a gap between what can be simulated and what is reality. This offers ways and avenues for the future. Further, with different types of applications, different demands emerge. For example, for a virtual reality system, the realism and the accuracy can be compromised to achieve a fast interactivity while for a CAD type system, a high degree of precision and accuracy is a must. And a similar argument holds for the animation. Therefore, the question is whether or not it is possible to build a multiresolution system (or a system with different levels of details) that would allow the automatic adjustment to the context of the system to be used. There has been some cross fertilization between textile engineering and computer graphics modeling methods, but we still have far to go before we can seamlessly blend the two aspects of modeling – macroscopic and microscopic. This encourages the employment of a multidisciplinary approach in cloth modeling research. Like many areas, the fundamental research in cloth modeling evolved from the university environment where the interest lies in experimenting some ideas and approaches. Recently, it has been an interest of industry to bring to production these prototypes and to distribute them to the concerned users. We hope this trend will continue.

This book introduces the problems and their solutions in cloth modeling and simulation. A collection of foundations which we consider important in this area are included. Historical evolution along with the state-of-the-art methods with examples are provided, which we believe will help the readers to understand the problem with its different components and their plausible solutions.

The book is the result of the contributions from the authors and the work of others on the important topic of cloth modeling or simulation. The authors hope and believe that the book will help interested beginners to start their research in the area and motivate researchers and developers in this area to further innovations.

1.1 A Brief Historical Background

Clothes synthesis has gone through several phases. First since it is basic to everything else, the most important was the determination of the mechanical properties of the fabric. Originally, the research in this area was directed to applications in industrial and manufacturing processes. The reference study, dating back to 1975, gave the experimental values for the main mechanical parameters of the fabric in terms of the behavioral curves, known as Kawabata curves. With these, the fabric could be modeled as a deformable surface exhibiting various properties, such as elasticity, viscosity and plasticity. Once the mechanical behavior was characterized, several techniques were developed to reproduce this behavior in computer models. The simplest approach consists of geometrically characterizing the shape of cloth and submitting it to mechanical constraints. The earliest trials in the mid 1980s featured simple rectangular pieces of fabric hanging from two fixed points or falling onto rigid objects. The techniques ranged from curve-fitting and spline approximation to the use of sweep surfaces, and the mechanical constraints included gravity, stretching and bending.

In 1987, Terzopoulos et al. proposed a new model for fabric behavior. The idea was to use a physically-based simulation engine, relying on the Lagrange equations of motion and elastic-surface energy. The solutions were obtained through the finite-difference schemes on regular grids. This allowed, for example, the accurate simulation of a flag or the draping of a rectangular cloth, and the method could distinguish cloth from stiff materials like metal or plastic.

The second phase focused on the specific aspects of clothes deformation, as in wrinkles for example. In the early 1990s, Aono proposed a model for simulating the propagation of wrinkles. Based on elasticity properties and d'Alembert's principle, the model accurately generated wrinkles in a piece of fabric, but was unable to model the draping of the clothes in more complex contexts, such as during collision. Several other investigations took the finite element approach: for regular shapes made up of a few hundred elements, results can be very precise. However, this technology requires excessive computation time for complex shapes, and unfortunately, garments inherently have complex shapes, and their geometries do not adapt naturally to the formalism of finite elements.

A new trend has been to exploit the particle systems. These are also physically-based, but are lighter and less computationally expensive/intensive than the Lagrangian models. A particle system can be described as a set of particles interacting with each other according to certain laws imposed by the problem. A particle system offers a viable solution to a problem if the change in the position of an element is known and the properties of its neighboring elements. One can observe such a system in various contexts from molecular dynamics to the calculation of colliding galaxies.

In chapter 2, we present some major cloth simulation models with their salient features. Ng and Grimsdale [HNG96] provide a good summary of these models. They categorize the models into three types: geometrical, physical, and hybrid. Geometrical techniques model the shape of the cloth without taking into account the cloth properties. Although these do not give realistic simulation, they are easy to compute. The physically-based techniques require solving a set of differential equations or a process of iteration, to find the state of the minimum energy. These may be computationally expensive (i.e., may require minutes to days to compute a small animation). However, these techniques should have an intuitive meaning and the control of the parameters, (e.g., specifying a larger mass will make the cloth look heavier). The hybrid methods combine the speed of geometrical methods and the improved realism of the physical techniques. A rough shape is determined using the geometrical method, and later refined using a physically based method. Most of the available methods in computer graphics attempt to model the macroscopic behavior of a cloth. This is primarily because of the set goals – to simulate cloth behavior rapidly with a reasonable realism. Secondly, representing each thread of cloth with its properties would be far too expensive to model. However, a cross-fertilization of the research in animation and textile engineering may give rise to the models which could be useful for both communities.

1.2 Problems

Cloth simulation and garment animation raise diverse scientific questions: not just the development of a technique or algorithm for solving a single kind of problem. They require a whole set of advances in a variety of fields: mechanical simulation, collision detection, geometric modeling, interactivity and others. There are many issues involved in the modeling and simulation of cloth. These issues are presented in a general sense. Later in the ensuing chapters, these issues are elaborated and discussed with appropriate examples.

1.2.1 Shape and Geometry

Shape is one of the most important clue in the simulation, particularly when visualization is a means to validate the simulation. For cloth simulation and garment design, like for other objects, one needs to answer the question: what is the best way to represent the shape of the object? There exist different ways to represent the shape and the geometry of objects in computer graphics: polygonal representation, high order surface representation such as parametric surfaces, and CSG, etc. The choice of the representation may not only have to consider the shape alone in a static and passive environment, but may also have to investigate what kind of behavior is being modeled, what the computational requirements of the simulation are, what the details to be shown are, and what rendering method is to be employed. For example, a mere representation of the form of a static garment or a piece of cloth may not be adequate when we also want its movement, folds and wrinkles. In fact since a cloth is flexible, it can attain different shapes in different situations, meaning it doesn't have a fixed shape. This suggests that the tools for modeling rigid objects (classical geometrical modeler) may not satisfy the needs of cloth modeling. In Chapter 2, we further explore the suitable geometrical representation of a cloth surface. Although one can envisage a cloth as a woven material with threads of primitives and therefore, the geometry of cloth being constituted by the shape and geometry of threads, for the current modeling tools, representing (or displaying) cloth as a thin surface is inadequate.

1.2.2 Behavior

In the real life situations, we notice the behavior of a cloth under different conditions, for example, as in flowing robes, draping, cloth folds, crumpling, tearing, etc. The behavior of a cloth is the manifestation of various properties of the cloth's material such as Young's modulus, bending modulus, Poisson's ratio, stress-strain curves, load-extension relationship, etc. Therefore, cloth simulation needs the study and analysis of these properties. Fundamental laws of mechanics are used for observing the behavior, e.g., the law of gravitation. An extended study of the behavior of the cloth with different models of its behavior is given in Chapter 2.

1.2.3 Interaction with Environment

Cloth in isolation has limited sense. A cloth's behavior is revealed as a consequence of interaction with its environment. This environment could be the wind – a piece of cloth looks very different in the wind – or other rigid or flexible objects causing collisions with the cloth. It is necessary to include these aspects into the modeling phase. The detection of collision of cloth with other objects or with itself is one important issue, and how the cloth reacts or responds to the collision is another issue. Very often we notice that the shape of the cloth touching an object, is different from where it is not. Collision detection and its response is an integral part of cloth simulation. The point is to decide which is the most appropriate, accurate and computationally tractable method.

1.2.4 From Cloth to Garment

One important application of cloth is in making garments. In reality, a garment is an assembly of different pieces of fabrics. Similar methodology is needed to be developed in the virtual world where different pieces of clothes can be stitched. Such actions can be conceived as the constraints to the model of clothing. In addition, these garments are then worn by virtual actors who can move. This requires the garment to follow the shape and movements of the virtual actor's body. Building a system which supports garments design for virtual actors, also necessitates the consideration of the issues of user interface and interaction, and the user's perspective. Chapter 6 is devoted to addressing many such issues in conceiving and building such a system.

1.2.5 Rendering

The problem of rendering is still being explored. Not much has appeared in the literature on the issues about the rendering of clothes in particular. The methods adapted are generally the classical shading models. Yasuda et al. [YAS 92] have reported a shading model for cloth objects, where they consider anisotropic reflection that accounts for the microscopic textile structure and weaving style. Since the main emphasis of this book is on simulating the behavior of cloth and clothing, we consider that rendering does not lie within the scope of this book. However, some of the recent activities related to adding details like small and fine wrinkles to cloth without the overhead of computation have been included in the chapter on wrinkles. In fact, the latter still remains more of a modeling issue as opposed to a rendering issue.

1.3 Garment Design and Simulation System: An Example

The advances in technology, computing power and cloth simulation research led to the next step. Now that simulating simple rectangular pieces of garment is possible, the challenge is to find a way to create a complex garment. This requires dedicated methodology and software. As for dressing virtual actors, one approach is to extract garments directly from the shape of the body, based on the interpolation between points selected on the body. However, the most intuitive and natural approach takes its inspiration from the traditional garment industry, where garments are created from two-dimensional patterns and then seamed together. The pioneers in this field, Lafleur et al. [LAF 91], Yang and Magnenat-Thalmann [YAN 91], Carignan et al. [CAR 92], have been undertaking studies in this direction since the early 1990s.

We briefly outline here the system conceived and developed in MIRALab, University of Geneva, for garment design and cloth simulation. This is to demonstrate a case study for illustrating the ideas, concepts and methodologies for building such a system. There are now other systems based on similar ideas, some of which are listed in the Appendix.

Such a system contains different components and modules (Fig. 1.1). The system has two software components: an editor to design garment patterns and a 3D garment simulator. There are several modules in each component. In particular the 3D simulator has the modules for mechanical model, collision engine, rendering, and user interaction. Within the 3D simulation, user specification and interventions are required for various tasks – positioning of patterns, setting material and physical parameters, seaming and assembling of garments, animation, and cutting and modifying the garment.

As mentioned earlier, the system is inspired by what happens in reality. The garment is made from 2D patterns of cloth surfaces. These patterns are constructed through an editor, which allows the specification of the 2D measures. The patterns constructed are discretized into a triangular mesh. The planar patterns are then placed around a 3D virtual body using manipulators. Once the patterns have been placed around the body, a mechanical simulation is invoked to make the patterns approach along the seaming lines. As a result, the patterns are attached and seamed on the borders as specified, attaining the shape influenced by the shape of the body. Thus the garment is constructed around the body. The mechanical simulation then gives the animation of the garment on a virtual actor's body, accounting for the collision response and friction with the body surface. The final visual look of the cloth is displayed through its material properties. The surface attributes like the material (diffuse) color, shininess, and texture, which are primarily the rendering parameters, can be defined in the system. It may be desired that the cloth is cut and then re-stitched to make it fit or adapt to the body shape after removing or adding the material. The geometric representation of the cloth surface i.e., discretization into polygons guides the processes of cutting, removing, and reconstructing the garment.

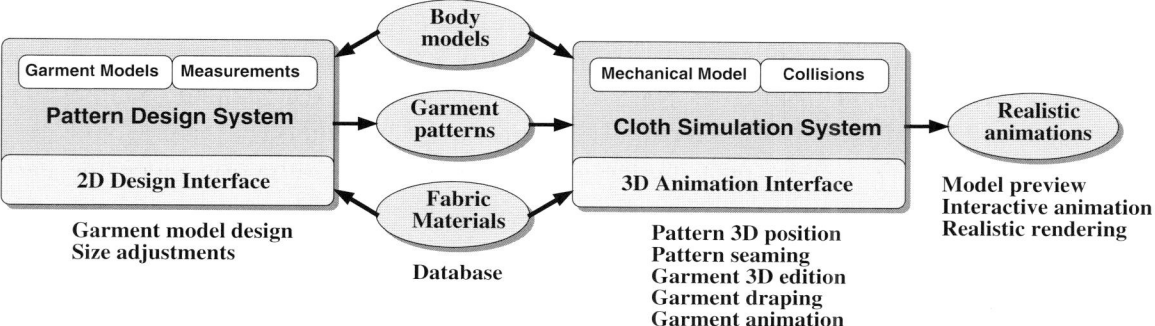

Fig. 1.1: The garment design and simulation framework.

2 Simulation Models

At the heart of a cloth simulation system, a mechanical model animates the cloth surfaces so that they behave like real fabrics.

This chapter first introduces the basic concepts of mechanical simulation, and then describes the different ways of simulating cloth materials. The details are then provided for implementing an efficient simulation system.

2.1 Introduction

Of all the branches of physics, electromagnetism, thermodynamics, quantum physics, relativity and mechanics, only the latter is necessary for the problems of cloth simulation. And while "classical" mechanics, developed in the 17th and 18th centuries by Newton, Euler and Laplace, has been extended from the infinitesimal (quantum mechanics) to the very large scales (relativistic mechanics), cloth is appropriately simulated at neither scales of atoms or of galaxies. Classical "Newtonian" mechanics is the natural framework for the consideration of the familiar objects we encounter in everyday life, such as cloth and fabric garments.

2.1.1 Dynamics

The part of mechanics which studies how objects evolve and move in time under the influences of forces and constraints is called dynamics. In kinematics, which is the mathematical study of motion, three essential quantities are:

- Position, *usually represented by a coordinate vector in 3D space.*

- *Velocity*, the first-order derivative of position with respect to time.
- *Acceleration*, the second-order derivative of position with respect to time.

Dynamics require the consideration of the *mass* as well as the quantities relating the mass and the motion of the object:

- *Force*, which generates acceleration on objects.
- *Energy*, from which forces are derived.
- *Momentum*, product of mass and velocity relating the "amount" of material movement.

The *fundamental law of dynamics*, also known as Newton's second law, is the equality between acceleration and force divided by mass. This law has various integral or differential formulations, being applicable to discrete particles as well as to continuous materials.

Other essential components of dynamics include *laws of conservation*, derived from Newton's third law, which state that as a system evolves, certain quantities remain constant, such as total energy and mechanical momentum.

While the movement of an object is locally and globally subject to the laws of dynamics, additional laws govern the deformations of the object itself. These depend on the properties of the material the object is made of, for example: elasticity, viscosity and plasticity. The form of these *behavioral laws* and the values of their parameters, are obtained mainly from experiments. Together with the laws of dynamics, they form a complete mechanical model of the system to be simulated.

2.1.2 Designing a Mechanical Simulation System

2.1.2.1 The Simulation Loop

The aim of mechanical simulation is the virtual reproduction of the mechanical behavior of a cloth object interacting with its environment. The object only exists as a virtual representation in computer memory. It is described through a *geometric representation* which models the shape to a given accuracy. At a given time, the current *state* of the object is defined by its *position* and *velocity*. From these geometrical characteristics, the current deformation state is computed. The behavioral laws describing the material are then applied on this state to obtain the current, internal *energies* and *forces* exerted on the object, and the possible external forces and constraints. From this, the evolution of the system is obtained using *the laws of dynamics* and *mechanical conservation*, taking into account the object mass and density. This evolution is finally integrated to obtain the new state of the object at subsequent times (Fig. 2.1).

A practical mechanical simulation system usually implements the loop described below for computing the evolution of simulated objects in time.

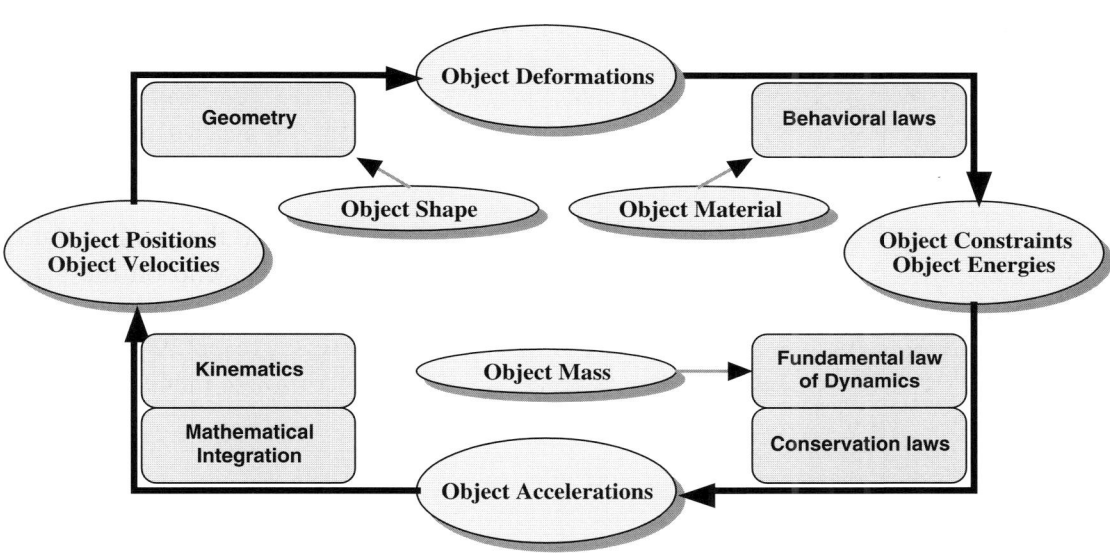

Fig. 2.1. A simplified view of the components of a mechanical system.

2.1.2.2 Components of a Mechanical Simulation System

There are several issues in building up a cloth simulation system:

- *Material Analysis*: The main mechanical properties of fabric materials and their reactions to given deformations. (For instance, measuring the elasticity of a fabric sample depending on its elongation).

- *Mechanical Modeling*: Approximation of the mechanical behavior by a set of behavioral laws that can be expressed using analytical and mathematical relations, such as the constraints and deformations of internal forces in the material, with a given set of parameters that specify the characteristics of the material to be simulated. (For instance, modeling the elasticity force -elongation relation with a mathematical curve defined by a given set of parameters).

- *Geometrical Modeling*: Definition of an adequate, geometric representation of the cloth designed to represent the shape in a given accuracy, using an easily manipulated set of geometrical data. (For instance, representing a cloth object with a polygonal mesh divided into small triangles).

- *Simulation Scheme*: Definition of an efficient, geometric and mathematical framework, specifying the integration of the mechanical model with the laws of dynamics. (For instance, defining how the elasticity laws will apply on the triangles of the mesh for computing strains, stresses, energies and acceleration on the object surface).

- *Numerical Integration*: Implementation of an efficient numerical integration for computing the evolution of the system, using the mechanical laws describing the system. (For instance, using the finite-difference and Runge-Kutta methods to compute the evolution of the object position from the mechanical values of the surface).

All these issues should be addressed keeping in mind that the quality of a good mechanical system is defined by the tradeoff between accuracy and simulation efficiency, as well as the robustness necessary for dealing with a wide range of situations.

The issues described above define the structure of this chapter, which deals with the material analysis (Part 1.1), mechanical modeling (Part 2.3), mechanical simulation (Part 1.1), and numerical integration (Part 1.1).

2.2 Mechanical Properties of Fabric Materials

The mechanical properties of a fabric material account for how its reaction to the given stimuli, such as the imposed deformations, constraints, or force patterns. While any number of parameters may be defined for modeling the behaviors that may occur in some applications, a standard set of parameters is used for reproducing the most important mechanical characteristics of fabric materials. In this section, the experimental characterization of these parameters is discussed, along with the discussion of fabric materials and an introduction to the theory of elasticity for deformable surfaces.

2.2.1 Fabric Mechanical Parameters

The mechanical behavior of a fabric is inherent to the nature and the molecular structure of the fiber material constituting the cloth, as well as the way these fibers are arranged in the fabric structure.

2.2.1.1 Fabric Structure

Fabric fibers in the cloth surface can be organized in several ways. The main structures are as follows:

- *Woven Fabrics*: Threads are orthogonally aligned and interlaced alternately using different patterns (such as plain or twirl) (Fig. 2.2).

- *Knitted fabrics*: Threads are curled along a given pattern, and the curls are interlaced on successive rows (Fig. 2.3).

- *Non-woven fabrics*: There are no threads, and the fibers are arranged in an unstructured way, such as paper fibers.

The woven fabrics are the most commonly used structure in garments. They are relatively stiff, thin and easily produced, and they may be used in a variety of ways in many kinds of designs. In contrast, the knitted fabrics are loose and very elastic. They are usually employed in wool or in underwear.

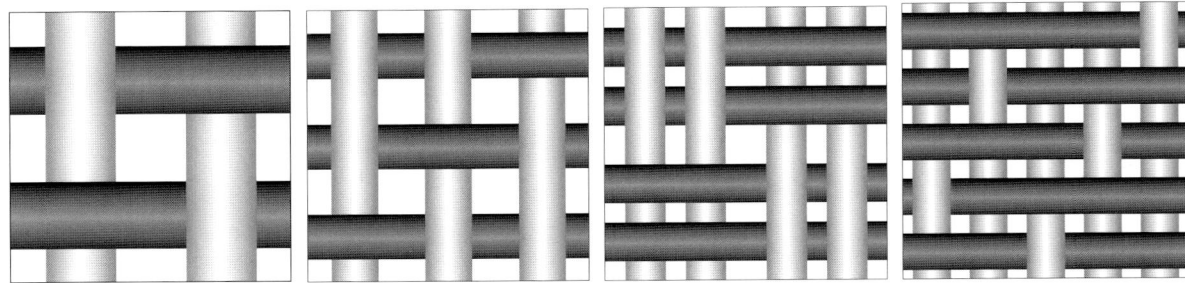

Fig. 2.2. Different woven fabric patterns: Plain, Twirl, Basket, Satin.

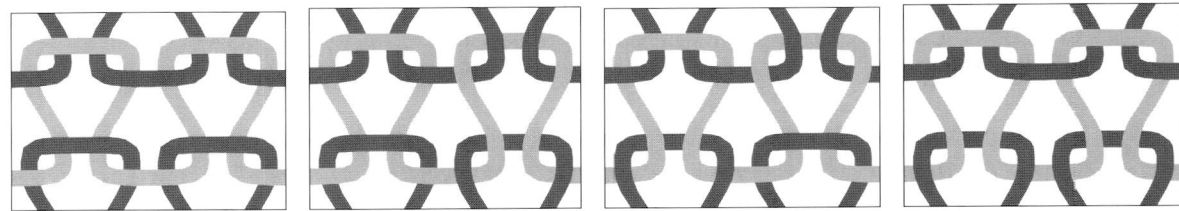

Fig. 2.3. Several basic knitted fabric patterns.

The fabric structure greatly influences the mechanical behavior of the fabric material, which is mainly determined by the following properties:

- *The nature of the fiber*: Wool, cotton, synthetic
- *Thread structure*: Diameter, internal fiber and yarn structure
- *Thread arrangement*: Woven or knitted, and particular pattern variation
- *Pattern properties:* Tight or loose

These properties are critical to the stiffness, the ability to bend, and the visual appearance of the material.

2.2.1.2 Basic Mechanical Properties

The mechanical properties of deformable surfaces can be grouped into four main families:

- *Elasticity*, which characterizes the internal forces resulting from a given geometrical deformation.

- *Viscosity*, which includes the internal forces resulting from a given deformation speed.
- *Plasticity*, which describes how the properties evolve according to the deformation history.
- *Resilience*, which defines the limit at which the structure will break.

A. Working hypotheses

Most important are the elastic properties which contributes mainly to the mechanical effects in the usual contexts where cloth objects are used. The deformations are often small and slow enough to make the effect of viscosity, plasticity and resilience insignificant. One major hypothesis is that the *quasistatic models* in the domain of *elastic deformations* will suffice for our models.

Depending on the amplitude of the mechanical phenomena under study, the curves expressing the mechanical properties exhibit shapes of varying complexity. If the amplitude is small enough, these shapes may be approximated by straight lines. This *linear domain* hypothesis is a common way to simplify the characterization and modeling of mechanical phenomena.

It is common in elasticity theory to consider that the orientation of the material has no effect on its mechanical properties (*isotropy*). This, however, is inappropriate for cloth, as its properties depend considerably on their orientation relative to the fabric thread.

B. Elasticity

Elastic effects can be divided into several parts:

- *Metric elasticity*, deformations along the surface plane.
- *Curvature elasticity*, deformations orthogonally to the surface plane.

Metric elasticity is the most important and the best studied aspect of fabric elasticity. It is usually described in terms of strain-stress relations. For linear elasticity, the main laws relating the strain ε to the stress σ involve three parameters:

- *The Young modulus E*, summarizing the material's reaction along the deformation direction.

- *The Poisson coefficient* ν, characterizing the material's reaction orthogonal to the deformation direction.

- *The Rigidity modulus G*, pertaining to the oblique reactions.

Along the direction **i** and orthogonal to the direction **j**, these relations, named *Hook's Law, Poisson Law and Simple Shear Law* respectively are expressed as follows:

$$\varepsilon_{ii} = \frac{1}{E_i}\sigma_{ii} \quad \varepsilon_{jj} = \frac{\nu_{ij}}{E_i}\sigma_{ii} \quad \varepsilon_{ij} = \frac{1}{G_{ij}}\sigma_{ij} \tag{1}$$

Cloth materials are two-dimensional surfaces for which the two-dimensional variants of the elasticity laws are suitable. They are not isotropic, but the two orthogonal directions defined by the thread orientations can be considered as the main orientations for any deformable properties. In these *orthorombic* cloth surfaces, the two directions are called *warp* and *weft*, and they have specific Young modulus and Poisson coefficients, E_p, ν_p and E_t, ν_t respectively. The elasticity law can be rewritten in terms of these directions as follows:

$$\begin{bmatrix}\sigma_{pp}\\ \sigma_{tt}\\ \sigma_{pt}\end{bmatrix} = \frac{1}{1-\nu_p\nu_t}\begin{bmatrix}E_p & \nu_t E_p & 0\\ \nu_p E_t & E_t & 0\\ 0 & 0 & G(1-\nu_p\nu_t)\end{bmatrix}\begin{bmatrix}\varepsilon_{pp}\\ \varepsilon_{tt}\\ \varepsilon_{pt}\end{bmatrix} \tag{2}$$

The energetic considerations imply the above matrix to be symmetric, and therefore the products $E_p \nu_t$ and $E_t \nu_p$ are equal. For simulating isotropic materials, we only consider a single Young modulus $E = E_p = E_t$, and also a single Poisson coefficient $\nu = \nu_t = \nu_p$. The rigidity coefficient **G** should also be taken equal to **E / (1+ ν)**.

A similar formulation can be obtained for the bending elasticity. However the equivalent of the Poisson coefficient for bending is null. The relation between the curvature strain τ and stress γ is expressed using the flexion modulus **B** and the flexion rigidity **K** as follows:

$$\begin{bmatrix}\tau_{pp}\\ \tau_{tt}\\ \tau_{pt}\end{bmatrix} = \begin{bmatrix}B_p & 0 & 0\\ 0 & B_t & 0\\ 0 & 0 & K\end{bmatrix}\begin{bmatrix}\gamma_{pp}\\ \gamma_{tt}\\ \gamma_{pt}\end{bmatrix} \tag{3}$$

These are the actual parameters that are used in most studies of the properties of fabrics when dealing with linear elasticity. Their determination is carried out experimentally by performing simple deformations on fabric samples.

2.2.2 Experimental Analysis of Fabric Properties

The first formal studies of the elastic properties of fabric materials include, among others, [PEI 37] [ABB 51] [LOV 54] [CHU 60] [CPR 60] [DAH 61] [BEH 61] [MOR 62] [KIL 63] [OLO 64] [GRO 66] [CUS 68] [KAW 73] [SKE 76] [GRO 78]. While these are mainly concerned with the metric elasticity, more recent studies have focused on the buckling properties [DEN 76] [AMI 86] [AMI 89] [AMI 91] [CLA 90] [GOS 90], the behavior of particular fabric materials [LLO 78] [MAN 92] [GON 93] [BAI 95] [YIC 96], and the modeling techniques [KNO 79] [LEA 85] [ANA 91] [CHE 95] [VLA 95] [HUJ 96] [CHE 96].

A reference study used in many computer graphics applications is [KAW 75]. In this paper, different experimental tests are presented for characterizing the main mechanical parameters of the fabric materials, as behavioral curves which can then be approximated analytically and integrated into a mechanical model of the material.

2.2.2.1 The Kawabata Experiments

The *Kawabata Evaluation System for Fabric* is a reference methodology for the experimental observation of the elastic properties of a fabric material. Using five experiments, fifteen curves are obtained, which then allow the determination of twenty-one parameters for the fabric, among which are all the linear elastic parameters described above, except the Poisson coefficient.

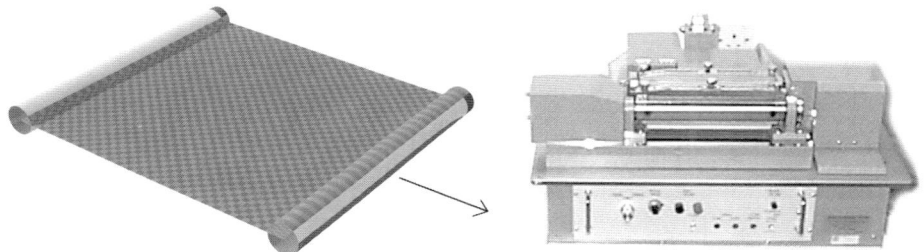

Fig. 2.4. The tensile test, and the KES-FB1 machine.

- The *Tensile Test* involves the extension of a standard (5 cm width, 20 cm length) rectangle of cloth material at a constant speed of extension (0.1 cm/s or 0.2 cm/s), with two opposite edges fixed (Fig. 2.4). After the deformation limit is reached, the traction is reversed at the same speed. From this test, the rest elongation (E0), the maximal elongation

(EM), the elongation ratio (EMT = EM/E0-1), the traction energy (WT), the recovery energy (WT'), the resilience (RT = WT/WT'), and the linearity (LT = WTlinear/WT) can all be computed.

- The *Shearing Test* is similar to the tensile test, but the movement is performed transversally (Fig. 2.5). From this test, the shearing stiffness (G) taken at 2.5° deviation and the two hysteresis amounts (2HG) taken at 0.5° and 5.0° deviation, can be computed.

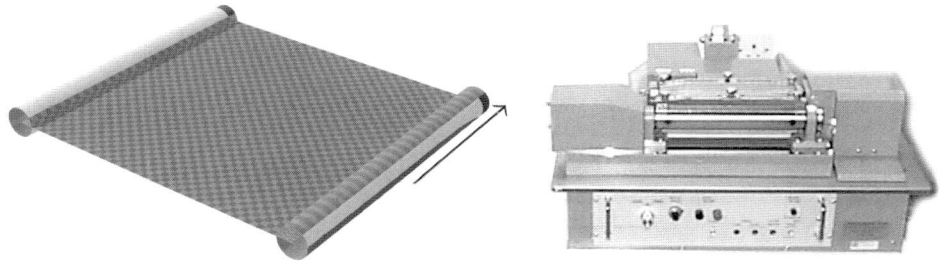

Fig. 2.5. The shearing test, and the KES-FB1 machine.

- The *Bending Test* involves a thin fabric rectangle (1 cm width, 20 cm length) fixed along its longest edge (Fig. 2.6). One edge is rotated along its direction and the distance between the two lines of attachment is adjusted to preserve the curvature as being a cylinder section. From this test, the flexion stiffness (B) at 1 cm curvature radius and the hysteresis (2HB) for the same curvature can be computed.

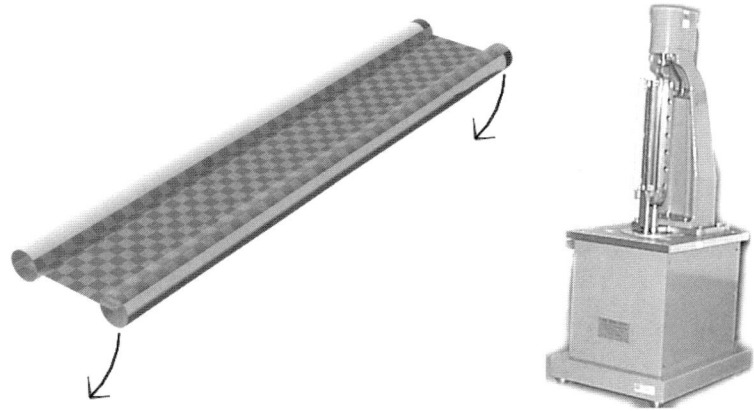

Fig. 2.6. The bending test, and the KES-FB2 machine.

2.2 Mechanical Properties of Fabric Materials

- The *Compression Test* compresses a cloth sample between a flat surface and a 2 cm2 cylinder (Fig. 2.7). From this test, the rest thickness (T0) for 0.05 KPa pressure, the compressed thickness (TM) for 5 KPa pressure, the compression energy (WC) during the compression, the recover energy (WC'), the compressibility ratio (EMC = 1-TM/T0), the resilience (RC = WC/WC'), and the linearity (LC = WClinear/WC) can be computed.

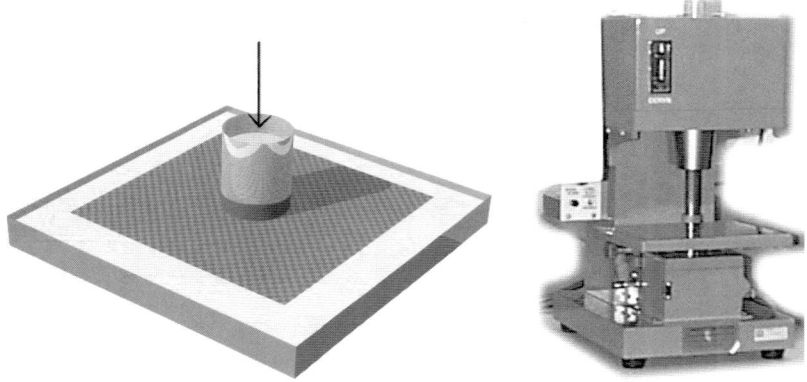

Fig. 2.7. The compression test, and the KES-FB3 machine.

- The *Friction Test* measures the roughness and the friction on a fabric surface of constant tension, using one and ten rods of 0.5 mm section and 5 mm length respectively, applied with a force of 0.5 N (Fig. 2.8). From this test, the roughness (SMD), the friction coefficient (MIU) and its variation (MMD) between the two cycles can be computed.

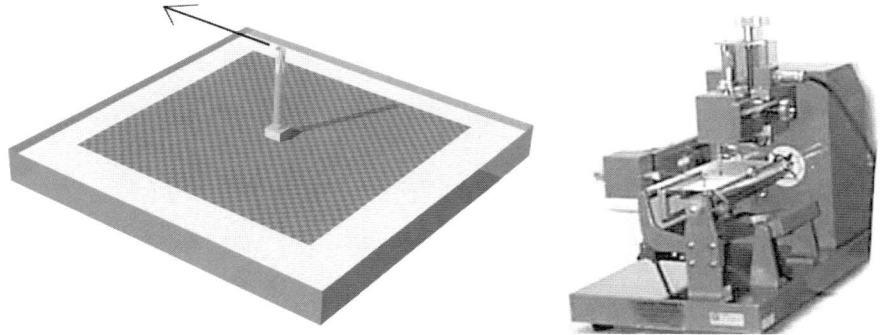

Fig. 2.8. The friction test, and the KES-FB4 machine.

Only the first three tests are widely used in the fabric industry, for determining the properties of the fabric in the weft and the warp directions (Fig. 2.9, 2.10, 2.11).

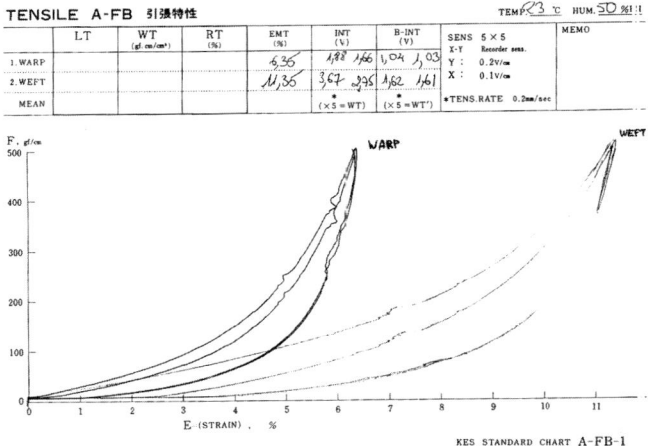

Fig. 2.9. Experimental Kawabata curves for the tensile test.

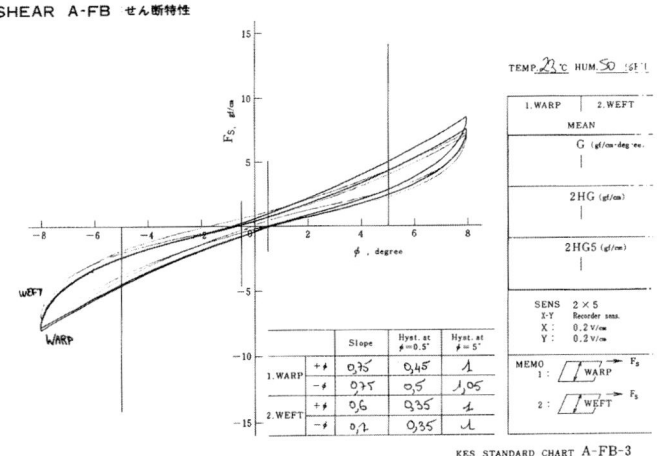

Fig. 2.10. Experimental Kawabata curves for the shearing test.

2.2 Mechanical Properties of Fabric Materials

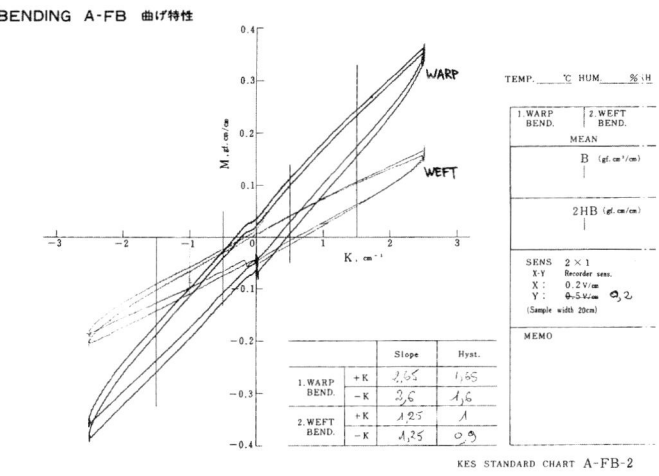

Fig. 2.11. Experimental Kawabata curves for the bending test.

2.2.2.2 Some Mechanical Properties

For a plain wool-polyester fabric of 125 g/m2 density, experimental tests yield the following approximate values:

Young modulus, Warp	3600 N/m
Young modulus, Weft	3200 N/m
Young modulus, diagonal	1200 N/m
Rigidity modulus	35 N/m
Poisson coefficient, Warp	0.18
Poisson coefficient, Weft	0.16
Flexion modulus, Warp	5.1 µNm
Flexion modulus, Weft	4.4 µNm
Flexion modulus, diagonal	3.7 µNm
Flexion rigidity	1.5 µNm

While high variations may be observed between different fabric materials, and particularly for knitted fabrics, these values constitute "average" values for common fabric types. However, for most common fabric materials, the following ranges are observed:

Young modulus, Warp	2000-6000 N/m
Young modulus, Weft	1000-5000 N/m
Rigidity modulus	20-60 N/m
Flexion modulus, Warp	5-15 µNm
Flexion modulus, Weft	4-10 µNm

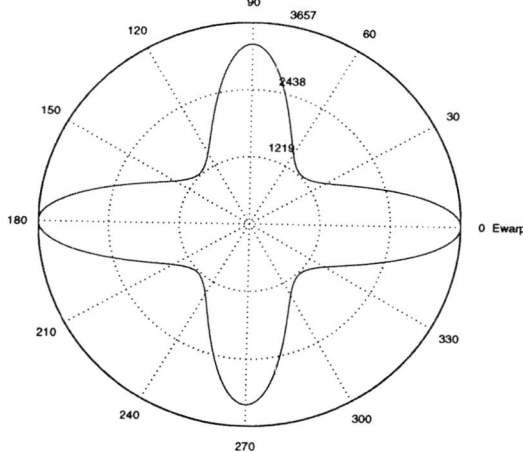

Fig. 2.12. Typical variation of the Young modulus for woven fabric according to the angle.

2.2.2.3 Other Experiments

While Kawabata measurements and similar systems summarize the basic mechanical behaviors of a fabric material, the visual deformations of cloth, such as buckling and wrinkling, are a complex combination of these parameters with other subtle behaviors that cannot be characterized and measured directly.

In order to take these effects into account, other tests focus on a more complex deformations. Among them, the *draping test* considers a cloth disk of a given diameter, draped onto a smaller horizontal disc surface. The edge of the cloth will fall around the support and produce wrinkling. The number and depth of the wrinkles can be measured and used as the validation test for simulation models.

Tests have also been devised for measuring other complex deformations of a fabric material, mostly related to the bending, creasing and wrinkling.

2.3 Implementing Mechanical Models

The mechanical behavior of a fabric can be studied experimentally on the fabric samples, as presented in the previous section. Curves of various physical properties are thus obtained. The most important parameters are the Young's modulus which measures the elongation, the elasticity, and the flexion modulus measuring the ease with which the material can be bent. Other parameters representing a more complex, mechanical effects can also be defined and measured. No matter how much data of this type is available, however, for carrying out simulations, a precise analytic description is needed, which for the internal forces of a material usually models constraint-deformation relations. This formalization is the topic of Part 2.3.1.

These relations can then be combined with the universal laws of mechanics to obtain the equations governing the evolution of the mechanical system, to be discussed in Part 2.3.2. The solution of this analytical system can be carried out using various schemes, as described in Part 2.3.3.

2.3.1 Defining Behavior Laws

In order to proceed to a formal simulation of an object, its mechanical behavior must be simplified to its most relevant parameters and expressed as a set of relations among the geometrical and mechanical values of the material that can be easily manipulated: *the mechanical model*.

2.3.1.1 The Mechanical Parameters

For cloth simulation, only the major *elasticity parameters* are retained:
- *Young modulus*, the main elasticity parameter.
- *Rigidity modulus*, expressing the shearing rigidity.
- *Poisson coefficient*, significant for highly stretched cloth.
- *Curvature modulus*, measuring the ability to wrinkle.

These are quasi-static parameters, meaning that their values do not depend on the actual deformation speed. However, a rapid movement can be taken into account, such as in the case of the fabric significantly elongated and then suddenly released. In this situation, the energy dissipation in the deforming material can be significant, producing additional constraints opposing to the motion. Such viscosity effects are negligible for simulations of small and slow deformations, such as the draping problems, but should be considered for highly dynamic situations involving the constraint discontinuities on the material.

Viscosity parameters are defined in the same way as the elasticity parameters, but depend on the rate of change of the strain rather than on the strain itself. They have not been studied much by the cloth industry as they are not relevant to the most applications that do not involve transitory motion of the cloth. For mechanical simulation however, they are needed, as reaching the stability in the simulation implies the passing through all the stages of the transitory motion. And the viscosity is essential for dissipating mechanical energy to reach equilibrium. The major viscosity parameters are defined for elongation, shearing and bending deformations, and they generally create efforts that oppose the corresponding motion.

Finally, some highly deformed materials do not return to their initial equilibrium point if a large deformation has been applied and then released. Plasticity also dissipates mechanical energy and materializes itself as a hysteresis phenomena in the property curves when the deformation increases and then decreases. While the deformation does not usually require plasticity as it remains within the ranges where such phenomena can be neglected, applications requiring large deformations should take them into account.

2.3.1.2 Mechanical Modeling

The parameters outlined above describe the curves that must be reproduced in the mechanical simulation system. However, storing the whole curve for each parameter is usually not suitable, as the amount of data is huge and the complexity of handling it in mathematical expressions is inconvenient. Any additional accuracy to be expected from the use of exact curve would be dwarfed by the inaccuracy inherent in the numerical simulation process.

A simplified mechanical model is obtained by reducing these curves into simple mathematical expressions. Depending on the desired accuracy, several methods are available:

- *A linear model*, in which the property is proportional to the deformation. These models involve only one coefficient for each property and are the simplest to work with. Linear models are usually applicable when deformations remain small.

- *A polynomial model*, where the property is represented by a higher order function, represented by the corresponding coefficients. These models are suitable for deformations of greater amplitude and remain relatively simple to handle in mathematical expressions.

- *An interval model*, where the curve expressing the property is approximated over successive intervals, usually as linear, sometimes as higher order spline curves. These models are suited for highly nonlinear properties containing important discontinuities.

- *A discrete model*, where the curve is completely discretized and stored in a data table, for a high accuracy. This is seldom of interest for cloth simulation models.

The choice of representation depends on the accuracy required, the expected deformation range, and the kind and the amount of mathematical operations expected to be applied to this data. For instance, while the derivative of a linear function is the coefficient itself, computing the derivative of an interval or of a discrete model may be much more complex.

2.3.1.3 Environmental Parameters

A simulated cloth has to interact with its environment. The most obvious external force exerted on the cloth is the universal gravity, which acts as to accelerate the cloth towards the ground. This acceleration is usually **9.8 m/s^2**. Gravity cannot be neglected in usual cloth simulation contexts.

Aerodynamic effects result from the interaction between the cloth and the surrounding air. These interactions are usually modeled as the viscosity forces proportional to the speed difference between the cloth and the air, and depend on the local surface orientation. These forces are also highly dependant on the actual shape of the cloth, as well as on all the possible aerodynamic turbulences arising at any distance of the surface.

Aerodynamic effects usually cannot be neglected for a freely moving cloth, which is light compared to the airflow forces. While a full aerodynamic simulation of the cloth including the motion of the air in the surrounding environment, is very difficult to compute, it is usually sufficient to implement the simple, linear, anisotropic, viscosity forces exerted on the cloth surface. These are only a very rough representation of reality, but practically their effects during the cloth movement attains a good degree of visual realism including the dynamic air draping. For a more rapidly moving air, such as wind, varying the airflow speed according to the pseudo-random functions with adjusted variation frequencies, can simulate the turbulence effects in a visually realistic way.

Clothes, however, do not generally move freely in the air. Garments are usually worn by bodies, and their shape is determined mainly by the contact and interaction with the underlying surfaces. These forces are usually taken into account when dealing with the collision response between simulated objects, and are essential for all simulations involving virtual garments on synthetic virtual characters.

Collision forces include reaction forces acting in the direction orthogonal to the contact surface and preventing the interpenetration of the objects. The tangential component is usually a dissipative force opposing the speed difference between the objects. This friction force is also highly nonlinear. It is essential to include the reaction and the friction forces in the simulation of garments since they are worn particularly when motion is involved.

2.3.2 Fundamental Laws of Mechanics

Whatever is the mechanical model representing a cloth, its evolution is governed by the fundamental laws which apply universally to the simulation systems. These laws must be combined with the relations modeling the behavior of materials described in the previous section to obtain the analytic expressions for the evolution of the mechanical system. For everyday-sized objects, such as those in cloth simulation, the rules of classical (Newtonian) mechanics are good approximations for these universal laws.

2.3.2.1 Newton's Law

The main law of dynamics relates the force exerted on a point mass to its acceleration. Newton's Second Law is usually formulated as follows:

$$f(t) = m \frac{d^2 x}{dt^2} \qquad (1)$$

Where **x** is the position of the point mass and **f** is the sum of the forces applied to it.

This law can be extended to non-point masses by considering the resultant action on the mass center and the rotational momentum around it.

Newton's Second Law may also be used to describe to local notion of an infinitesimal particle. The forces exerted on this element include the external forces as well as the internal forces resulting from the deformations of the material. From such representation, we can derive the Lagrange equations.

2.3.2.2 Conservation Laws

Dynamic properties evolve in predictable ways. Derived from Newton's law, conservation laws apply to motion, rotational momentum, and mechanical energy.

Energy conservation implies that in a given mechanical system, the internal energy evolves according to the work of the external forces exerted on that system. For a purely mechanical system, energy is made up of potential energy resulting from the work of the internal conservative forces and kinetic energy resulting from the speed of the material mass.

Internal mechanical energy may also be dissipated by non-conservative forces, such as viscosity or plasticity effects. Dissipated mechanical energy is usually turned into thermal energy. More marginally, other energy forms, such as chemical energy or electromagnetic energy, can be converted into mechanical energy, but this is unlikely in the case of cloth simulation.

Conservation of mechanical momentum is another aspect of mechanical conservation deriving from Newton's law. Its main effects in a mechanical system on which no external forces are acting, are the conservation of motion momentum (the total mass of the system times the speed of its mass center) and rotational momentum (the inertia momentum of the system around its mass center times the angular rotation speed).

These laws manifest themselves in collision problems, where they must be respected whatever the collision configuration and the amount of mechanical energy dissipated in it may be.

2.3.3 Defining a Simulation Scheme

In implementing a mechanical simulation system, the behavioral laws of the material have to be combined with the mechanical laws in a single framework that works on an appropriate geometrical representation of the mechanical entities to be simulated.

2.3.3.1 Numerical Simulation

Combining the equations of material behavior with mechanical laws yields complex systems of mathematical equations, usually partial differential equations or other types of differential systems. Mathematics provide analytical solutions only for a limited class of simple equations, which would only solve very elementary situations involving simple models, and which have no interest for usual cloth simulation contexts. For complex cloth simulations, such solutions are not available, and the only practical solution is to implement numerical methods.

The numerical solution of a system of differential equations requires discretization and explicit computation of the physical values at precise points in space and time. Space discretization can either be accomplished through numerical solution techniques, such as in models derived from continuum mechanics, or be part of the mechanical model itself, as in the particle system models. Time discretization results from the numerical computation of a sequence of states during the time period. Interpolation of the successive states provides an approximation for the entire trajectory.

There are several schemes for performing mechanical simulation, differing mainly on where the discretization takes place in the process. The two major families are the following:

- *Continuum mechanics*, which studies the state of material surfaces and volumes through quantities varying continuously in space and time. Each physical parameter of the material is represented by a scalar or vector value continuously varying with position and time. Mechanical laws can then be represented as a set of partial differential equations which hold throughout the volume of the material. While the mechanical representation of the object only depends on the model itself, numerical resolution often requires the discretization of the equations in the volume space.

- *Particle systems*, which discretize the material itself as a set of point masses ("particles") that interact with a set of "forces" which approximately model the behavior of the material.

2.3 Implementing Mechanical Models

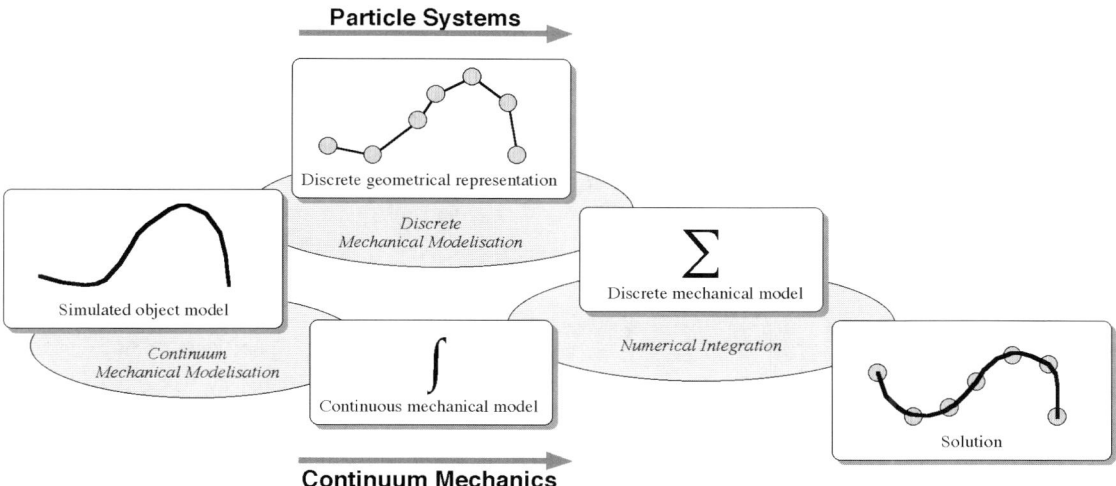

Fig. 2.13. A mechanical simulation carried out with particle systems and continuum mechanics.

The difference between these two schemes is that a particle system is a discrete model built on a related discrete surface representation, whereas continuum mechanics define a continuous model which is then discretized.

Aside from these mechanical simulation techniques, we can also define *geometrical simulation techniques* which, instead of computing the system position and evolution using mechanical laws, only attempt to reproduce it in a realistic way by imitating the expected phenomena geometrically. While such models are unable to deal with "unexpected situations" for which the result has not been explicitly foreseen, they can be efficient for limited contexts for which the object deformations are deterministic within a well-defined range, using very little computation.

2.3.3.2 Geometrical Cloth Surface Representations

Geometrical discretization is a necessity, not only because numerical solution requires discrete data, but also because it is a convenient way to describe the shape and the motion of the cloth as a compact and easy-to-manipulate set of data.

In order to simulate cloth efficiently, a good structural framework for describing its geometry is needed. This description must be accurate enough to capture all the significant details of the geometry, while minimizing the total amount of geometrical data to be handled.

These data should also be efficiently accessible so that they can be integrated into a mechanical model and into an animation system.

A. Polygonal Meshes

The polygonal mesh is the simplest data structure for representing geometrical surfaces. The surface is discretized into flat polygons, separated by edges, themselves connected by vertices. The vertices are associated with discrete positions representing the sampled geometry. The topological structure of a polygonal mesh corresponds to a locally planar graph.

For a flat surface, the polygons serve to subdivide it into different regions which may have different properties or functions. For curved 3D surfaces, polygons are necessary for rendering the curvature through discretization. The size and shape of the polygons are chosen to correspond to the desired accuracy of the representation of the "ideal", smoothly curved surface. The smaller the polygons, the more accurate the mesh, but also the more data are needed to represent them.

Several kinds of polygonal mesh can be defined. While the most general meshes may be made up of any kind of polygons, it is often useful to restrict them to contain only triangles or quadrangles. This may be useful in performing certain geometrical computations on the mesh elements For example, mechanical computations, use the same formula designed specifically for elements of the given fixed topology.

While it is possible to work with meshes having irregular structures (unstructured meshes), imposing the condition of a constant number of edges around each vertex leads to regular meshes, having a globally constant topology. Regular meshes can be triangular (six edges per vertex), quadrangular (four edges per vertex), or hexagonal (three edges per vertex). These meshes allow us to take advantage of the local symmetries in performing geometrical computations. Furthermore, global numbering and indexing schemes can be established in order to provide random access to any element in the mesh without performing search or traversal operations.

Along with these topologically regular properties, geometric properties may be considered as well. A mesh is geometrically and perfectly regular when its elements have all the same shape and size. Strictly speaking, this is only possible for topologically regular meshes. For irregular meshes, if rough size and shape uniformity is feasible, then a degree of geometrical regularity can be attained. This geometrical regularity allows to factorize certain geometrical calculations in the mesh.

Mesh anisotropy prevails when global, geometrical properties vary depending on the direction of the mesh surface. Elongated mesh elements are the major cause of anisotropy. However, regular meshes may also be considered as anisotropic, since global element alignments represent "preferred" directions on the mesh.

Polygonal meshes may be deformed simply by moving their vertices to the new surface positions. This "direct access" to the surface geometry makes working with polygonal mesh animations simple and straightforward. However, describing a smoothly curved surface needs some geometrical consistency and regularity among several vertices, which can be difficult to maintain. Furthermore, extracting certain geometrical properties, such as curvature, cannot be carried out precisely, and has to be done by approximation between several mesh elements.

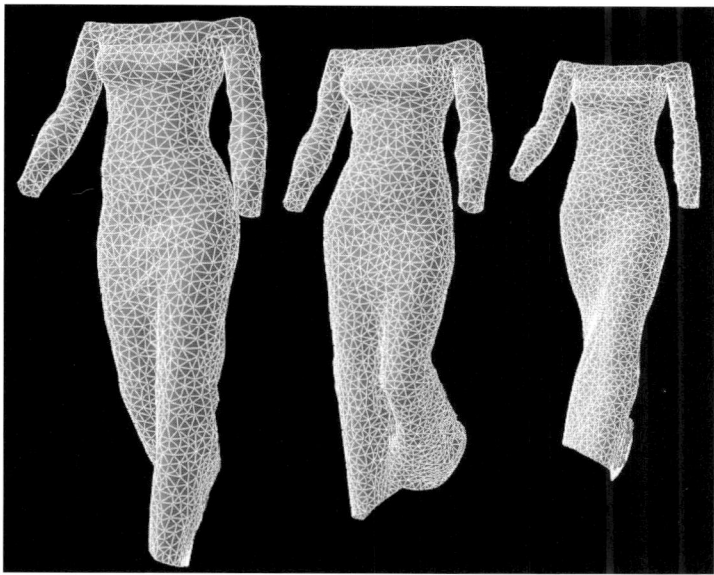

Fig. 2.14. A garment represented as a polygonal mesh (triangular, unstructured, globally anisotropic).

B. High-Order Surfaces

In order to reduce the amount of geometrical data to be managed for describing a smoothly curved surface, high-order surfaces can be used. They are described by curved surface primitives that fit given curvatures more accurately. A curved surface is described by a set of curved patches, with a reduced number of control points carrying the geometrical information.

The patches may be described by explicit or implicit mathematical expressions which have various curvature and continuity properties. Among them, spline and Bezier patches, NURBS, polynomial and rational surfaces, and many of their variations. The patches may also be defined implicitly by a subdivision algorithm which constructs intermediate points hierarchically through a geometrical construction until a given accuracy has been reached.

The definition of the patches generally requires that they have a given topology, such as being triangular or quadrangular. Surface continuity between the patches has also to be maintained.

While only a reduced number of control points are required to control the shape of the surface, it is much more difficult to control the global shape since each control point implicitly controls a whole surface region. The higher the order is, the fewer control points are required, but the more difficult it is to control the surface and to render sharp and irregular details that do not fit the smooth curvature of a patch. Most of these representations also usually determine an implicitly defined polygonal mesh which is needed for most operations requiring explicit geometrical data, such as visualization and rendering.

For mechanical simulation, one major interest of high-order surface is that curvature is contained in the patches and can be computed analytically from the patch parameters. This eases the definition of continuum model systems which can directly consider this curvature for the computing bending energies and forces.

C. Hierarchical and Progressive Meshes

In order to overcome the limitations of the previous techniques for highly variable contexts where portions of the mesh may be almost flat, interspersed with highly curved portions, or with irregular and sharp deformations, an adaptive topology is often required.

The best approach is to subdivide the mesh adaptively, depending on the surface curvature and acceptable geometrical error of the mesh representation. Different "levels of detail" may be considered, either upward by grouping bigger polygons into bigger and rougher domains, or downward by subdividing mesh polygons into smaller ones.

Hierarchical schemes may be applied on any surface description, either directly on polygonal meshes, or on the patches of a high-order description. For the latter case, subdivision schemes can efficiently be integrated into a hierarchical mesh description scheme.

2.4 Mechanical Simulation Systems

The goal of mechanical simulation is to produce a model with which we may simulate the basic properties of fabric rapidly but realistically. Whatever the mechanical model chosen, an adequate implementation using state-of-the-art algorithms and numerical methods has to be defined for reaching this goal.

2.4.1 A Good Simulation System

Efficient algorithms are always the result of algorithmic compromises that balance qualities of the results with the computation times. Numerous qualities can be considered for cloth simulation systems, which have to be considered with respect to their application contexts and respective computation time requirements.

2.4.1.1 Qualities

The major qualities of a good mechanical simulation system are:

- *Scope*: The simulation system should support the mechanical behavior and the properties to be simulated. The simplest models only support some basic form of linear elasticity, while advanced models can deal with anisotropic and highly nonlinear behaviors related to elasticity, viscosity, plasticity in elongation or curvature, including advanced aerodynamic effects and possibilities for various dynamic constraints.
- *Accuracy*: The mechanical system should be simulated in a very accurate way in whatever possible context. Depending on the application (computer graphics or mechanical

engineering) the requirements on accuracy can be very different, ranging from visual realism to quantitative accuracy of some mechanical states.

- *Robustness*: The simulation system should be able to compute accurately the mechanical system whatever the context, which can vary along the simulation, and no particular situation should cause the simulation to fail. The major problems usually result from numerical instability caused by inadequate space and time discretization in the numerical algorithms.

- *Speed*: Obviously, speed is one of the major value of a simulation system, and the "money" you will use for "buying" the qualities mentioned above.

Computation speed may become a constraint, of variable impact depending on the application.

- For *offline computation systems* that do not require user interaction, the total computation time and the amount of time that the user can afford to wait for getting the results of a simulation are the constraint in the design sequence. While not very constraining for static models where only a final position has to be computed (for example, a draping problem), this may become an issue for the computation of an animation requiring several thousands of frames. Speed is also an issue in a design process based on trial-and-error, limiting the number of possible tests in a certain amount of time.

- For *interactive applications* where the user interacts with the cloth being simulated, the computation time between two frames is more critical. The affordable time is determined by the user's perception of the effects of his interactions which is usually also related to the perception of evolution and movement. While real-time animation is usually not a requirement, the frame rate should be high enough (usually at least five frames per second) for motion perception, and the reactivity of the model to user interaction should not be delayed more than the duration of one frame.

- For *real-time applications* where the timeline of the computation has to match the actual time, the time of the computation is strictly bounded, and the simulated phenomena should be computed at the speed they would actually occur. This is usually the hardest requirement to meet in terms of computation speed. Unlike interactive applications, there is no requirement based on the frame rate. However, most real-time applications are usually meant to be interactive or at least to display their results directly as being computed. An adapted frame rate related to the internal time discretization and good user perception of the motion, is then necessary.

2.4.1.2 Compromises and Choices

It is always possible to build a very accurate and general simulation system through very complicated and detailed models, and by performing the simulation on very refined, geometrical representations, but always at the expense of speed.

A. Simulation Accuracy

It is not very difficult to define an accurate mechanical model, as long as we are willing to give up computational efficiency. The major difficulty is in fact to find the best tradeoff between the accuracy and the speed so that the model fulfills our goal (realistic cloth animation for computer graphics) most quickly, wasting as little time as possible.

Inaccuracy in simulation results from several factors:

- *Coarseness of the surface discretization*: The topology and smoothness of the triangular mesh makes it a more or less accurate representation of the surface shape and deformation.

- *Approximations in the mechanical model*: The "real material" is never modeled exactly, and its behavior is approximated by simplified mechanical laws which does not take into account several nonlinear behaviors, particularly for highly deformed domains, as well as local variations in the mechanical structures along the surface.

- *Accuracy of the simulation method*: The simulation process is numerical and iterative, and its accuracy is closely related to the discretizations in the numerical model and particularly to the chosen timestep.

The literature often emphasizes the accuracy of the mechanical model. The major causes of inaccuracy, however, are rather found in the surface discretization, not only because it is a geometrical approximation, but more importantly because it is highly dependent on the actual behavior of the model. This is particularly true in a situation with a high degree of deformation, such as cloth simulation, where the size of the wrinkle folds may attain the size of the discretization elements. For instance, if a rough triangle mesh is modeled to be inelastic for in-plane deformations, then this will hinder the surrounding mesh from bending, even if according to the model, only weak forces should be required to bend it.

B. Major tradeoffs

Obviously, the computation speed lays at one side of the tradeoff possibilities, and simulation accuracy at the other side. The correct algorithmic choices are to be based on the purpose of the application:

- Real-time and interactive applications are fitted to hard computation time requirements, and simplified models that compute quickly are necessary. The computation time should also not be altered by the variable mechanical contexts that might occur during the simulation. This is usually done for computer graphics by keeping in mind that these applications usually only require visual realism, more than quantitative accuracy of the deformation amounts.

- Computer design and simulation applications require some quantitative reproduction of the deformation phenomena, and thus an adapted model that is accurate enough to simulate them precisely. Depending on the considered objects to be simulated (for example, a simple cloth square of a full garment), this is usually incompatible with interactive and real-time applications.

- Application involving highly variable situations and user interaction also have the requirement of robustness, for being able to deal with any situation that may arise, even if they are not physically valid. This complicates the mechanical model which should cope with extended geometrical deformations, and the numerical resolution scheme which should converge as quickly as possible back to "normal" deformations and not diverge or exhibit instabilities.

C. Robustness Considerations

A major quality of a mechanical simulation system is to be accurate: Given a realistic mechanical system and some realistic mechanical parameters, the result of the simulation should be realistic and reflect as exactly as possible the expected evolution of the model.

Robustness also relates to the ability of the model to deal with unexpected situations that might be a little beyond the limits of realism of a mechanical model. For instance, user manipulation of a geometrical object is purely geometrical and can lead to deformations that are dynamically not correct (unrealistic deformations, infinite accelerations,...). Computing exact mechanical response from these situations is obviously quite a nonsense, as they would actually produce similarly unrealistic effects that might lead to inconsistent and irreversible results and numerical instability.

Nevertheless, a realistic behavior cannot be expected if the geometrical deformations itself are not realistic. A robust system is expected to be able to cope with extreme situations, possibly by altering the simulation away from the original mechanical model, in order to produce a moderate response which effect is to converge back to a realistic situation as quickly as possible. A good compromise is for the forces to simulate the reality as long as the deformations are kept at a reasonable level, but to remain "unrealistically" low when deformations go beyond usual values.

D. Mesh Refinement Considerations

As stated above, the discretization of the geometrical model is an important factor of the accuracy and simulation speed which should be chosen adequately to the accuracy of the considered mechanical simulation scheme. It is highly related to the expected deformations of a surface region and particularly to curvature deformations (folds and wrinkles). For instance, accurate bending will only be simulated accurately by a precise mechanical model if its geometrical representation contains at least a few dozens of polygons across the binding section. However, modeling all the wrinkles of a garment in this way would require several hundred thousands polygons for the whole surface, which is computationally not realistic with the current technologies. A more realistic garment simulation would only use objects containing a few thousands of polygons and thus, unable to relate precisely the cloth surface curvatures.

The optimal discretization of a cloth object should be determined with narrow consideration of the expected accuracy of the geometrical model, particularly for curvature, and the related accuracy of the mechanical model that will simulate these deformations.

While bending and wrinkling patterns are often roughly predictable on the cloth surface simulated in a precise context, an optimized mesh would be adapted to this context and refined in the surface regions most likely to be curved, with possibly anisotropic refinement along the curvature direction. For more variable contexts, adaptive and dynamic rediscretization schemes may be implemented.

2.4.2 Geometrical Models

A simple approach to cloth modeling is to geometrically characterize the shape of the cloth surface under given mechanical conditions and to reproduce this accurately on the computer model.

2.4.2.1 Principles

Geometrical models constitute an intermediate simulation paradigm where the evolution of the simulated system is modeled by laws and behaviors derived from geometrical descriptions and their derived approximations.

For cloth animation, geometric models derive the cloth motion and deformation of the cloth from geometrical curves and functions that are parametrized by time so as to satisfy a number of criteria, including most obviously the conservation laws for surfaces and momentum, as well as the collision effects with other objects and external factors such as gravity and wind.

A variety of mathematical surfaces can be used to model the cloth shape, such as various kinds of Bezier or spline surfaces which model curved surfaces in a continuous way. Discrete surface representations may also be considered, such as polygonal meshes.

Surface area conservation is a key consideration in cloth simulation as it is mainly responsible for making cloth simulation realistic. The major visual effect is wrinkling behavior. When a surface is deformed, the metric length of any arc drawn on the surface should remain more or less constant, provided that metric rigidity is high relative to the applied forces. The main consequence of this is the appearance of wrinkles as the surface gets compressed along one direction. Geometric models can incorporate these considerations to generate wrinkling patterns on deformed surfaces.

The main interest of geometrical simulation models for cloth simulation application is to have a computationally efficient and highly controllable model which can perform the simulation well in certain predefined contexts. Since the geometrical deformed state of the cloth, which is part of the model, is directly computed from the simulation parameters, it can be closely controlled by tuning the model so that the context it performs best corresponds to the expected behavior. Furthermore, hysteresis effects on the evolution of the system can be minimized because the dependence on initial conditions can be suppressed.

The most important use of geometrical models are applications in very specific contexts where the expected behavior and evolution is well known and easily integrated into the model. An efficient and straightforward computation can then deduce the evolution of the state of the system directly from these geometrical rules. These models offer high controllability and allow easy and predictable design of animation sequences. However, they cannot reproduce highly variable situations such as those encountered in general garment applications, without unrealistically simplifying the expected response. Geometrical models are thus very efficient for simple problems, such as wrinkle formation on local surface areas of the cloth. However, very general applications using arbitrary cloth shapes submitted to arbitrary and complex, mechanical and environment contexts might involve less predictable trajectories which cannot be reproduced by such models.

2.4.2.2 History

Geometrical models were the first techniques to be used in computer graphics for cloth simulation, as these techniques do not require the huge amount of computation that mechanical simulation necessitates.

Weil [WEI 86] produced the first simulations of hanging cloth surfaces by fitting catenary curves between the points of attachment of a recursive subdivision of the cloth surface. Spline approximation was then performed for smoothing the final surface.

An extension of this work is presented in [TAI 91], which models the wrinkles of a fabric rectangle hanging between two points under additional mechanical constraints, such as stretching, bending and gravitational forces.

Another approach is to build the cloth surface using sweep surfaces, such as presented in [DHA 93], where the sweep deformation is determined by certain mechanical calculations.

While simulating fabric behavior is the most common approach to cloth simulation, another completely different way of constructing dressed characters is to base the garment shape using aspects of the body shape. The work described in [HIN 90] presents the first solution using this approach and produces the cloth surfaces as a set of fabric panels generated by interpolating a user-defined set of points on the body surface.

A more advanced approach is to deform an offset of the underlying skin to simulate the cloth surface, which can then be wrinkled according to the deformation. This technique is described in [HNG 96], where sinusoidal wrinkle deformations are generated along the lines on a cloth surface which is originally defined as an offset of the underlying body skin. The wrinkle lines are either automatically determined or manually edited.

2.4.3 Continuum Mechanics Models

A continuum mechanic model describes the mechanical state of an object using the continuous expressions defined on the geometry. For deformable surfaces, such expressions are usually the surfacic deformation energy related to the local surface deformation (elongation, shearing, curvature), formulated as differential expressions. Mechanical laws are directly derived from them, providing the strains exerted on infinitesimal surface elements.

The main advantage of continuum mechanical techniques is that they provide accurate models of the material properties derived directly from mechanical laws. They are inherently capable of reproducing the nonlinearities of most viscoelastic models. Furthermore, object representation is constant, and the discretization needs only be performed for numerical solution, which can be adapted dynamically. Besides the heavy computing requirements of continuum mechanics techniques, they also suffer from several drawbacks which can render them inappropriate for certain applications. For instance, the formal and analytical description they require for the mechanical behavior of the material cannot easily be altered to represent the transitory and nonlinear events. Hence, phenomena such as frequent collisions or other highly variable geometrical constraints cannot be conveniently taken into account.

While highly adapted to the accurate computation of the dynamics of objects having well-defined mechanical constraints and relatively stable mechanical contexts, continuum mechanical approaches are less promising for the rapid simulation of highly deformable materials involved in numerous collisions, such as cloth simulation

2.4.3.1 Lagrange Equation Models

The Lagrange equations are the basis of the most common continuum mechanical models. It is initially used by Terzopoulos et al in [TER 87] for the simulation of deformable surfaces and is the starting point of many current models.

A. Theory

Such model considers the equation of motion of an infinitesimal surface element, expressed from the variation of internal energy produced by the particle motion. The equation of motion is derived from variational calculus and described in the Lagrange form:

$$\frac{\partial}{\partial t}\left(\mu(a)\frac{\partial r(a,t)}{\partial t}\right)+\gamma(a)\frac{\partial r(a,t)}{\partial t}+\frac{\delta\varepsilon(r)}{\delta r}(a,t)=f(r(a,t),t) \qquad (1)$$

where **r(a,t)** is the position of **a**, the particle of material with coordinates α_1 and α_2 on the surface Ω at time **t**. $\mu(a)$ and $\gamma(a)$ are the mass and damping densities at the position of the particle **a**. $\varepsilon(r)$ is the instantaneous elastic deformation potential energy of the surface.

The mechanical behavior of the material should be expressed as the local deformation energy related to the actual material deformation and expressed locally for any surface point. The first step is to compute the local deformation properties of the surface. Most of the time, the model would allow a separate consideration of elongation and curvature deformations. In that case, the elastic surface energy is represented by two components **G** and **B**, derived from the elongation and curvature elasticity deformation, namely the metric tensor of the first fundamental form and the curvature tensor of the second fundamental form:

$$G_{ij}(r(a,t))=\frac{\partial r}{\partial \alpha_i}\cdot\frac{\partial r}{\partial \alpha_j} \qquad B_{ij}(r(a,t))=\frac{\frac{\partial r}{\partial \alpha_1}\times\frac{\partial r}{\partial \alpha_2}}{\left|\frac{\partial r}{\partial \alpha_1}\times\frac{\partial r}{\partial \alpha_2}\right|}\cdot\frac{\partial^2 r}{\partial \alpha_i \partial \alpha_j} \qquad (2)$$

The internal energy is then derived from these expressions. The mechanical behavior of the material is integrated at this point in its mechanical deformation energy expression. In the general case, the curves relating the deformation energy with respect to any kind of elementary deformation has to be expressed. In the particular case of a linear and isotropic elastic model considering only metric elongation and curvature deformation, the model uses a simplified representation which computes the energy as follows:

$$\varepsilon(r)=\int_\Omega \sum_{i,j=1}^{2}\left(\eta_{ij}\left(G_{ij}-G_{ij}^0\right)^2+\xi_{ij}\left(B_{ij}-B_{ij}^0\right)^2\right)d\alpha_1 d\alpha_2 \qquad (3)$$

where η_{ij} and ξ_{ij} are weighting functions which control the elongation and curvature rigidities of the surface, respectively, and which are related to the metric and curvature elasticity parameters of the material.

The expression (4) is then integrated in the Lagrange equation (2), which is turned into a differential system which has to be solved for obtaining the evolution of the deformable surface.

$$\frac{\partial r}{\partial \alpha_1}(m,n) = \frac{r(m+1,n)-r(m-1,n)}{2\Delta_1} \quad \frac{\partial^2 r}{\partial \alpha_1^2}(m,n) = \frac{r(m+1,n)+r(m-1,n)-2r(m,n)}{\Delta_1^2}$$

$$\frac{\partial r}{\partial \alpha_2}(m,n) = \frac{r(m,n+1)-r(m,n-1)}{2\Delta_2} \quad \frac{\partial^2 r}{\partial \alpha_2^2}(m,n) = \frac{r(m,n+1)+r(m,n-1)-2r(m,n)}{\Delta_2^2} \tag{4}$$

$$\frac{\partial^2 r}{\partial \alpha_1 \partial \alpha_2}(m,n) = \frac{\partial^2 r}{\partial \alpha_2 \partial \alpha_1}(m,n) = \frac{r(m+1,n+1)+r(m-1,n-1)-r(m+1,n-1)-r(m-1,n+1)}{4\Delta_1 \Delta_2}$$

Such system cannot be solved analytically and has to be processed numerically using surface discretization along the material coordinates α_1 and α_2. The most convenient way to discretize the problem is to use a regular grid defined along the material coordinates α_1 and α_2. In such a grid, each node of the grid **r(m,n)** can be expressed in its coordinates (α_1, α_2) = (**m Δ_1, n Δ_2**). The partial derivatives are then expressed using the finite differences as:

These expressions yield the elongation and curvature deformation using formula (2) and the corresponding energy with formula (3) for each grid vertex. The differential expression of this energy for each grid vertex using the discrete expression of the Lagrange equation (1) finally yields a sparse linear system that can be solved using a numerical method, such as the Gauss-Seidel method.

The major problems concerning such methods are related to the constraints on the equation formulations and also on the regular grid structure:

- The continuous formulation of the model complicates the integration of local effects and constraints, such as geometrical and variable constraints related to collision response.

- The regular grid structure constrains the global shape of the surface to be simulated. Describing a complex geometrical shapes can only be performed using the definition of approximate boundary elements, increasing the system complexity and approximation.

However, the formulation of the model does not include any hypothesis on the surface description. It is possible to increase performance using advanced surface representations, such as recursive quadtree meshes for which the resolution is dynamically adapted to the expected deformations. Moreover, a continuous scheme is highly suited for the surface representations that include surface curvature in and analytical way, such as spline or Bezier patches. The computation of the deformation energy of such patches is highly simplified, as the shape can be expressed analytically from the geometrical parameters of the patch without any form of discretization.

B. Developments in Continuum Mechanics Models

The first major simulation system was developed by Terzopoulos [TER 87] for simulating cloth and deformable surfaces. It used the Lagrange formulation described above for simulating viscoelastic surfaces.

Terzopoulos has extended his model to various applications where deformable objects are simulated using physically based animation, described in detail in [TER 88]. These include cloth simulation, other applications showing simple surfaces with geometrical or collision constraints as well as flag animations and cloth tearing.

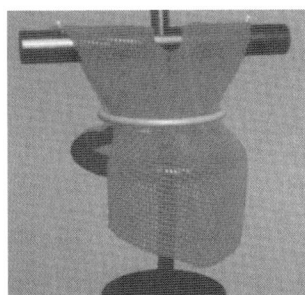  

Fig. 2.15. Various cloth simulations
(Reprinted from [TER 88] – © Springer-Verlag, The Visual Computer, Issue 4, 1988)

This model has been used and further developed for garment simulation on virtual actors, using adapted elastic models and collision response, as described in [LAF 91] and [CAR 92]. This work has shown a real integration of the cloth simulation system into a framework for building and animating garments on virtual actors.

A more recent implementation of Terzopoulos's model is described in [LIU 96]. This involves drapings of rectangular cloth surfaces constituted by regular meshes. The Lagrangian description is integrated using finite differences on a regular grid for simulating a viscoelastic surface. The interest of this work is its improved collision response management which constrains the displacement of the cloth along the object surfaces in contact when the exact collision time has been determined. The collision detection algorithm is a simple algorithm which only optimizes the detection process using bounding boxes around mesh triangles.

A particular implementation of Terzopoulos's model was also presented in [LLI 93] and [LLI96]. Its particular interest was the modeling of the interaction between the cloth and an air flow using Reynold's averaged Navier-Stokes equations. A steady air flow was considered in [LLI 93] and an unsteady one in [LLI 96], which included an advanced model of air velocity variation. Although the computation times are quite acceptable, the model was restricted to simple cloth objects composed of regular grids of a few hundred elements, and the mechanical context was very restrictive.

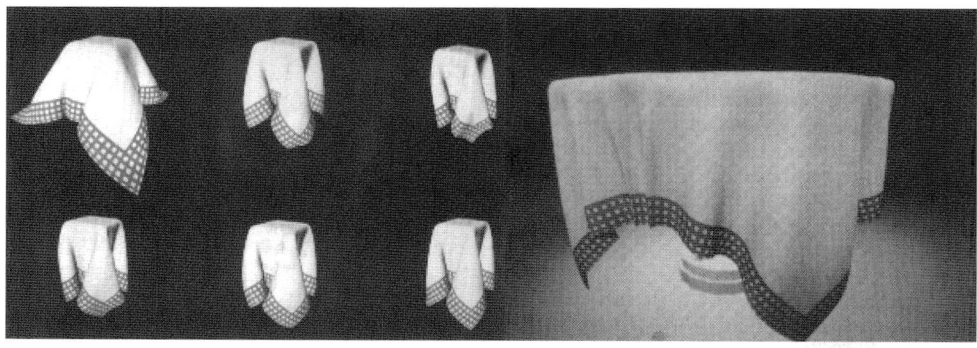

Fig. 2.16. Cloth draping (Reprinted from [LIU 96] – © Springer-Verlag, The Visual Computer, Issue 12 1996).

A more specialized model was presented in [AON 90]. It considered wrinkle propagation in a piece of cloth under given mechanical constraints. The cloth was modeled as a perfectly, linearly elastic material described by its Young modulus and its Poisson coefficient in equilibrium state at all times according to D'Alembert's principle. The stain-stress behavior equations were derived by adding to these conditions the additional assumption that the cloth never deforms along the surface normal direction. As a result, this model accurately represents wrinkle propagation on a deformed simple cloth surface, but is unable to produce the drapings of a cloth under complex mechanical contexts, such as collisions.

"Flashback" is one of the first films to simulate a complete garment on a virtual actor. It was produced at MIRALab on 1990 as described in [LAF 91]. The film is a short sequence showing a virtual Marilyn in a dress with a wide skirt. Air currents from a subway vent lift the skirt, showing draping effects. The small, physically simulated paper squares are also scattered by the wind.

2.4 Mechanical Simulation Systems

The virtual actor does not exhibit any movements, except for arm motion which does not interfere with the cloth. Only the moving part of the cloth was modeled, using a cone shaped surface fixed at the waist. Above the waist, the dress is basically the surface part of the body model.

The fabric is modeled as a simple viscoelastic surface, represented by its mass, elongation and curvature elasticity, and viscous damping. Additional forces include air speed and viscosity, and gravity. The model is embodied in Lagrange equations, adapting the work of Terzopoulos [TER 97]. Integration is carried out using a simple, finite difference scheme on the cloth surface discretized into a regular mesh. No real, simulation, timestep management is implemented.

Fig. 2.17. Flashback (see also color section, plate A).

An algorithm for collision detection was adapted from [MOO 88] and applied to a truncated body consisting of the pelvis and the legs only. Collision response was modeled by a repulsion force varying with distance according to an exponential law, which takes effect starting from a threshold contact distance, and repels the fabric with a given damping factor. No friction model had to be implemented since the cloth was mainly floating in the air without prolonged contact with the body.

"Flashback" represented the first successful attempt to dress and animate the skirt of a virtual actor. It used simple and ad-hoc solutions to solve the problems of cloth simulation in the particular context of the film sequence. All technical aspects of cloth software have since been improved, and so has the cloth design procedure, leading to the first real cloth software introduced by MIRALab in 1992 and developed during ensuing years.

"Fashion show", described in [YAN 91], is a good example of a sequence produced in 1992 with this new approach. It features garment animation on walking characters along with numerous other innovations related to virtual actor animation and modeling.

The mechanical model for "Fashion show" is derived from the same Lagrangian formulation [TER 87] which was used for "Flashback". An elastic damping factor has been introduced, however, as proposed in [PLA 88]. A new dissipative term takes into account the viscosity generated by the deformation itself, rather than the general "air viscosity" of the original model. As a result, the viscosity of the material is accurately modeled. The mechanical model is described in detail in [CAR 92].

Collision response has been greatly improved. In order to prevent bouncing artifacts inherent to the strong contact repulsion forces used in the previous model, the normal speed component is annulated according to the momentum conservation laws in order to simulate perfectly inelastic contact. Furthermore, the tangent speed component is also used to compute a friction force simulating a simple Coulombian model, which is then integrated in the dynamic model.

2.4 Mechanical Simulation Systems

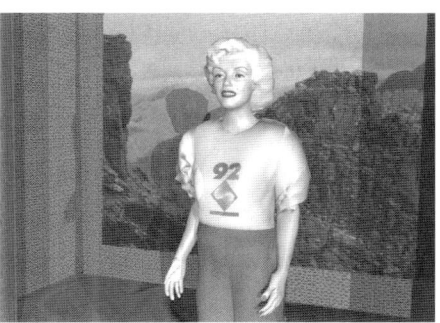

Fig. 2.18. Various garment models made using the 1992 MIRALab software
(see also color section, plates B and C)

Collision detection has also been improved. An octree-based algorithm speeds up proximity detection for collisions and self-collisions. To save additional time, optimizations were added according to the context: collisions were only detected between selected regions of the garment with the corresponding body part of the virtual character. Furthermore, though implemented, recourse to self-collision detection was not necessary in most scenes. This avoided computation a speed penalty, not worthwhile for collision types that appear only marginally on simple garments. More details on the collision detection algorithm used, can be found in [YAN 93].

A 2D pattern design process has been implemented in this system. The garment is built from a set of 2D fabric polygons, which are then assembled around the body using 3D physical simulation. Attracting forces are added between specific components of the pattern to bring and hold them together. These forces correspond to "seaming lines and points" between the garment components. Similar forces maintain the garment on the body while it is moving. This garment design process is detailed in [WER 93].

2.4.3.2 Finite Elements

Finite elements are a powerful way of integrating continuum mechanics models. At the difference of the previously described model which discretizes the mechanical equations on a grid representing the surface using finite differences, finite elements compute mechanical energies within a predefined discretization.

A. Theory

A discrete element of the surface is basically defined as an interpolation function over a patch (usually a triangle or a quadrangle). This interpolation function has a given order (bilinear, trilinear, quadrilinear) and an associated set of parameters (degrees of freedom) that give the actual shape to the interpolation surface over the element. The higher the order, the more accurately the element would fit the actual surface shape, but also the more degrees of freedom. Beside polynomial functions, other shape functions can also be used.

From the mechanical properties of the material is computed the energy, related to the deformation of the surface for given values of the interpolation parameters. Depending on the kind of mechanical simulation to be performed, these values have to be processed globally on the whole system (for example, energy minimization for computing an equilibrium position).

Surface continuity between the interpolation surface of adjacent elements imposes constraint relationship on the degrees of freedom of these elements. All these relationships are summarized in a huge and sparse linear system defined on all the degrees of freedom and completed by additional constraints (boundary conditions) which can be, for example, constraining the motion of some edges of the surface. The huge linear system is built by assembling successively, the contributions of all the elements of the surface. This operation is eased by using elements defined as regular meshes, for which some mechanical parameters as well as the neighboring relationships are uniform.

For performing the simulation, the huge and sparse linear system has to be solved. This is done using optimized, iterative techniques such as the conjugate gradient method. Several factors influence the performance, such as the matrix conditioning which can be improved by an adequate numbering of the elements that reduces the diagonal band width of the sparse matrix.

While finite element methods are very efficient for simulating accurately complex mechanical behaviors over well-defined mechanical systems, their computation requirements are, however, far beyond what can be afforded for fast simulation in interactive applications. Furthermore, they do not allow an easy and flexible integration of constraints that can evolve dynamically, such as the effects of collisions which makes this technology quite unsuitable for the simulation of highly deformable surfaces that may bend highly and produce numerous wrinkles and highly variable contact patterns with neighboring objects.

B. Developments in Finite Elements for Cloth Simulation

Finite elements have only had a marginal role in cloth simulation [COL 91] [GAN 91] [GAN 95] [EIS 96]. The work presented in [EIS 96] is restricted to rectangular cloth surfaces for which an accurate nonlinear elastic model is built from experimental curves of fabric characteristics obtained using the Kawabata methodology [KAW 75]. The study focuses on the model accuracy by precisely simulating fabric behavior and comparing the bending and buckling properties with those inferred from real fabric experiments for a range of values of the mechanical properties.

The accuracy of finite element models is clearly demonstrated by this study. Finite element methods have also been the best choice for simulating precisely elastic solids in mechanical engineering. However, the limitations of this methodology are evident: first, the computation time is 'excessive for use in complex "real-world" garments' [EIS 96], and the study was limited to simple squares of material containing only a few hundred regular elements. Second, accurate modeling of highly variable constraints is difficult to integrate into the formalism of finite elements, and this sharply reduces the ability of the model to cope with the very complicated geometrical contexts which can arise in the real-world garment simulation on virtual characters.

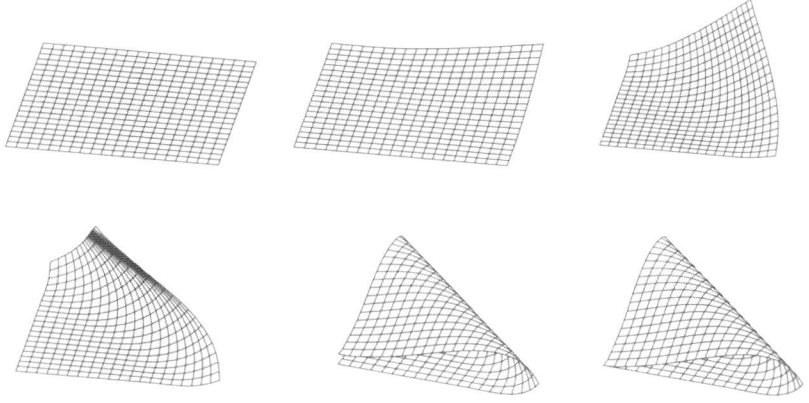

Fig. 2.19. Finite-element simulation (Reprinted from [EIS 96] – © 1996 IEEE)

2.4.4 Particle System Models

Instead of considering the mechanical properties of the material volume as a whole, another approach would be to discretize the material itself as a set of point masses ("particles") which interact with a set of "forces", and thus model approximately the behavior of the material.

Particle systems are used to simulate a wide range of phenomena, ranging from models of crowds in which each particle is an autonomous entity reacting to its environment such as gas or fluid flow, and to the deformation of solids where the particles constitute a discretization of material volume. The latter application is characterized by the interaction involving only neighboring particles which are linked together in a relatively fixed topology, whereas the others do not maintain constant neighbor particle relations (free particles).

In computer graphics applications, curved surfaces are often represented by polygonal meshes. A convenient way to build a particle system from this kind of description is to consider each vertex of the mesh as a particle and the edges or polygons as the interaction forces among several particles.

The biggest advantage of particle systems is their simplicity. It is easy to implement a spring-mass system which effectively simulates the deformation of a polygonal mesh that represents an elastic surface. As the positions, velocities, and forces of each particle appear explicitly in the equations, any kind of nonlinear effect or time-varying geometrical constraint may be implemented, such as the responses to object collisions. It is, however, more difficult to build this kind of model, one that is capable of accurately simulating certain complex viscoelastic behaviors. Furthermore, the numerical solution of particle systems involves ordinary differential equation systems whose solutions become stiff as the rigidity of the simulated objects increase, leading to the numerical instabilities requiring small simulation timesteps. Despite being appropriate for simulating efficiently and highly deformable objects or surfaces such as cloth, the particle systems should be avoided for modeling elastic solids with predefined constraints.

2.4.4.1 Description

Implementing a particle system is the most common way to animate cloth that is represented by polygonal meshes. The geometrical discretisation corresponds to the discretisation of the mechanical model. Each vertex of the mesh is a particle representing a small surface region of the object. The particle interacts mechanically with the neighboring particles in various

2.4 Mechanical Simulation Systems

ways, depending mostly though, on the kind of mesh and on the elasticity representation chosen.

A. Principle

The usual way to numerically simulate a mechanically based particle system is to directly integrate Newton's second law for a mass particle over all the particles:

$$F(t) = M \frac{d^2 P}{dt^2} \tag{5}$$

where **P** is the particle position and **F** is the sum of the forces applied to the particle, and **M** its mass.

The forces exerted on each particle depend on the current state of the system, which is represented by the position and the speed of all the particles. These forces usually represent all the mechanical effects on the system, which include internal elasticity and viscosity forces, gravity and aerodynamic effects, and different kinds of other external constraints. However, some particular kinds of geometrical constraints can also be integrated geometrically, by altering directly the position or the speed of particles.

B. Particle System Representations

The mechanical behavior of the material is implemented as interactions between the particles. These interactions are usually limited to the neighboring particles for simulating basic elasticity behaviors.

Mass-Spring systems are the simplest way to design a volume model using a particle system. In this approach, each particle represents a point mass, a part of the material discretization which is linked to its neighbors by a "spring" representing the elastic behavior of the material. The springs tend to keep the particles at their initial resting positions.

Various types of springs are available for representing the usual mechanical parameters (Fig. 2.20). Using regular grids, metric, shearing and bending elasticities can be modeled using elongation springs as well as flexion springs. While metric elasticity is usually defined by elongation springs along the lattice edges, the shearing elasticity can be modeled either by lattice angle springs or by diagonal elongation springs. In the same way, curvature elasticity may be defined either by flexion springs between opposing edges or by elongation springs between opposed vertices.

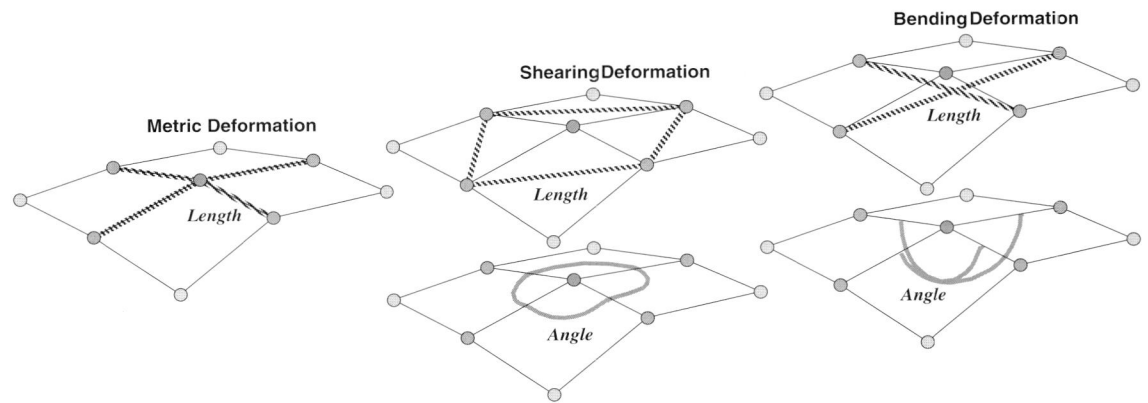

Fig. 2.20. Using lengths or angles for measuring deformations in a square particle system grid.

Using elongation springs only clearly simplifies the model, as this simple kind of spring element can be easily modeled. This will not, however, be accurate for high deformations. These change edge orientations significantly and also interfere with too "normal" metric elasticity, a combination that makes precise modeling of strain-stress behavior difficult.

Flexion springs can model the shearing and particularly, the curvature elasticity more accurately. However, this requires more intensive computation and makes use of surface orientation information which cannot be always precisely computed.

More complex formulations exist that consider not only the mesh edges, but also the interactions between all the particles of a full polygon or even a more extended group of polygons. Such representations are necessary for reflecting accurately all the elasticity behaviors of the surfaces. Accurate curvature representation usually needs several polygons for an accurate evaluation. In the case of irregular meshes, such models are often required, as there are no geometrical symmetries to be exploited.

2.4.4.2 History

Particle systems have often been used for simple simulations involving basic mechanical rules. Some applications for computer graphics are detailed in [REE 83]. These systems, however, have appeared only quite recently in the domain of cloth simulation.

2.4 Mechanical Simulation Systems

One of the first particle systems which was used for simulating cloth was described in [KUN 90]. The system is a hybrid simulation model. It involves physical simulation using a spring-mass system as well as the geometrical modeling of fabric wrinkles derived from the singularity theory. The particle system is made up of a grid where each node is linked to its neighbors with springs. The relation of a node to its four nearest neighbors along the grid lines and the four nearest diagonal neighbors account for metric elasticity, and the angle between the two opposite grid line neighbors is treated for curvature elasticity. The simulation is carried out through a relaxation process which successively selects one random node and moves it a small distance along an arbitrary direction. The position is retained if the elasticity energy is decreased by the move. This kind of quasi-static scheme converges quite slowly and is unsuited for computing the animations with a significant amount of cloth motion, which would require a fully dynamic scheme.

Wrinkles are modeled on the cloth using "characteristic points", which appear, disappear and change according to the laws of local wrinkle evolutions. Changes in the wrinkles are calculated from the assumptions about the behavior of the mechanical context. Though this approach may efficiently model wrinkles in contexts where the global cloth shape and mechanical context are already known and well-defined, it would not be feasible to apply it in the more general situations encountered with garment simulation.

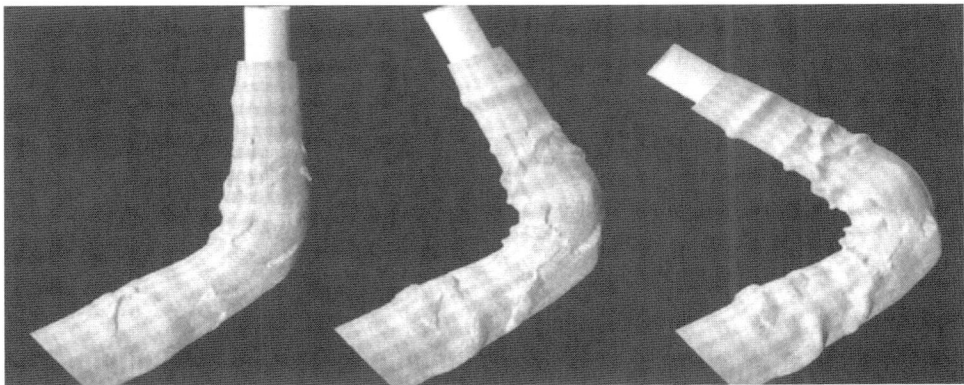

Fig. 2.21. A cloth on a bending arm (Reprinted from [KUN 90] – © Springer-Verlag, Computer Animation'90 proceedings, 1990).

In a similar wrinkle modeling study [TSO 91], the particular case of a cylindrical cloth surface is simulated under different mechanical loads. Wrinkles appear following diamond-shaped patterns, in which the elastic forces and the fabric shape are modeled using splines.

This very specific model simulates the crumpling of fabric around a deformed cylinder in a quasi-static way.

Another early particle-system based cloth simulation was described in [SAK 91]. A regular grid was used for modeling a cloth surface, on which elastic, viscosity and plasticity forces were modeled. Numerical integration was performed using the simple Euler method. Collision detection was optimized only with bounding boxes around the mesh elements. Collision response included friction. The results were limited to static scenes of hanging cloth and cloth draped on a human shape.

Key developments in the area of cloth simulation with particle systems are detailed in [BRE 92], and improved in [BRE 94]. In this work, the main motivation to use particle systems was to simulate a small-scale fabric structure, where continuum mechanics approximations had proven unsatisfactory. Energy approximation models were built taking into considerations, the fiber structure of the fabric. The corresponding parameters were adjusted so as to model the Kawabata curves [KAW 75] for a set of materials, such as cotton or wool. The simulation process was carried out in two steps, the first simulating the particles moving freely under external forces such as gravity, the second minimizing the particle interaction energy and performing the velocity correction accordingly.

The model described in [BRE 94] was designed to simulate the fabric material very accurately, taking into account precise mechanical data to perform the simulation. The results were quite convincing (Fig. 2.22). The computation time, however, for a week of CPU time on a RS6000 workstation for draping a square cloth on a cube, is highly excessive compared to the material particle grid size, 50x50 elements.

2.4 Mechanical Simulation Systems

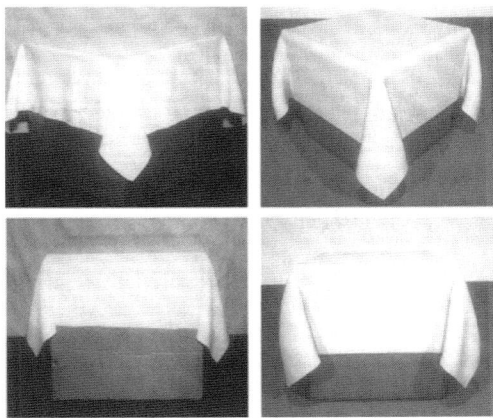

Fig. 2.22. Draping of real fabric (left) and simulation using particle systems (right) (From [BRE 94], reproduced by permission of the authors)

A particle system for cloth simulation in current use is described in [PRO 95]. The cloth is modeled as a regular grid of square elements. The particularity of this spring-mass model is the use of springs to represent all the mechanical properties, such as the metric elasticity, shearing and bending elasticity. Each particle is connected to its four nearest neighbors in the grid directions with "structural" springs which reproduce the material's metric elasticity. Four "flexion" springs connect the particle to the second nearest neighbors in the grid directions. Finally, four "shear" springs connect the particle to its nearest diagonal neighbors. Additional gravity, damping, and surface normal viscosity forces are also implemented. The system is numerically integrated using Euler's method. A special feature of this model is a limit on the frequent deformations occurring around constraint regions by a geometric limitation on the distance between the particles.

More recent, related work by the same team [PRO 95] simulated simple garment assemblies on static virtual bodies. Collision detection was implemented using an adaptation of the hierarchical bounding box algorithm [VOL 94]. Collision response was assured by a simple "gluing" of the colliding elements according to the mechanical conservation laws in order to prevent bouncing.

One efficient implementation of a particle-system cloth simulation system [EBE 96] builds an accurate representation of the fabric material properties (tension, shearing, bending) using the experimental Kawabata curves, for which the nonlinear and hysteresis properties are taken into account and modeled into piecewise linear functions. The cloth surface is discretized into a grid of square elements. Tension energy is computed by the distance from one particle to its four nearest neighbors, whereas the shearing and bending energy are modeled by the angles between the crossing diagonals. Additional forces are gravity, air resistance, and friction when there is a contact with a solid object. A Lagrangian formulation of the mechanical model is then integrated, using either the Burlich-Stoer method or the Runge-Kutta method with adaptive timestep. Performance tests clearly show the superiority of the Runge-Kutta integration, which can produce one frame of animation of a cloth composed of a few thousand particles in tens of minutes on a R8000 SGI Indigo2.

The efficiency and general performance of this implementation of a particle-system based cloth animation seem far better than the solution proposed in [BRE 94]. However, the simulation is restricted only to rectangular cloth draping around simple and immobile objects, situations for which the mechanical context is much simpler than for garments on a virtual body.

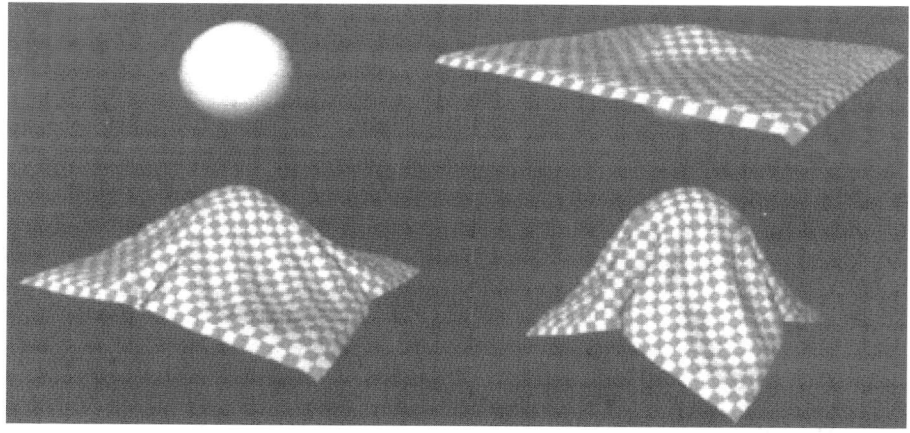

Fig. 2.23. Cloth draping using particle systems (From [EBE 96] – © 1996 IEEE)

A number of new contributions using particle systems have recently been proposed to the field. In [DER 98], an advanced subdivision surface model has been proposed to generate smooth surfaces with controllable blending properties. A cloth simulation system has been built on top of it, using the curvature of the smooth surface through a square grid representation of the surface patches. Edge spring energies represent the main contribution to the metric material elasticity, and the product of the diagonal spring energies is used for producing realistic wrinkling behaviors. Additional rigidity threads, defined as a sequence of vertices, add customized stiffness contributions to stiffen specific garment regions. The collision detection algorithm takes advantage of the subdivision patch structure through an object-based bounding-box hierarchy. While within the patches, a surface-based quadtree structure defines the bounding-box hierarchy, and the hierarchy between the different patches is built through an automatic upward hierarchisation process similar to the one described in [VOL 94]. As the surface topology and local structure remains constant, such surface-based hierarchy can be kept constant and does not need to be reconstructed as the object moves. These collection of techniques have led to the convincing results demonstrated in the animation sequence "Geri's game".

An efficient garment simulation system using an integrated particle system with the backward Euler step method, is presented in [BAR 98]. While this technique involves much more complex operations than the traditional forward and explicit methods, it does overcome the inherent numerical instability of particle systems, particularly for stiff materials and refined discretizations, and thus allows the use of large simulation timesteps. This technique also involves the inversion of a huge, sparse, and linear system, which can be carried out using the conjugate gradient method. This also requires a symmetric system matrix and thus, an appropriate way to consider constraints and collision response. Results show good performance due to the enlarged timesteps.

Fig. 2.24. "Golden Camera Awards", from [VOL 97] (see also color section, plate G).

Two different implementations of particle systems for animating garments on virtual characters are explored in [VOL 95] and [VOL 97]. While the former performs a full planar deformation evaluation on triangular surface elements for computing the forces exerted on the particles, the latter uses a simplified approach enhancing the basic edge spring-mass model to render the basic elastic properties of a deformable surface more accurately, using the system described in the following section.

2.4.5 A Fast Particle System for Irregular Meshes

Particle systems are prime candidates for cloth simulation models, as they are fast and versatile, facilitate implementation of various behavior equations, and allow direct access to the system state (interaction with the object's position and speed) for enforcing constraints and manipulations.

There are many particle systems which have been described in the literature, that implement accurate, elastic, linear model featuring precise elasticity, viscosity, and plasticity parameters.

How accurate do we really need to be? Do we need to determine the deformation state of each triangle in all its details, pursuing the complex, time-intensive, geometrical computations to completion for obtaining the exact deformation state required for complex mechanical models?

As for the other extreme, the simplest and the fastest particle-system based mechanical model is certainly the simple spring-mass model, where the surface is discretized into simple masses linked to their respective neighbors by springs, forming a structure with the topology of a triangular mesh. The springs are considered to have their rest length at the original position of the surface and upon deformation, produce a force proportional to their elongation along their current orientation.

This section details an adapted particle system model that is able to represent quite accurately the major elastic parameters of elastic surface, such as the Young modulus and the Poisson coefficient, while remaining simple enough to be implemented almost like a simple spring-mass system.

2.4.5.1 The Simple Spring-Mass System: Efficiency and Weaknesses

The simple spring-mass model may be the simplest and fastest particle system that can be implemented for the mechanical simulation of elastic surfaces. However, this model is clearly inadequate for cloth animation, as it produces unrealistic deformations, mainly due to:

- An unrealistic Poisson coefficient for high elongation.
- A collapse of elastic response upon high compression.

2.4 Mechanical Simulation Systems

The most visible results of these artifacts are the partial or complete loss of transversal surface wrinkling during states of high deformation.

A spring-mass model is, however, numerically stable. The model has no singular configurations where some spring forces result from a zero division, hence there are no geometrical deformation configurations where constraints reach infinite values. Whatever the deformations at a given moment, the forces will always have "reasonable" values. Such a model therefore has the ability to recover efficiently from numerical inaccuracies.

2.4.5.2 Improving the Spring-Mass Model

A model which avoids the drawbacks of the simple spring-mass model, but which also remains simple enough for being implemented in a fast simulation system, is described in [VOL 97] as follows.

A. In-Plane Elasticity

Let's consider a triangle (P_a, P_b, P_c) in which deformations have elongated its edges from rest length (L_a, L_b, L_c) to the current length (l_a, l_b, l_c), as illustrated here (Fig. 2.25):

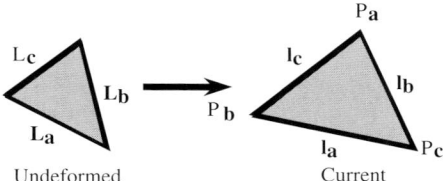

Fig. 2.25. Deforming a triangle.

The current edge lengths are found as follows.

$$l_i = \|P_j - P_k\| \quad \begin{matrix} i \\ j \\ k \end{matrix} = \begin{pmatrix} a & b & c \\ b & c & a \\ c & a & b \end{pmatrix} \tag{6}$$

The cosine (c_a, c_b, c_c) of the current angles are also computed. At this point, an extra constant parameter $\alpha = 1$ point is introduced. It will be used later for tuning the Poisson coefficient of the model (Part.B).

$$c_i = \alpha \frac{l_j^2 + l_k^2 - l_i^2}{2 l_j l_k} \qquad (7)$$

In the simple spring-mass model, the three edges produce a force, usually proportional to their elongation from rest length. Obviously, the system reaches the equilibrium when the three edges reach their rest length.

The expected displacement **d_i** in each edge direction is computed from the elongation of the edge in its corresponding direction, as follows:

$$d_i = l_i - L_i \quad i = (a,b,c) \qquad (8)$$

The spring forces are then computed directly from the displacements:

$$F_i = \frac{R_i}{L_i} d_i = \frac{R_i}{L_i}(l_i - L_i) \qquad (9)$$

R_i is a strength factor linked to the surface elasticity as well as a "shape factor" of this edge in the triangle (quite often, the rest length of the associated triangle height).

This model is quite easy to compute, but it does not reflect the actual forces when a "full material" triangle gets deformed. Each deformed edge will produce a force component along its direction which is usually not the principal deformation direction. The resulting effect is an extra orthogonal deformation similar to the one produced by the Poisson coefficient. This may produce unrealistic effects especially when the triangles are not equilateral (irregular meshes or high deformations). In particular, high compression does not lead to high deformation resistance in the compression direction, but rather along the orthogonal direction to which the edges become parallel (Fig. 2.26).

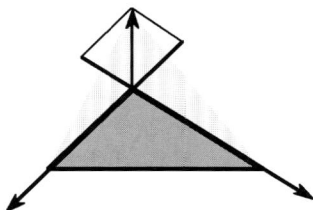

Fig. 2.26. Vertical compression stretches the triangle horizontally.

The main idea of the improved model is to recompute the individual elongation contribution of each edge of the triangle, by taking into account, the interdependence of the displacements that would be generated by each of them in their respective directions. Thus, the combined effect of the edge forces based on these corrected displacements would produce a more accurate constraint situation.

As shown in the following figure (Fig. 2.27), if we suppose that the length of edge **J** varies by an amount **dj**, its extremities **Pi** and **Pk** will be displaced in its direction by half of the distance **dj**. The elongation contribution to edge **I** is then the displacement of the point **Pk** multiplied by the cosine of the angle between the two edges, **ck**. We linearize the problem by assuming that the edge angles do not vary significantly. We note **(i, j, k)** as all the permutations of **(a, b, c)**.

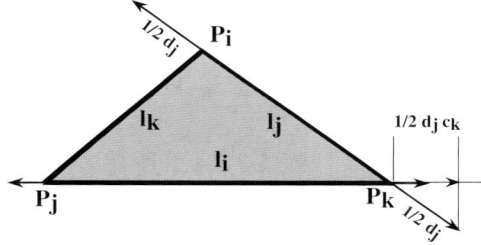

Fig.2.27. Computing the elongation effect of the edge **J** on the direction of the edge **I**.

As the final length variation of the edge **I** is expected to equal **li-Li**, this is equaled to the sum of the elongation contributions of the three edges **I**, **J** and **K** so that they would individually lengthen by an amount **di**, **dj** and **dk**. Doing this on the three edges simultaneously yields a linear system of three equations with three unknowns **(da, db, dc)**:

$$d_i + \frac{1}{2}c_k d_j + \frac{1}{2}c_j d_k = l_i - L_i \quad \begin{matrix} i \\ j \\ k \end{matrix} = \begin{pmatrix} a & b & c \\ b, c, a \\ c & a & b \end{pmatrix} \tag{10}$$

The 3-equations 3-unknowns system (10) is analytically solved, yielding the values of **(da, db, dc)**, that, if applied altogether, contribute to deforming the triangle to its equilibrium state, and the equivalent spring forces are computed from the material elongations:

$$F_i = \frac{R_i}{L_i} d_i = \frac{R_i}{L_i} \frac{\left(c_i^2 - 4\right)\left(l_i - L_i\right) - \left(c_i c_j - 2c_k\right)\left(l_j - L_j\right) - \left(c_i c_k - 2c_j\right)\left(l_k - L_k\right)}{c_i^2 + c_j^2 + c_k^2 - c_i c_j c_k - 4} \tag{11}$$

This assumption has been proved experimentally not to have much of an effect on the behavior of the simulated elastic material in most of the usual situations in cloth simulation.

Finally, and for any model, the acceleration contributions from the triangle applied to its vertices are computed from (7) or (11) or by:

$$P_i'' = M_i^{-1}\left(\frac{F_j}{l_j}(P_k - P_i) + \frac{F_k}{l_k}(P_j - P_i)\right) \begin{matrix} i \\ j \\ k \end{matrix} = \begin{pmatrix} a & b & c \\ b, c, a \\ c & a & b \end{pmatrix} \tag{12}$$

B. Controlling Stability and the Poisson Coefficient

To preclude any "infinite force" configuration, the α coefficient was introduced in (7), representing a linear interpolation factor between a simple spring-mass system ($\alpha = 0$) and the model described above ($\alpha = 1$). By setting $|\alpha| < 1$ any position configuration is prevented from leading to infinite forces. Furthermore, the forces remain continuous without singularities at the vertex positions, increasing the quality of the simulation.

With $\alpha = 1$, our model simulates a fabric material with a null Poisson coefficient. The simple spring-mass model simulates a material with an unrealistically high Poisson coefficient, which, moreover, is highly dependent on the shape of the triangles. In addition to stability, the α coefficient allows us to control the Poisson coefficient of the simulated fabric, which otherwise would require more calculations since it would have to be integrated explicitly in the force computation formulas.

C. Implementing the Improved Model

The advantage of this model is its simplicity, as it is able to compute realistic elastic forces even in irregular triangle meshes. It involves very few vector operations, directly computing force contributions along the edge direction without the need of any local coordinate system.

Its implementation is straightforward. It uses the same framework as the simple particle system model. Extra computation only involves finding the triangle angles using formula (7) and then replacing the force computation formula (9) by the more complete formula (11).

This kind of model is a good replacement for simple spring-mass models in simulation systems where it is desirable to preserve the basic elastic properties of elastic surfaces and to avoid paying the price for full surface deformation computation.

2.4 Mechanical Simulation Systems

D. Working with inverse masses

Dynamics in particular the mechanical simulation of a particle system, usually involves the mass of the particle to be considered. Newton's law finds the acceleration of a particle by dividing the total applied force on this particle by its mass.

A particle of null mass has no physical meaning: it would have an infinite acceleration. However, a particle with infinite mass is a meaningful way to model a particle constrained to have no acceleration despite applied forces, namely a geometrically constrained particle such as a fixed particle.

When using the inverse mass in mechanical computations, constrained particles could simply be represented as having null inverse masses without any modification or without any particular case to be considered when describing the mechanical model. Furthermore, in the acceleration computation, mass division turns into inverse mass multiplication, which can be computed more efficiently and never introduces singularities into the calculations.

In all formulas described in this section, constrained particles can simply be handled by considering that $\mathbf{M}_i^{-1} = \mathbf{0}$. This scheme can even be generalized to particles constrained to move along particular directions by replacing in the above formulas the $\mathbf{M}_i^{-1}$ scalar values by hermitian inertia matrices having null eigenvalues for the eigenvectors along the constrained directions, and eigenvalues equal to the inverse mass along unconstrained directions. For instance, for constraining a particle $\mathbf{i}$ of mass $\mathbf{m}_i$ to move along the direction defined by the normalized $\mathbf{X}$ vector, the matrix $\mathbf{M}_i^{-1} = \mathbf{m}_i^{-1} \mathbf{X} \mathbf{X}^T$ would be used in the above formulas. For constraining it to move along the plane orthogonal to that direction, the matrix $\mathbf{M}_i^{-1} = \mathbf{m}_i^{-1} (\mathbf{I} - \mathbf{X} \mathbf{X}^T)$ would be used. An unconstrained particle is also obviously handled with a scalar matrix $\mathbf{M}_i^{-1} = \mathbf{m}_i^{-1} \mathbf{I}$. A similar scheme was proposed in [BAR 98] for constraining particle motion in their implicit simulation system.

Similar techniques are applicable in solid mechanics using inverse inertia matrices whose singularities model geometrical constraints in translational and rotational motion.

2.4.5.3 Curvature Elasticity

The above model only deals with in-plane elasticity. Another kind of elasticity, involving surface curvature and bending, has to be considered. This elasticity which only produces weak effects when the cloth is considered on a large scale, cannot however be neglected for local deformations, such as the wrinkles, and must be included in the model.

For a perfectly elastic, anisotropic material, the surface should exhibit curvature elasticity for the surface thickness: local compression and elongation strains occur in the inner and outer sides, of the curved surface and thus generate curvature stress. This can be computed for a material volume making use of a 3D elastic model, but is impossible for a 2D elastic model of the material as a surface. A separate curvature elasticity model is required for simulating this response in 2D, which actually originates in the nature of the textile fibers and thickness of the fabric.

A. Curvature Response

The obvious way to compute curvature elastic response is to produce forces that oppose the surface curvature. A surface curvature force moment has to be generated in the curved areas of the surfaces. While the formulation of such an effect may be easy in a continuum mechanical model where the second-order derivatives efficiently measure curvatures, its implementation in discrete meshes is more problematic.

Whichever solution is chosen, a rough mesh can never describe a highly curved surface accurately. Therefore, the inherent surface deformations occurring in the curved regions degrade the accuracy of any attempt to measure the surface curvature as a local mesh property. When edge angles between mesh polygons become significant, any curvature measurement should be considered as only an approximation to the real average curvature in that region.

The most common way to measure the curvature in an irregular triangular mesh is to consider the angle Θ formed by two triangles **(A C B)** and **(B D A)** about an edge **(A B)** (Fig. 2.28). The resulting curvature force moment is then given by forces **Fa, Fb, Fc, Fd** applied to the vertices **A, B, C, D**, respectively.

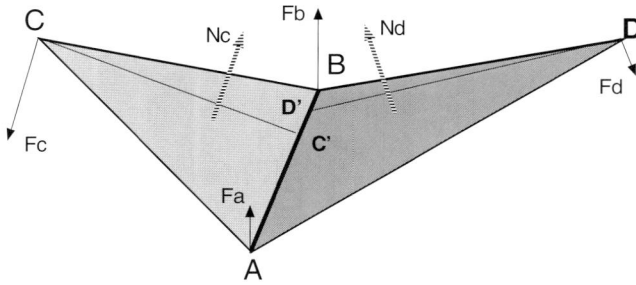

Fig. 2.28. Computing curvature forces on the vertices surrounding an edge of a polygonal mesh.

The angle Θ can be determined through its sine and cosine using triangle normal vectors **Nc** and **Nd** according to the following computation:

$$\cos(\Theta) = Nc \bullet Nd$$
$$\sin(\Theta) = \frac{(Nc \wedge Nd) \bullet (B-A)}{|B-A|} \tag{13}$$

For computational ease, these trigonometric functions should not be expanded. From these values we compute the required force moment **M(Θ)** to be produced around the edge in question as detailed in the following section.

The two forces **Fc** and **Fd** generate opposed force moments around the edge, whose global effect is to "unfold" the two adjacent triangles. By expressing their momentum around the **(AB)** axis, they must comply with the following expressions:

$$\frac{((C-C') \wedge Fc) \bullet (B-A)}{|B-A|} = M(\Theta)$$
$$\frac{((D-D') \wedge Fd) \bullet (A-B)}{|A-B|} = M(\Theta) \tag{14}$$

Since the two forces **Fc** and **Fd** should be aligned to the respective triangle normals **Nc** and **Nd**, they are computed as follows:

$$Fc = \frac{M(\Theta)}{|C-C'|} Nc$$
$$Fd = \frac{M(\Theta)}{|D-D'|} Nd \tag{15}$$

The two vertex forces, **Fc** and **Fd**, generate the required force moment representing the curvature elasticity that opposes the bending of the polygons around an edge. However, the forces **Fa** and **Fb** applied to the vertices **A** and **B** are required to comply locally with the conservation laws, around the considered edge. The most important factor is the equilibrium of all the forces:

$$Fa + Fb + Fc + Fd = 0 \tag{16}$$

Additional constraints to assure zero total force momentum finally lead to the following expressions:

$$Fa = \frac{(C'-B)\bullet(B-A)}{|B-A|^2}Fc + \frac{(D'-B)\bullet(B-A)}{|B-A|^2}Fd$$
$$Fb = \frac{(C'-A)\bullet(A-B)}{|A-B|^2}Fc + \frac{(D'-A)\bullet(A-B)}{|A-B|^2}Fd$$
(17)

The computation of these expressions can be simplified using intermediate values already calculated during the determination of **C'** and **D'**.

For the whole surface, the curvature elasticity response is computed by adding the forces created around all the mesh edges adjacent to two triangles (non-boundary edges).

B. Nonlinearity and Angle Inversions0

The computation of the force moment **M(Θ)** from the edge angle Θ should be based on the material curvature elasticity Γ, as well as on the "shape factor" Ψ which takes into account the configuration and mass of the vertices surrounding the triangle. This will ensure a similar curvature response whatever the discretization size. Roughly speaking, the shape factor should be proportional to the length of the edge in question and to the inverse square of the triangle heights.

A linear curvature elasticity would mean a curvature force momentum proportional to the edge angle:

$$M(\Theta) = \Gamma\Psi\Theta$$
(18)

This formula is however, highly unpractical. First, it requires the explicit calculation of the angle Θ using computationally expensive inverse trigonometric formulas and also, does not render an adequate response for large curvatures, that is when Θ nears $\pm\pi$.

Rather than trying to accurately model a fabric curvature response for such large angles which, in any case, are themselves only rough approximations to the real surface curvature, we should aim at a robust curvature response in these situations, which effectively prevents surface crossings.

2.4 Mechanical Simulation Systems

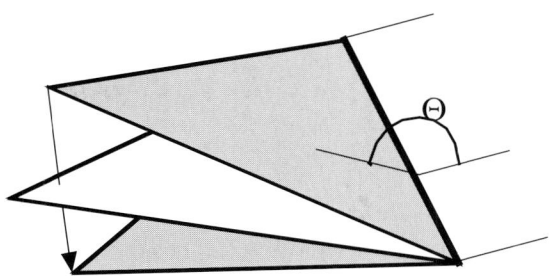

Fig.2.29. A curvature crossing occurring along an edge.

The limiting behavior of Θ close to $\pm\pi$ deserves special consideration: it reflects the situation where the surface is bent to a U-like shape. Normally, self-collision would prevent further bending where the surface might "cross" along the concerned edge (Fig. 2.29). However, the situation cannot be integrated into a general self-collision response scheme, as the surfaces are not geometrically colliding and the geometry around a "crossed" edge remains locally consistent.

Two different solutions may be considered:

A. When a curvature crossing occurs, the angle Θ goes "beyond" $\pm\pi$, and $|\Theta| > \pi$. As the angle Θ is only geometrically measured in the $[-\pi,\pi]$ interval, a tracking system has to be implemented to add or subtract 2π terms to reach the actual angle. One way is to assume that between two successive states, the change in angle should be less than π. In that solution, the response would cause the edge curvature to cross back to the original state.

B. The only angle directly measured in the $[-\pi,\pi]$ interval is the Θ angle. Any crossing is then "forgotten". In order to limit crossings from occurring, the response has to take on large values as the angle Θ approaches $\pm\pi$, creating a "potential wall" stopping the increase in the angle before crossing occurs.

Theoretically, the first solution would be the best one, as it would ensure that the global geometrical mesh configuration reverts to its initial state. Practically, this is not true, as "real" self-collisions start to occur in neighboring mesh elements. Either these self-collisions would prevent the crossing from occurring, or they would prevent the system from crossing back if a crossing had already occurred. Furthermore, the history of the system would have to be known to compute the curvature angles, which is impractical in many situations, and would seriously complicate mesh storage and calculations.

The second solution is then to be preferred, as only a suitable response has to be computed. Retaining a linear behavior similar to (18) for small angles, we introduce a parameter **g** for tuning the height of the potential wall and construct the response as follows:

$$M(\Theta) = \Gamma\Psi\frac{(1+2g)\sin(\Theta)}{1+g(1+\cos(\Theta))} \qquad (19)$$

The function shape is shown in Fig. 2.30. The expressions (18) and (19) exhibit the same behavior for small angles regardless of the value of **g**. As the angle increases when, approaching $\pm\pi$, the response reaches a maximum whose value is adjusted by means of the parameter **g**, and which acts like a force derived from a potential wall. However, for numerical stability, some response must be ensured even if a crossing occurs through the $\pm\pi$ boundary value where the response drops to zero. For practical implementations, only the sine and cosine angle values computed from formula (13) are used.

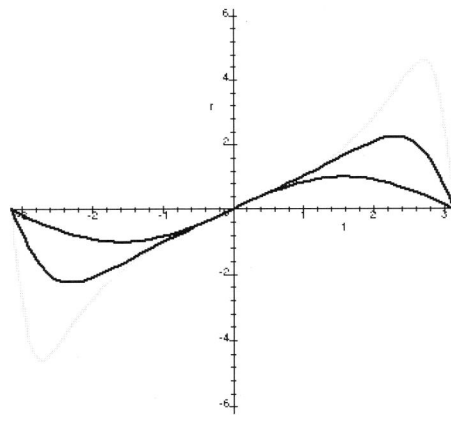

Fig. 2.30. Force Moment-Angle curvature response, shown with different boundary parameters values.

While this angle limiting technique prevents most curvature crossings around the edges, another type of curvature crossing around vertices may still occur (Fig. 2.31). This could only be prevented by means of expensive geometrical evaluations around each vertex, and the minor benefits this would entail might not be worthwhile.

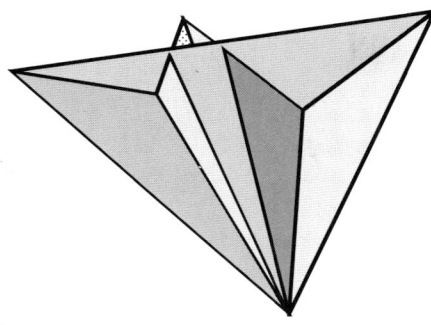

Fig. 2.31. Local curvature crossing occurring around a vertex.

C. Curvature and Elasticity in a Polygonal Mesh

The use of polygonal meshes to describe highly deformed surfaces introduces artifacts likely to interfere both with the rendering quality and the mechanical simulation based on the mesh. To a greater extent than the shape deformation resulting from the rough description of the curved parts, these artifacts affect the accuracy of the modeling of curvature elasticity for large deformations.

The problem arises mostly in the situations involving irregular triangle meshes. An irregular triangle mesh composed of a network of rigid inextensible rods (the edges) articulated with other edges at their extremities (the vertices) is in fact, more or less undeformable. Except for certain regular mesh configurations, curving a triangle mesh necessitates changes in the edge lengths in the curved region (Fig. 2.32).

This change in edge length may be negligible when the curvature radius is large compared to the size of the mesh elements, but a high degree curvature is likely to compress the edges crossing the curved regions orthogonally, as the parallel edge lengths remain roughly unchanged. As a consequence, the edge elasticity, used to model in-plane elasticity will interfere with the curvature elasticity.

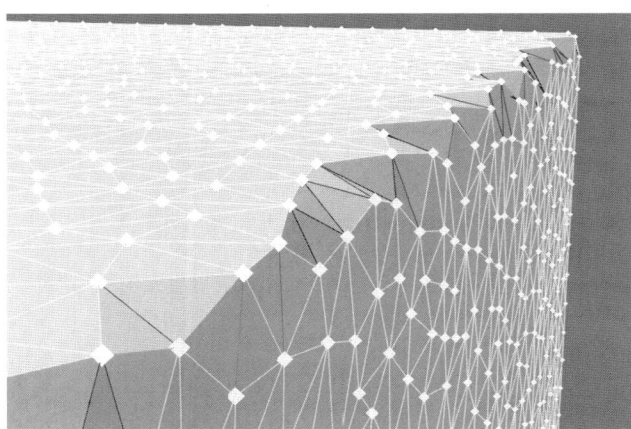

Fig. 2.32. High mesh curvature generates compression (dark edges).

A model allowing surface curvatures of the same scale as elements, cannot simply model curvature elasticity through polygonal angle control. This problem is particularly important for models with high in-plane rigidity, which interferes with curvature stiffness. Altering the edge rest lengths according to the estimated curvatures measured at their endpoints would approximately compensate for this. This method, however, would involve non-trivial geometric computations for only a partial gain in accuracy.

Working with regular meshes could overcome this problem to a limited extent, as these can be bent in certain directions without altering the edge lengths. In addition, these models can tolerate slightly rougher meshes for an equivalent curvature description. They do however, introduce anisotropic behaviors in the curvature elasticity that can, for example, produce abnormal wrinkling patterns.

2.5 Numerical Integration

The mechanical model equations cannot be solved analytically, and the simulation has to be carried out using a numerical process. Implementation of efficient numerical techniques is a key issue for an efficient simulation system.

In some models derived from continuum mechanics, and particularly for optimized techniques, the numerical resolution is embedded in the model, as for example with finite element methods. Other methods apply a discretization scheme to convert the analytical system into a set of equations that have to be solved numerically. (For example using finite differences.)

For particle system models, the system state and evolution are described by the position and evolution of the particles. The discretization of the mechanical laws on the particles usually produce a system of ordinary differential equations that has to be solved numerically along time evolution.

Except the very simple "school" problems that consider elementary mechanical systems with one or two degrees of freedom and linear mechanical models, it is quite impossible to analytically resolve the differential equation systems describing the evolution of mechanical systems. Numerical resolution approximates the solution by a form of extrapolation from timestep to timestep, using the derivatives as evolution information. One of the main drawbacks of numerical simulation is the *simulation error* which accumulates from step to step. Optimized numerical methods can perform the numerical resolution by efficiently minimizing this error and the resulting simulation inaccuracy. This section will focus on this particular techniques that can be directly used with the particle system described in the previous section.

2.5.1 Integration Techniques

Solving differential equation system is a very wide topic in numerical analysis, covering a large range of equation families. For mechanical simulation using particle systems, the problem can usually be reduced to the resolution of second order ordinary differential equation system where the variables are the particle positions along the evolving time.

2.5.1.1 Modeling as a First Order System

Let **P(t)** be the position vector of the entire system at time **t**, whose size is three times the total number of vertices (we're working with three dimensional coordinates in the Euclidian space). **P'(t)** and **P"(t)**, the first and second derivatives with respect to **t**, are the speed and the acceleration vectors, respectively. As detailed earlier, the mechanical model computes

P"(t) from **P(t)** and **P'(t)** at a given time **t**. The role of the numerical integration is to compute the state of the system after a given timestep **dt**.

The most intuitive method is to perform two successive integrations: compute **P(t+dt)** from **P(t)** and **P'(t)** and compute **P'(t+dt)** from **P'(t)** and **P"(t)**. There are, however, several drawbacks with this. The main problem is the accumulation of error during successive integrations, leading to potential instability artifacts after several timesteps.

A better solution is to consider the state of the system as being represented by the position **P(t)** *and* the speed **P'(t)**. Define a vector **Q(t)** to be the concatenation of **P(t)** and **P'(t)**. The size of this vector is six times the number of vertices. Then **Q'(t)** is the concatenation of **P'(t)** and **P"(t)**.

With this operation, we reduce our problem to a first order differential equation, for which numerous integration techniques exist. Our task is now to compute **Q(t+dt)** from **Q(t)** and **Q'(t)**.

Solving the first-order ordinary differential equation obtained this way, is a common problem of numerical analysis, well covered in the literature. Numerous integration techniques exist, of different complexities and having optimal accuracy and efficiency in different contexts.

2.5.1.2 Explicit Integration Methods

Explicit integration methods are the simplest methods available for solving first-order ordinary differential systems. They consider the prediction of the future system state directly from the value of the derivatives. The most well-known techniques are the Runge-Kutta methods. Among them, the Euler method considers the future state as a direct extrapolation from the current state and the derivative. Higher order and more accurate methods also exist.

A. Runge-Kutta Family Methods

The "intuitive" way of computing the increment of a function from its first derivative, is to set the average speed of function **(Q(t+dt)-Q(t))/dt** equal to the computed speed **Q'(t)**. Thus, we compute:

$$Q(t+dt) = Q(t) + Q'(t)dt \tag{1}$$

2.5 Numerical Integration

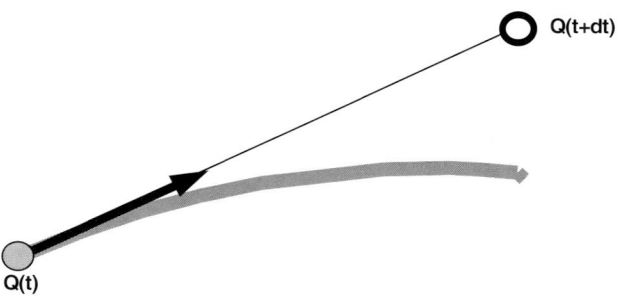

Fig. 2.33. The first-order Euler step.

This method, called Euler integration, is a first-order method, meaning that for each step, the simulation error is proportional to **dt²**. Only one derivation, at the initial time **t**, is required.

Controlling the simulation error is however, essential in our application, not only for accuracy, but more especially for the stability of the simulation. To reduce the error, we can use a smaller timestep **dt**, which proportionally increases the computation time.

Increasing the order of the simulation is another way to improve accuracy. This can be done by computing intermediate values, thus diminishing the errors from previous orders.

In the second-order Midpoint method, the simulation error is proportional to **dt³**. Two derivations are required, successively at times **t**, **t+dt/2**. The final result benefits from an intermediate computation in the middle of the interval. The computation is:

$$Q1(t+dt/2) = Q(t) + Q'(t)\,dt/2$$
$$Q(t+dt) = Q(t) + Q1'(t+dt/2)dt \qquad (2)$$

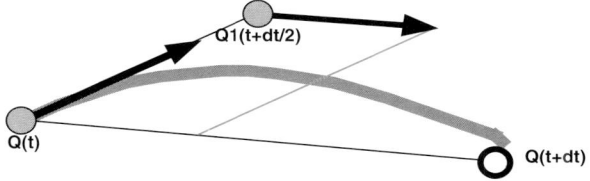

Fig. 2.34. The second-order Midpoint step.

The fourth-order Runge-Kutta method has a simulation error proportional to dt^5. It computes three intermediate values, the first in the middle of the interval as in the midpoint method, the second also at the midpoint but using the information from the first, and the third at the end of the interval using information from the second. The final result is a weighted sum of the intermediate values at the end of the interval. Four derivations are therefore required successively at times **t**, **t+dt/2**, **t+dt/2**, and **t+dt**. The computation is:

$$Q1(t+dt/2) = Q(t) + Q'(t)\,dt/2$$
$$Q2(t+dt/2) = Q(t) + Q1'(t+dt/2)dt/2$$
$$Q3(t+dt) = Q(t) + Q2'(t+dt/2)dt$$
$$Q(t+dt) = Q(t) + \bigl(Q'(t)/6 + Q1'(t+dt/2)/3 + Q2'(t+dt/2)/3 + Q3'(t+dt)/6\bigr)dt$$

(3)

In a typical cloth simulation situation, the fourth-order Runge-Kutta method has proven to be far superior to the second-order Midpoint method which itself is significantly more efficient than the first-order Euler method. Though computationally more expensive than the Midpoint and Euler methods for each iteration, the larger timestep which can be used makes it worthwhile, especially considering the benefits in stability and accuracy.

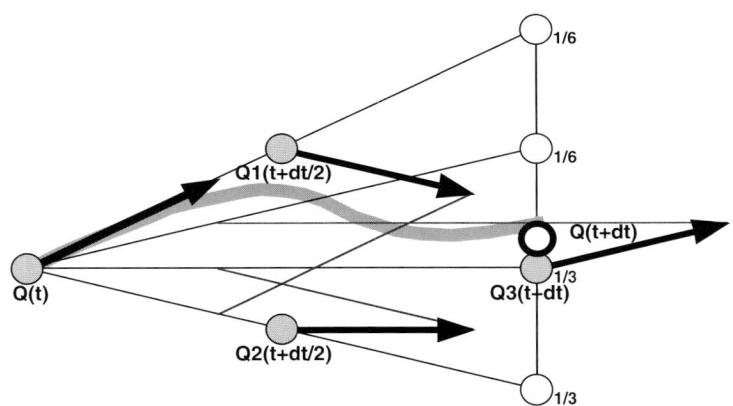

Fig. 2.35. The fourth-order Runge-Kutta step.

For taking advantage of this performance, an efficient, adaptive control algorithm is however, required for tuning the timestep in order to remain within the optimal values.

B. Timesteps, Accuracy and Order of Integration

As any numerical processes, the Runge-Kutta methods described above are approximations of the actual solution and give their result within an error range which depends on several factors: the size of the timestep, the order of integration, and the regularity of the functions governing the differential system.

The first-order Runge-Kutta method approximates the solution within the timestep using a linear (first-order) function, actually given by the derivative at the initial position. Higher order methods use higher order polynomial functions to perform the approximation, which are more likely to fit precisely the solution in a given range of the timestep.

Increasing order, however, does not translate indefinitely into increasing precision. The situation is analogous to polynomial interpolation, where fewer points are needed to interpolate a function with a polynomial of higher order, but only with smooth functions that can be effectively approximated by these polynomials. This is not the case of highly irregular and discontinuous functions for which such approximation is not valid. Furthermore, trying to represent a discontinuous function using high-order regular functions may actually lead to catastrophic artifacts near the discontinuities. Simulating these functions using low order or even linear functions using small timesteps, highly increase the robustness and reduce the errors in such situations.

High-order methods obviously also require more computation for each timestep. The time consuming aspect in mechanical simulation is the computation of the mechanical model in order to obtain the derivative **Q'** from the state of the system **Q**. As seen above, one integration step requires one mechanical computation for the first-order Euler method, two for the second-order Midpoint method, and four for the fourth-order Runge-Kutta method, and computing time is proportional to these requirements. Thus, in comparison with Runge-Kutta, we could afford computation steps half of the size with Midpoint and quarter of the size with Euler for equivalent computation time.

Is the precision gained by increasing the order of the method worth the extra computation? High order methods combine the data from several points to increase the order of accuracy of the solution. The simulation accuracy improves with the order of the method as the timestep decreases (provided that the actual solution to be simulated has similar regularity order), yielding very accurate simulation for small timesteps. This increase of precision allows to increase the timesteps for a given accuracy, which usually also compensate for the extra computation (for example, the fourth-order Runge-Kutta would allow timesteps more than four times bigger than the first-order Euler).

Unfortunately, as the timestep increases, the inaccuracy of large timesteps is degraded with the same order than the one of the method. This imposes a particularly tight control of the suitable timestep for high order methods.

The optimal order of integration has to be determined according to all these considerations. While the first-order Euler method is too inaccurate for usual problems (but might be considered for highly discontinuous situations), the fourth-order Runge-Kutta method is usually a very good compromise for applications of cloth simulation using usual elastic models. The integration methods above the fourth order are not usually considered, though they could easily be implemented because of their potential lack of robustness in nonlinear situations, and also because of other constraints on the timestep of on the mechanical model, such as collision detection and response.

C. Error Evaluation

The evaluation of the computation error is a good way to control the adequacy of the timestep which is used for the computation. It is possible to embed, within the computation of the solution for next step **Q(t+dt)**, the computation of the possible error interval **q(dt)** which provides a way of judging the appropriateness of the timestep size **dt**.

Derived from the fourth-order method described above, a convenient way of doing this is to use a derivation of the fifth-order Runge-Kutta algorithm detailed in [PRE 92], modified for computing the error for comparison with an embedded fourth-order evaluation. Using six derivation stages instead of four, we gain an order of accuracy as well as the error evaluation. The computation is:

$$\begin{aligned}
Q1(t+dt1) &= Q(t) + (r10 Q'(t)) dt \\
Q2(t+dt2) &= Q(t) + (r20 Q'(t) + r21 Q1'(t+dt1)) dt \\
Q3(t+dt3) &= Q(t) + (r30 Q'(t) + r31 Q1'(t+dt1) + r32 Q2'(t+dt2)) dt \\
Q4(t+dt4) &= Q(t) + (r40 Q'(t) + r41 Q1'(t+dt1) + r42 Q2'(t+dt2) + r43 Q3'(t+dt3)) dt \\
Q5(t+dt5) &= Q(t) + (r50 Q'(t) + r51 Q1'(t+dt1) + r52 Q2'(t+dt2) + r53 Q3'(t+dt3) + r54 Q4'(t+dt4)) dt \\
Q(t+dt) &= Q(t) + (r0 Q'(t) + r1 Q1'(t+dt1) + r2 Q2'(t+dt2) + r3 Q3'(t+dt3) + r4 Q4'(t+dt4) + r5 Q5'(t+dt5)) dt \\
Q(dt) &= (s0 Q'(t) + s1 Q1'(t+dt1) + s2 Q2'(t+dt2) + s3 Q3'(t+dt3) + s4 Q4'(t+dt4) + s5 Q5'(t+dt5)) dt
\end{aligned} \quad (4)$$

There exists several sets of constants, depending on the chosen algorithm variation. The Cash&Karp constants may be considered:

2.5 Numerical Integration

y \ x	rx0	rx1	rx2	rx3	rx4	rx5	dtx = •rxy
r1y	1/5						1/5
r2y	3/40	9/40					3/10
r3y	3/10	-9/10	6/5				3/5
r4y	-11/54	5/2	70/27	35/27			1
r5y	1631/55296	175/512	575/13824	44275/110592	265/4096		7/8
ry	37/378	0	250/621	125/594	0	512/1771	1
ry-sy	2825/27648	0	18575/48384	13525/55296	277/14336	1/4	1

Although 50% more expensive to compute than the traditional fourth-order Runge-Kutta method, this estimation does increase the accuracy. But the major benefit is the error evaluation which enables us to take full advantage of the efficiency of the method by optimally controlling the timestep.

Besides controlling the timestep as described in the following subsection, the computation error can also be used to reduce the effect of computation errors which usually result from unwanted mechanical energy accumulation in the structure. The idea is to "correct" the current state of the system after the simulation step, to a position within the error interval so as to put the system in its minimal energy configuration within this interval. This would involve a position correction for minimizing elastic deformation energy and a speed correction for minimizing deformation kinetic energy. This process should ensure an overall decrease in the mechanical energy, preventing occurrences of instability.

D. Timestep Control

The most suitable timestep depends on the structure of the simulated problem (in our case, the topology and the rest position of the spring-mass mesh), its mechanical properties, and its actual state. It also changes in the course of the simulation. The integration technique should allow variable timesteps to be used for simulating a given system in any state, accurately. There is no good method for evaluating the theoretical optimal timestep other than monitoring the simulation error for each step as described above.

A numerical technique, based on the simulation error prediction, can be used for that purpose. The magnitude of this interval is a useful and pertinent information on whether the time step used was well-adapted for the computation of this iteration. An adequately normalized value of this error interval can control adjustments in the timestep through a mechanism based on the threshold values (Fig. 2.36).

The threshold mechanism uses three user-defined constants **Em**, **En**, **Ep** and attempts to keep the current maximum simulation error between two values, **Em** and **Ep**.

- If the current error is above **Ep** (the error is excessive and the last step should be recomputed), the timestep is divided by a given constant and the last simulation step is recomputed with this new timestep.

- If the current error is above **En** (the error is significant and the simulation timestep should be reduced), the timestep is divided by a given constant.

- If the current error is below **Em** (the simulation timestep can be increased without the risk of instability), the timestep is multiplied by a given constant.

The threshold constants are set empirically:

- **Ep** is set to a value that completely prevents unrealistic results and instabilities from occurring.

- **En** is set below **Ep** to prevent visual inaccuracies.

- **Em** is set below **En** to ensure significantly high values of the timestep.

We allow an interval between **Em** and **En** to ensure that the timestep does not change constantly, whereas the interval between **En** and **Ep** ensures correct simulation accuracy. The timestep multiplication constants have to be tuned accordingly.

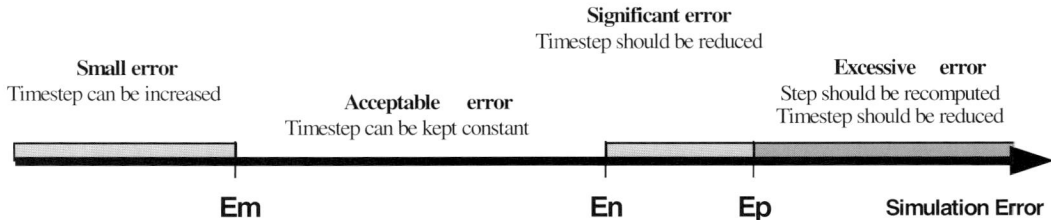

Fig. 2.36. Simulation error and timestep control.

E. Other Explicit Methods

Many other techniques exist in the literature for the solving first-order, ordinary differential systems.

2.5 Numerical Integration

The major families of techniques have different strategies for further reducing the integration error, sometimes at the expense of numerical robustness. Among them, the Burlish-Stoer method and its variations based on the Richardson extrapolation, which tries to guess the "limit value" of the result while the timestep decreases to **0**, by comparing and extrapolating the evolution of the computed solution as the size of the computation timestep changes.

While these methods are very efficient for functions that are more or less derived from analytic expressions, they are not very robust for handling discontinuities such as those encountered with the collision models.

2.5.1.3 Implicit Integration Methods

Inaccuracy is by far the only consideration for determining the appropriate timestep. As it will be detailed in the next subsection, numerical stiffness is another issue in particle simulation. Certain integration methods try to avoid integration inaccuracies which produce simulation instability. The main idea is to use the backward (implicit) integration steps which differ from the usual forward (explicit) integration steps in finding the value at time **t+dt** that would produce the value at the time **t** by applying time-reversed derivatives.

A. Principles

The most basic implementation of implicit method is the Euler step, which considers finding the future state for which "backward" Euler computation would return to the initial state. It performs the computation not using the derivative at the current timestep, but using the predicted derivative for the next timestep. The inverse Euler step uses this predicted derivative for the "backward" computation of the step:

$$Q(t) = Q(t+dt) - Q'(t+dt)dt \tag{6}$$

which is equivalent to:

$$Q(t+dt) = Q(t) + Q'(t+dt)dt \tag{7}$$

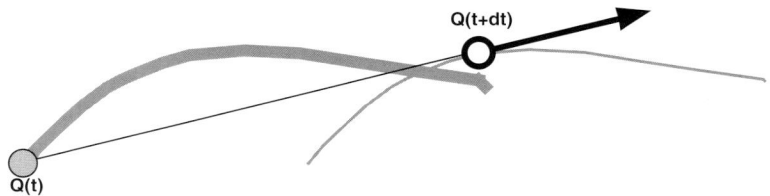

Fig. 2.37. The inverse Euler step.

The derivative at time **t+dt** is not known and has to be approximated. Knowing the evolution of the derivative as the state of the system changes, it is possible to make a first-order approximation for any state. Supposing that the derivative only depends on the state of the system **X(t)**, we have:

$$Q'(t+dt) = Q'(t) + \frac{\partial Q'}{\partial Q}(t)(Q(t+dt) - Q(t)) \tag{7}$$

Because of this linear approximation, such integration method is often called a *semi-implicit integration method*. Substituting equation (7) into equation (6), we get:

$$\left(I - \frac{\partial Q'}{\partial Q}(t)dt\right)Q(t+dt) = \left(I - \frac{\partial Q'}{\partial Q}(t)dt\right)Q(t) + Q'(t)dt \tag{8}$$

I being identity, and we finally get:

$$Q(t+dt) = Q(t) + \left(I - \frac{\partial Q'}{\partial Q}(t)dt\right)^{-1} Q'(t)dt \tag{9}$$

As detailed in Part.0, integration error does not diverge towards instability phenomena with this method. By supposing that the linear approximation of the derivative is valid within the evolution range of the system state, a huge timestep **dt** brings the system quickly to an equilibrium state where the derivative is null. By this way, the system is stabilized for whatever timestep used.

This stabilisation is actually obtained by resolving a linear system relating the evolution of the derivatives. While this does not cause any problem for a scalar differential equation system, the **Q** vector considered for the problem of cloth simulation is quite huge, proportional to the number of particles of the system. Hence, the partial derivative matrix of all degrees of freedom of the system (the Hessian matrix) is indeed quite a huge matrix that has to be computed. Finally, the matrix inversion required in equation (9) has to be carried out.

Hopefully, the structure of the matrix is close to the relationship structure between the particles. In the context of particle simulation, the particles are only interacting with a roughly constant number of neighbors, and therefore the matrix is sparse. In this context, rather than carrying out the matrix inversion, it is profitable to solve a linear system expressed as follows:

$$\left(I - \frac{\partial Q'}{\partial Q}(t)dt\right)(Q(t+dt) - Q(t)) = Q'(t)dt \tag{10}$$

If the interaction between each particle is symmetric (typically, if the particles have identical mass), the matrix is symmetric and positive. This allows to take advantage of the powerful conjugate gradient method for resolving this system iteratively [PRE 92]. In cases that do not satisfy these requirements, the less efficient biconjugate gradient method can be used [PRE 92]. Different tricks also allow the use of the conjugate gradient method by walking around this requirement, as for example discussed in [BAR 98]. In a further step toward simplification, considering linear models on regular structures allows to simplify the expression of the matrix, such as suggested in [DES 99]. Such simplifications may lead to considering this matrix as a constant. In this way the inverse of equation (9) would be expressed as a constant, suppressing the need of linear system solution. However, such inverse is not sparse. An approximate, sparse inverse would then be considered, which only expresses the relations of particles within a given neighborhood range. While performing all those possible simplifications, attention should be paid to the effect of the considered approximations that may either lead to a static system or degrade the original stability of the system.

All implicit methods are more stable, but are not necessarily more accurate than their explicit counterparts. They give better results only on the assumption that giving a result close to the equilibrium is better than giving a result simply by extrapolation. Apart from the inverse Euler method, more accurate, higher order methods also exist, such as the Rosenbrook method. [PRE 92] contains more details about available integration techniques and related references.

B. Implementing an Implicit Method
We briefly detail the implementation of an implicit integration method based on the inverse Euler step, in order to illustrate the main issues to be considered.

The inverse Euler step of Equation (10) can be rewritten by separating the position and the speed components as follows:

$$\left(I - \begin{bmatrix} \partial P'/\partial P & \partial P'/\partial P' \\ \partial P''/\partial P & \partial P''/\partial P' \end{bmatrix} dt \right) \left(\begin{bmatrix} P(t+dt) \\ P'(t+dt) \end{bmatrix} - \begin{bmatrix} P(t) \\ P'(t) \end{bmatrix} \right) = \begin{bmatrix} P'(t) \\ P''(t) \end{bmatrix} dt \quad (11)$$

The partial derivative sub-matrices, **dP'/dP** and **dP'/dP'**, have respectively null and identity values. The sub-matrices **dP"/dP** and **dP"/dP'** relate respectively, the elasticity and the viscosity force variations. Turning into an equation system and rearranging lead to:

$$P'(t+dt) = P'(t) + \left(I - \frac{\partial P''}{\partial P'}dt - \frac{\partial P''}{\partial P}dt^2 \right)^{-1} \left(P''(t)dt + \frac{\partial P''}{\partial P}P'(t)dt^2 \right)$$
$$P(t+dt) = P(t) + P'(t+dt)dt \quad (12)$$

The main difficulty now is to compute the first part of the equation which is equivalent to solving a linear system. Hopefully, the matrix of the system is generally sparse and positive, allowing efficient resolution methods such as the biconjugate gradient method [PRE 92]. However, the conjugate gradient method converges as quickly with half of the computation per iteration, but requires the system matrix to be symmetric. In the context of a particle system, while the interaction between particles create symmetric force patterns, symmetry is broken by interaction between particles having unequal masses.

By noting **F**, the force exerted on the particles, and **M**, the global mass matrix being a diagonal (thus symmetric) matrix containing the masses of the particles M_i in the corresponding diagonal elements, Newton's law is expressed as **P"(t) = M⁻¹ F(t)**. Hence, we have:

$$P'(t+dt) = P'(t) + \left(I - M^{-1}\frac{\partial F}{\partial P'}dt - M^{-1}\frac{\partial F}{\partial P}dt^2 \right)^{-1} \left(M^{-1}F(t)dt + M^{-1}\frac{\partial F}{\partial P}P'(t)dt^2 \right) \quad (13)$$

The matrices **dF/dP** and **dF/dP'** being symmetric, global symmetry can be recovered by multiplying the expressions by the global mass matrix. Hence, we get:

$$P'(t+dt) = P'(t) + \left(M - \frac{\partial F}{\partial P'}dt - \frac{\partial F}{\partial P}dt^2 \right)^{-1} \left(F(t)dt + \frac{\partial F}{\partial P}P'(t)dt^2 \right) \quad (14)$$

It is important to note that as discussed in Part.2.4.5.2, by assigning to a particle, a null inverse mass **Mi⁻¹ = 0**, it is possible to constrain it so it would not react to external forces. In the same way, it is possible to constrain a particle to move along specified directions by using inverse mass matrices that are singular along the constrained directions. Constrained particles however cause problems in the formulation of the **M** term of expression (14) (con-

2.5 Numerical Integration

strained particles have "infinite mass"). In the developments of [BRE 98], a special filtering scheme has been adapted in order to circumvent this problem. Another way to deal with the problem is to perform an adequate preconditioning of the system, as detailed below.

The biggest difficulty in implementing the implicit methods is the resolution of a sparse linear system, which usually implies the appropriate data structure for managing huge sparse matrices and operations on them. The conjugate gradient algorithm can however, remove this difficulty in the case of particle systems involving sets of simple interactions between reduced number of particles.

Calling **H**, the system matrix appearing in equation (14) to be inverted, and **Y**, the second member of the equation, we intend to find the vector **X** solution of the equation **H X = Y**. The conjugate gradient algorithm, applicable if **H** is symmetric and positive, can be expressed as follows:

```
β ← 0;   X ← 0;   R ← Y-HX
Iterate {
    α ← RᵀR;   if (β ≠ 0)   T ← R+(α/β)T   else   T ← R
    β ← TᵀHT;  R ← R-(α/β)HT;   X ← X+(α/β)T
    β ← α
} until (β < ε)
```

The algorithm iterates until the error factor gets below a value ε that should reflect the desired accuracy and should be normalized homogeneously according to the timestep, particle masses, and the typical distances of the system. Usually, a certain number of iterations are necessary to "propagate" the force effects through the same number of neighborhood interactions, and the number of iterations can in practice, be limited by a value related to the mesh size.

The implementation difficulty lies in the handling of the sparse matrix **H**. The interactions between the particles exactly reflect the structure of this matrix, and taking advantage of this fact removes the need of storing an explicit sparse matrix structure for applying the Conjugate Gradient method. In this algorithm, the sparse matrix operations are restricted to the vector product **HT** and to the quadratic product **TᵀHT**. When knowing exactly the elementary force interactions exerted between the particles, the vector products can be computed easily by adding all the corresponding contributions.

Among these forces, external forces independently exerted on the particles only account for a diagonal component **Hi** in the sparse matrix **H**. Defining $\mathbf{V_i} = -d\mathbf{F_i}/d\mathbf{P_i}$, $\mathbf{W_i} = -d\mathbf{F_i}/d\mathbf{P_i}'$ as the force **F$_i$** derivatives on position **P$_i$** and speed **P$_i'$** respectively for a particle **i**, we obtain the following product contributions for each particle:

$$(H_i T)_i = T_i \left(V_i dt^2 + W_i dt \right)$$
$$(T^T H_i T) = T_i^2 \left(V_i dt^2 + W_i dt \right) \quad (15)$$

Internal forces result from particle interactions that are modeled through various schemes. The simplest scheme to consider is a spring-mass system where interactions are defined between a particle couple **i, j**. The interaction force derivatives on position and speed are respectively $\mathbf{V_{ij}} = -d(\mathbf{F_i}-\mathbf{F_j})/d(\mathbf{P_i}-\mathbf{P_j})$ and $\mathbf{W_{ij}} = -d(\mathbf{F_i}-\mathbf{F_j})/d(\mathbf{P_i}'-\mathbf{P_j}')$. This contributes to a submatrix **Hij** containing four elements, at the intersection of the **i** and **j** rows and columns. We obtain the following product contributions for each interaction:

$$(H_{ij} T)_i = (T_i - T_j)\left(V_{ij} dt^2 + W_{ij} dt \right)$$
$$(H_{ij} T)_j = (T_j - T_i)\left(V_{ij} dt^2 + W_{ij} dt \right)$$
$$(T^T H_{ij} T) = (T_i - T_j)^2 \left(V_{ij} dt^2 + W_{ij} dt \right) \quad (16)$$

As a generalization of the two cases above, we can define an interaction **c** between multiple particles and a particle **i** being weighted by a coefficient **s$_i$** in the interaction. The interaction force derivatives on position and speed are respectively $\mathbf{V_c} = -d(\sum \mathbf{s_i F_i})/d(\sum \mathbf{s_i P_i})$ and $\mathbf{W_c} = -d(\sum \mathbf{s_i F_i})/d(\sum \mathbf{s_i P_i'})$. This contributes to a submatrix **H$_c$** and thus to the following product contributions for each interaction:

$$(H_c T)_{i \in C} = s_i \left(\sum_{j \in C} s_j T_j \right) \left(V_c dt^2 + W_c dt \right)$$
$$(T^T H_c T) = \left(\sum_{j \in C} s_j T_j \right)^2 \left(V_c dt^2 + W_c dt \right) \quad (17)$$

We clearly identify the relations (15) to be the relations (17) using one particle of weight +1, and the relations (16) to be the relations (17) using two particles of weights +1 and -1. This type of interaction can, for instance, be efficiently used when mechanical interactions have to be defined between any polygonal mesh elements (edges, polygons) rather than only on vertices.

We can see that the computation of these products can be performed efficiently, for each successive force contribution in the mechanical system, this process being directly embedded in the Conjugate Gradient algorithm. This is indeed likely to be more efficient than building explicitly the sparse matrix, as this process includes efficient factorization of constant values for contributions related to each interactions. Generalization to complex interactions between several particles, such as for models taking into account complete surface elasticity computed on the deformed polygons of a mesh, can be obtained in the same way.

C. Mechanical Parameters and Anisotropy

The **V** and **W** components defined above are submatrices of the size of the space dimension in which the simulation takes place. For usual 3D cloth simulation applications, this is **3**. The structure of these matrices are "constants" illustrating the variations of the corresponding force with respect to the position and the speed of a particle.

The structure of these matrices is symmetric and can be decomposed into *isotropic* and *anisotropic* components.

- An *isotropic component* relates a force variation identical in any direction. This contribution is proportional to the identity matrix **I**.

- An *anisotropic component* relates a force variation along a precise direction. If this direction is described by the normalized vector **X**, the contribution is proportional to the hermitian matrix $\mathbf{X}\mathbf{X}^T$.

Among the possible forces exerted on the particles, here are some examples of the main contributions:

- *Gravitation*: The resulting force $\mathbf{F}_{i\,grav} = \mathbf{M}_i\,\mathbf{G}$ exerted on a particle **i**, is constant, and there is no derivative contribution.

- *Air viscosity*: A simple air viscosity force $\mathbf{F}_{i\,air} = \mathbf{e}_i\,(\mathbf{P'}_{air}-\mathbf{P}_i')$ on a particle **i** can be modeled to be proportional to the speed difference between the air speed (wind) and the particle speed. Thus, it has an isotropic derivative component $\mathbf{W}_{i\,air} = -\mathbf{e}_i$. If this force is only exerted perpendicularly to the surface (along the direction of the surface normal $\mathbf{X}_i$ corresponding to the particle **i**), this would be an anisotropic component $\mathbf{W}_{i\,air} = -\mathbf{e}_i\,\mathbf{X}_i\,\mathbf{X}_i^T$.

- *Elastic force*: Simple spring-mass systems are based on the particle interactions between particle couples, usually as the form of linear elasticity relations $\mathbf{F}_{ij\,elast} = \mathbf{k}_{ij}\,(\mathbf{L}_{ij}-|\mathbf{P}_i-\mathbf{P}_j|)\,\mathbf{X}_{ij}$, where $\mathbf{X}_{ij} = (\mathbf{P}_i-\mathbf{P}_j)/|\mathbf{P}_i-\mathbf{P}_j|$ is the spring orientation and $\mathbf{L}_{ij}$ its native length. In this case, the force derivative contribution is $\mathbf{V}_{ij\,elast} = -\mathbf{k}_{ij}\,\mathbf{X}_{ij}\,\mathbf{X}_{ij}^T$. A spring viscosity force and the derivative contribution can be defined in the same way.

More complex interactions can be defined in similar ways. When implementing models resulting from continuum mechanics (as in [BAR 98]), discretization of the equations lead to expressions that can be handled in the same way.

A common way to simplify these computations is to consider only the isotropic derivative expressions. In [DES 99], along with the linearization of all interactions, this allowed to have a constant matrix H which did not depend on the state of the system, and whose inverse could be precomputed. This is a drastic simplification of the problem for which the "exact" force derivatives are usually anisotropic. However, it sometimes makes sense to alter some purely anisotropic components by adding to them some isotropic contributions. There are two reasons for this:

- In some situations, the anisotropy orientation may change drastically from one iteration to another. For instance, an anisotropic elastic force derivative of a spring is only valid for the relative lateral displacements of its extremities remains small compared to the current spring length. While an isotropic derivative approximation would overestimate the force evolution in case of lateral motion of the edge extremities, the anisotropic exact derivative evaluation leads to an underestimated force not taking into account this lateral displacement (Fig. 2.38). While the consequence of an overestimation is only a stabilization the system through an apparent additional damping, the underestimation has dramatic destabilizing consequences for the reproduction of lateral movements.

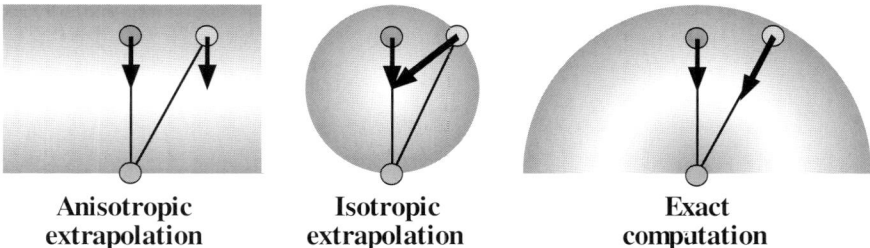

Fig. 2.38. Computing the force of a spring resulting from a displaced vertex (light) out of the force of an initial position (dark) using anisotropic extrapolation from the derivative at this point (left), isotropic derivative approximation (center), and exact computation (right).

- In some simple simulation models, such as those not including any curvature force or damping, global alignment of the particles may cause null derivatives to occur in a given direction orthogonal to all interactions. When anisotropic derivatives are used, this degeneracy causes a singularity in the resolution in that direction, as well as degenerating the equation system. Lateral forces do actually appear along these orthogonal directions if the particles are displaced (although only with a second-order evolution) and thus, are not represented by the first-order derivatives. For instance, the underestimated first-order approximation may lead to totally incorrect equilibrium evaluations in a spring-mass system with almost aligned springs (Fig. 2.39). This however has to be taken into consideration, as large displacements are to be expected in these directions.

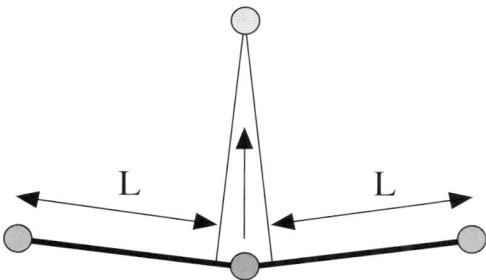

Fig. 2.39. In a spring-mass system containing almost aligned springs, with the spring rest length **L**, the computation of the equilibrium position (light) from the initial position (dark) using exact derivatives computed at this point is aberrant.

If any of these problems arise, mostly when dealing with simple spring-mass models that do not contain any curvature effects or any form of damping, a small isotropic component in the derivative computation is often sufficient to prevent instability to appear. While only considering isotropic components would, more than stabilization, cause excessive and unwanted damping in the system, a linear interpolation between the isotropic and anisotropic is often the best solution to implement.

D. Resolution Preconditioning

The Conjugate Gradient method is an iterative method that resolves simultaneously and symetrically the equations of the linear system. The result of the resolution converges to the result of the equation system as the number of iterations increases. The convergence rate on all unknowns and on all the equations may however, not be the same, depending on the relative importance of each equation and each unknown in the system. Preconditioning is a method to give more relative "importance" to certain unknowns and certain equations in the resolution by multiplying them prior to system resolution.

Sometimes, the accuracy requirement is not uniform for all the problems, and some regions of the mechanical system need more accuracy than others. If these regions are quite independent, the best optimization is to perform independently the system resolution for each region. When particles having various accuracy requirements are highly mixed in the system, the best solution is to alter the system resolution through preconditioning techniques. A diagonal preconditioning matrix **D** should be constructed, for which the diagonal elements are proportional to the relative accuracy required on the particles. Then, instead of solving the system for obtaining $\mathbf{X} = \mathbf{H}^{-1}\mathbf{Y}$ as above, we would rather compute $\mathbf{X} = \mathbf{D}^T(\mathbf{D}^T\mathbf{H}\mathbf{D})^{-1}\mathbf{DY}$. Dealing with the Conjugate Gradient algorithm described above, this basically means:

- Multiplying the second member of the equation by **D** before resolution.

- Multiplying the result by $\mathbf{D}^T$ after resolution.

- Replacing the computation of the products **HT** and $\mathbf{T}^T\mathbf{HT}$ by the products $\mathbf{D}^T\mathbf{H}(\mathbf{DT})$ and $(\mathbf{DT})^T\mathbf{H}(\mathbf{DT})$ respectively in the iterations of the Conjugate Gradient algorithm.

While only little complication is added to the computation due to the simple diagonal structure of **D**, this extra computation could be worthwhile only when very heterogeneous particle structures are used. Particular accuracy requirements are necessary on a reduced number of particles.

In our case, we take advantage of preconditioning for handling constrained particles, by removing the singularities resulting the **M** term appearing in equation (14) through its replacement by the product $\mathbf{D}^T\mathbf{MD}$ with **D** chosen for instance to be the inverse mass matrix $\mathbf{M}^{-1}$, the constrained particles being represented by null terms in this matrix.

When dealing with scalar particle masses, the best preconditioning matrix that is able to handle the constrained particle and solve efficiently the systems containing particles with very diverse masses, is defined by the square root of the inverse masses: $\mathbf{D}_{ii} = \mathbf{M}_i^{-1/2}$, again with null terms representing constrained particles.

E. Precomputed Matrix Inverses

The slowest part of the computation of implicit models is the resolution of the linear system involving the **H** matrix, carried out using the Conjugate Gradient method as described above. However, in some particular situations (notably linear force models and isotropic derivatives), the **H** matrix can be constant along the simulation steps. An idea resulting from that, proposed in [DES 99] is the possibility to pre-compute the inverse of the **H** matrix and substitute the linear system resolution by a simple matrix-vector multiplication.

Unfortunately, the inverse of a sparse matrix is most of the time not sparse. However, as the matrix inverse reflects the effect of a particle's state on any other particle of the system, we can suppose that the particles far away from each other only have minor effects on each other, and the corresponding terms of the matrix can be dropped.

It is easy to compute such a sparse inverse approximation by iterating the Conjugate Gradient method at a reduced number of times. The number of non-diagonal elements in each inverse matrix row or columns for a given number of iterations is basically the number of particles linked to a particle by the same number of successive interactions, which, in the case of a flat surface mesh structure, increases quadratically.

The interest of pre-computing the inverse of the **H** matrix can only be justified in small problems where the entire matrix can be computed, or in problems that allow enough approximations that a very reduced number of carefully computed elements of a sparse matrix inverse approximation can be used. However, the conjugate gradient method carries an inherent factorization scheme that allows to process, in a linear number of iterations, the contributions generated from a quadratic number of inverse matrix contributions in the case of a surface mesh structure, and therefore is preferable when high accuracy is required. The conditions required for having a constant **H** matrix also highly limit the accuracy of a model that would be computed using inverse the pre-computation.

F. Variations for Specific Applications

The draping problem is a specific issue where the interest is the final, rest configuration of the mechanical system which has to be computed as quickly as possible starting from an initial configuration. What is important is the final stable position of the cloth than its evolution.

A draping model is implemented as a quasi-static model where the speed is not taken into account. By removing the speed components in the equation (12), we obtain the following system:

$$P(t+dt) = P(t) + \left(I - \frac{\partial P''}{\partial P}dt^2\right)^{-1} P''(t)dt^2 \tag{18}$$

The "timestep" is here more a parameter relating the convergence speed than a parameter really representing time. Very high value can be used, but it may degrade the smoothness of the evolution if the system is significantly nonlinear. Using an infinite timestep, this method is actually equivalent to the resolution of an equation system using Newton's resolution method, and has the same convergence properties. This system is solved in the same way using the conjugate or biconjugate gradient method as described above.

On the other hand, some other applications require additional accuracy to reflect more accurately, the actual evolution and the motion of cloth, particularly in situations with free motion and draping. Instead of implementing a complex resolution method that will spoil the advantage of having frames quickly computed in real-time systems, we would rather prefer a "cheap" method that does not complicate the computations significantly. A good solution is to use a variation of the implicit midpoint step. This method considers the evolution during the former step for increasing the accuracy of the current step. Still, only one linear system resolution for each step, bringing the accuracy for very little additional computation. The implicit midpoint step is written as follows:

$$\left(I - \begin{bmatrix} \partial P'/\partial P & \partial P'/\partial P' \\ \partial P''/\partial P & \partial P''/\partial P' \end{bmatrix} dt \right) \left(\begin{bmatrix} P(t+dt) \\ P'(t+dt) \end{bmatrix} + \begin{bmatrix} P(t-dt) \\ P'(t-dt) \end{bmatrix} - 2 \begin{bmatrix} P(t) \\ P'(t) \end{bmatrix} \right)$$
$$= 2 \begin{bmatrix} P'(t) \\ P''(t) \end{bmatrix} dt - 2 \left(\begin{bmatrix} P(t) \\ P'(t) \end{bmatrix} - \begin{bmatrix} P(t-dt) \\ P'(t-dt) \end{bmatrix} \right) \quad (19)$$

One drawback of this method is the reduced robustness in the cases of stiff problems which again, may become prone to numerical instability. We found a good compromise by introducing a λ coefficient which allows to scale linearly and progressively, from the implicit Euler step (11) (λ set to **0**) to the implicit midpoint step (16) (λ set to **1**). After turning into an equation system and after rearranging similarly to (12), we obtain:

$$P'(t+dt) = P'(t) + \lambda(P'(t) - P'(t-dt)) + \left(I - \frac{\partial P''}{\partial P'} dt - \frac{\partial P''}{\partial P} dt^2 \right)^{-1} \left((1+\lambda) \left(P''(t) dt + \frac{\partial P''}{\partial P} P'(t) dt^2 \right) - 2\lambda(P'(t) - P'(t-dt)) \right) \quad (20)$$
$$P(t+dt) = P(t) - \lambda(P(t) - P(t-dt)) + (P'(t+dt) - \lambda P'(t-dt)) dt$$

This expression is not significantly more complicated to compute than the simple implicit Euler step and only requires the additional storage of the former step. For that reason, the computation of the first step of the simulation should be performed with $\lambda = \mathbf{0}$. For most problems, the most adequate values of λ range from **0.5** to **0.9**.

2.5.1.4 Maintaining the Simulation Stability

Numerical integration, like any other numerical process, is inaccurate. A small and controlled numerical inaccuracy is of no harm to the result, particularly in our case where only the visual aspects are important. However, numerical inaccuracy may produce a more serious side effect: the simulation may become unstable. In such a model, numerical errors accumulate with successive iterations and may diverge, eventually to near-infinite values without any resemblance to the physical reality. The model seems to "explode", and there is no hope of recovery.

We stated above that the accuracy could always be obtained at the expense of computation time. The opposite is unfortunately not always true. While many very simple mechanical models have enough realism for them to be integrated in the real-time computation systems, the major limiting factor is not further realism degradation, but numerical instability that is likely to arise.

As stated previously, it is this instability rather than the numerical inaccuracy itself, which quite often must be controlled in a simulation. The main reason for paying attention to the simulation accuracy is not for the visual realism, but to prevent the simulation from "exploding". While small, unrealistic artifacts would often go unnoticed in real-time simulation systems, a numeric explosion due to instability systematically leads to unrecoverable effects.

Understanding and controlling numerical stability in a particle system model is described in the following paragraphs.

A. Stability, Simulation Timestep and Internal Vibrations

Any mechanical system may be animated by several deformation patterns that combine into vibration modes. A particle system composed of masses and springs is not equivalent to the elastic surface because of additional vibration modes inherent in its discrete spring-mass structure. Each particle can vibrate individually, according to the effect of its adjacent springs.

An accurate mechanical simulation should be able to accurately simulate all the vibration modes of the system. While some of the modes reflect the overall elasticity of the material through the vibration patterns affecting large portions of the system, the local vibrations of individual particles are not relevant to the simulation, as they only result from the spring-mass discretization. Ideally, they would not occur in the simulation. Nevertheless, if the simulation cannot represent them accurately, they may well increase and produce instability rather than decrease to zero amplitude.

To simulate a vibration mode accurately, the simulation timestep should be related to the vibration frequency, so that the vibration pattern can be described accurately by the successive states of the simulation. For a globally accurate simulation, the timestep should be adapted to the maximum frequency of all the possible modes of the system. The higher this frequency, the smaller the timestep should be.

Unfortunately, the particle-scale vibration modes resulting from the discretization, have higher frequencies than the global-scale vibration modes due to the usual deformations of the simulated object. Furthermore, the particle vibration frequency is related to the element size of the discretization.

In a square grid with particles of mass **M** linked by springs of length **l** and metric elasticity coefficient **k**, the local vibration frequency of these particles is roughly proportional to $(k/(M\ l))^{-1/2}$. This system models an elastic surface of surface density M/l^2 and surface Young modulus k/l. The same surface modeled with elements half as large, requires particles of mass **M/4** linked by springs of length **l/2** and metric elasticity coefficient **k/2** (Fig. 2.40). The local vibration frequency of these particles is then twice that of the previous model.

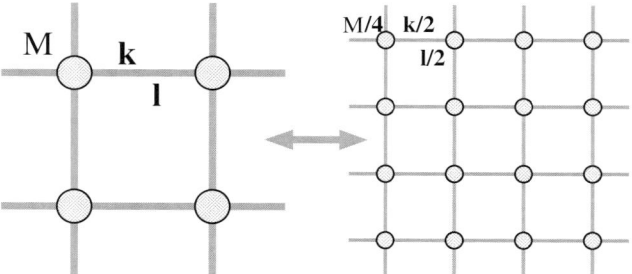

Fig. 2.40. Representing equivalent surface metric elasticity with two different spring-mass systems. **M** is the mass of the particles, **k** the metric elastic coefficient and **l** the length of the springs.

The allowable simulation timestep of a particle system simulation is then roughly proportional to the element size **l** for surfaces of equivalent mechanical parameters. Furthermore, as the number of elements to be processed is proportional to $1/l^2$, the total simulation time becomes globally proportional to $1/l^3$ for equivalent surface parameters. This is why fast simulation of particle systems requires discretizations to remain rough.

The practical limitation of the timestep also depends on the rigidity of the material and evolves proportionally to its square root (Fig. 2.41).

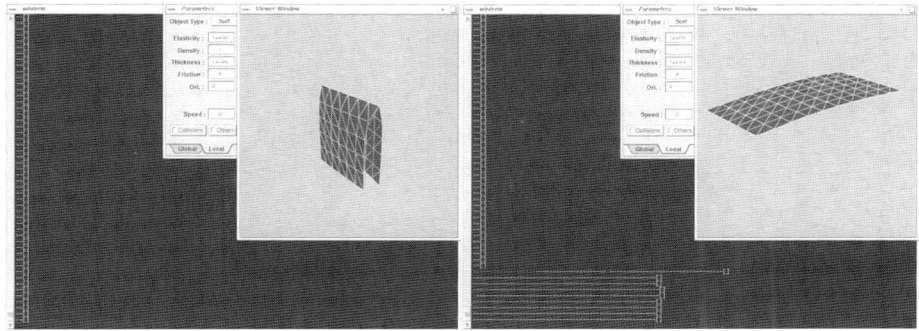

Fig. 2.41. Multiplying elastic stiffness by a 1000 factor implies performing the simulation with timesteps 33 times smaller.

The timestep value is determined by the least favorable region of the surface. This is reasonable since an instability is likely to appear locally in that region first if the stability conditions are not met, compromising the whole simulation. For surfaces involving different local contexts such as widely varying mechanical parameters or discretization sizes, a simulation system involving local timesteps could be considered.

B. Implicit vs. Explicit Integration Methods

As stated previously, implicit methods do not suffer from the instability problems as explicit methods do. For illustration, the following simple linear differential equation should be considered:

$$X(t) + k X'(t) = 0 \qquad (21)$$

The obvious analytical solution of this equation is:

$$X(t) = X(0) e^{-t/k} \qquad (22)$$

The solution starts from the initial value **X(0)** and converges to **0** with time. The convergence rate decreases with the value of the parameter **k** (Fig. 2.42).

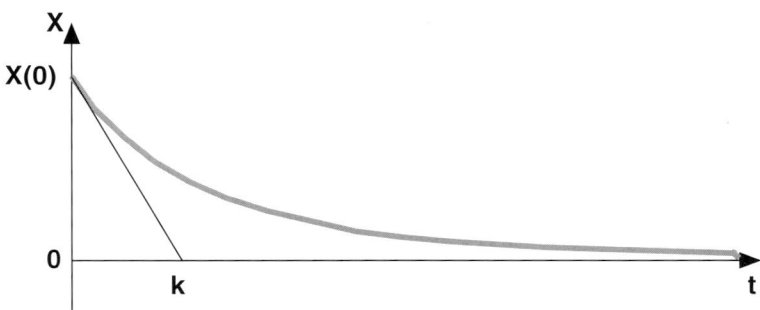

Fig. 2.42. The solution of the differential equation (11).

The Euler simulation of this equation is a succession of values **X_n** computed for each time **t_n = n dt** using equation (1) as follows:

$$X_0 = X(0)$$
$$X_{n+1} = X_n + X'_n dt = X_n \frac{k - dt}{k} \tag{23}$$

This succession of values will exhibit various behaviors depending on the relative values of the timestep **dt** and **k**. These cases arise (Fig. 2.43):

- If **dt** is smaller than **k**, the succession will converge to 0 progressively. The smaller **dt** is, the closer the succession is to the theoretical exponential curve.

- If **dt** is between **k** and **2 k**, the succession will converge to 0 by alternating positive and negative values. Vibration occurs. The higher **dt** is, the slower the convergence is.

- If **dt** is higher than **2 k**, the succession diverges and the values get bigger and bigger. This is numerical instability.

2.5 Numerical Integration

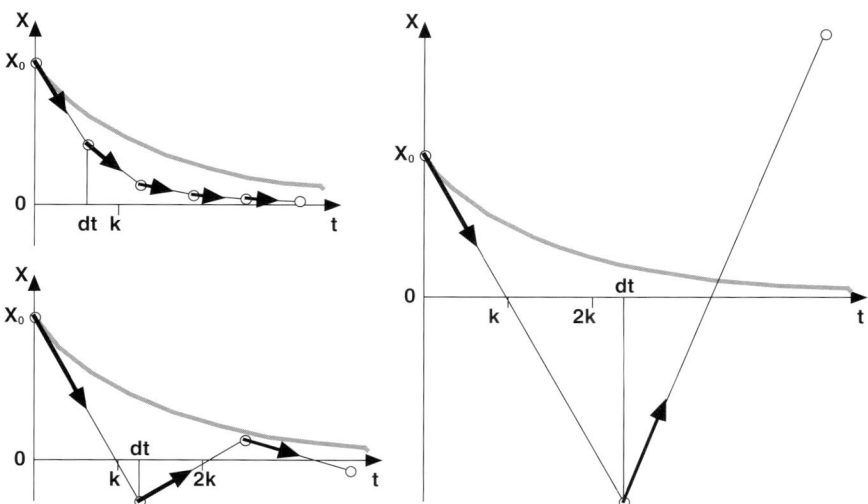

Fig. 2.43. The Euler step resolution of equation (11) depending on the timestep size: Stable, oscillating, and unstable situations.

This clearly illustrates the possible behaviors of all direct integration methods depending the timestep size **dt** relative to the "time constant" **k**. If the timestep gets too large, numerical instability does occur. Higher order methods allow higher timesteps, but do not prevent the problem.

Accurate simulation always implies that the timestep remains comparable to the time constant of the system. Unfortunately, for large systems, a local small time constant in one place of the system is enough to destabilize the whole system. The simulation efficiency of such stiff systems using explicit methods is constrained by this small local timestep for stability reasons, even if we do not care at all about the simulation accuracy for this particular region.

As stated previously, the implicit methods are the key for dealing with instability problems. Considering the resolution of system (21) using the inverse Euler method and equation (9), we obtain:

$$X_0 = X(0)$$
$$X_{n+1} = X_n + \left(1 - \frac{\partial X'}{\partial X}\bigg|_n dt\right)^{-1} X'_n dt = X_n \frac{k}{k+dt} \tag{24}$$

If **dt** is relatively small compared to **k**, the expression (24) behaves similarly to the expression (23). However, when **dt** becomes relatively big compared to **k**, the succession quickly converges to 0 which is actually the final limit of the evolution (Fig. 2.44).

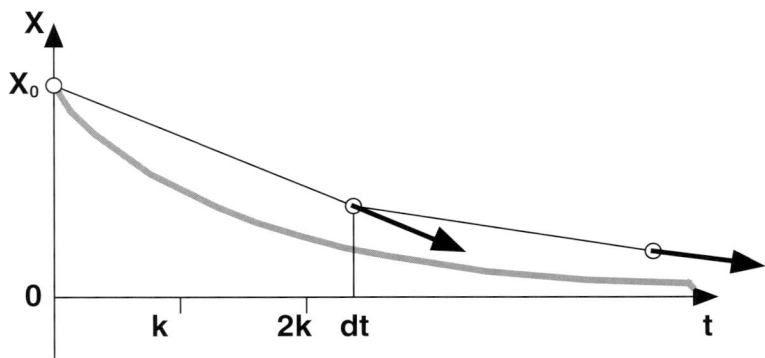

Fig. 2.44. Convergence of the backward Euler method with large timestep.

This example illustrates the superiority of the implicit methods in regard to numerical stability, as the derivative evolution evaluation is a good hint for guessing the equilibrium state of the system to which the simulation should converge to. A too large timestep will thus give a result closer to the equilibrium rather than a wrong extrapolated value. This does not however always mean more accuracy, as the dynamic phenomena arising with time constants smaller than the timestep, will totally disappear. Unfortunately also, the simple division shown in this 1-dimensional example (24) turns into a huge linear system to be solved when the problem dimensionality becomes high. The only and the major drawback of implicit methods is the linear system resolutions implied for problems with huge state vectors.

2.5.2 Choosing the Suitable Integration Method

For a given problem, the adequate integration method should be defined considering:

- The required accuracy of the simulation that may limit the timestep.
- The required accuracy for a given timestep, which is related to the accuracy order.
- The numerical stability issues that may also limit the timestep.

2.5 Numerical Integration

- Other factors limiting the timestep, such as some required high frequency phenomena to be retraced or accurate collision detection and response.

- The amount of time required for the computation of a timestep.

- The structure of the problem allowing certain computation tasks to be simplified.

Obviously, implicit methods have their advantages in most applications for computer graphics where numerical stability is the main issue. Most particle systems used for cloth simulation are stiff systems, where the important behavior to be reproduced is the global cloth motion, discarding the unwanted high-frequency phenomena related to particle vibration, which are only the result of the discrete structure. While explicit methods require to have timesteps adapted to the frequencies of these vibrations to prevent numerical instability, implicit methods can afford dealing with timesteps only adapted to the macroscopic behaviors of the cloth. Unfortunately, the computation time required for one implicit step is much higher than for most explicit methods.

Implicit methods are also not a universal panacea that resolves efficiently any kind of simulation. They are low in order meaning that despite their stability, the solution they propose is not necessarily an accurate solution, particularly when using large timesteps. Actually, they only ensure the stability by "guessing" the equilibrium state of the system (through additional computation requiring the knowledge of the state derivatives and system resolution) and converging to this guess when the timestep becomes large.

Many dynamical effects may disappear in these approximations, leading to disturbing artifacts such as excessive dampening. For instance, having a stiff hanging cloth rectangle, an implicit method will efficiently pull back the displaced vertices to their equilibrium positions with respect to their neighbors, but may completely fail to reproduce global draping effects resulting from gravity and weak curvature forces when using refined meshes. The reason is that when high curvature and complex global deformations are involved, the complex and non-linear evolution of the system to its equilibrium state cannot be computed only from the knowledge of the linear derivatives at the current state. The most observable effect are folds and wrinkles that seem not to evolve despite all the interactions exerted on the cloth. In some extreme cases, such a cloth would not even fall through its own weight.

You get what you pay for. Whatever technique you use for performing the simulation. In the case of explicit methods, you have to pay for accurate computation of the motion of every particle. This may take a lot of computational resources, but the result will be very accurate through the use of high-order methods describing the whole evolution completely. With implicit methods, you find a way to "cheat" the previous methods in order to allow higher computation inaccuracy without compromising numerical stability that may arise from the local dynamic properties of your mesh, and pay less for a more approximate result (but possibly realistic, as you care only for the macroscopic motion and not for all individual particles). This is obtained through an evaluation of the equilibrium position, so you have to pay some extra for this knowledge. The first-order approximation you get from the current state might not be valid through all the deformations you expect. Finally, as stated above, the resulting approximations are likely to prevent the reproduction of complex global dynamic motions of very refined meshes.

Different options can be considered depending on the nature of the application integrating the mechanical system:

- *Real-time and interactive systems*: its speed, more than the computation inaccuracy, is likely to deteriorate the visual perception and motion quality. Such a system usually needs timesteps to allow frame rates of at least five images per second. On the other hand, quantitative accuracy of the dynamic behaviors is not usually required, visual realism being enough. Simple particle systems do fine in these cases, using a fast and approximate integration method. Implicit method can be considered if the system is simple enough to implement simplifications that will reduce the computation time of each timestep for allowing a correct frame rate. This is usually obtained with the use of regular meshes and simple linear interaction between particles. Explicit methods should be considered when dealing with complex models and behaviors, or when very fast iterations are required on rough meshes.

- *Off-line visual simulation systems*: Such systems usually perform more accurate computations on refined models. The mesh size becomes an important factor, as well as its refinement and the numerical stiffness resulting from it. Implicit methods can be useful to deal with stiff systems rapidly, at the expense of accuracy. If the bottleneck is accurate, high-order explicit system should rather be considered, which can provide several orders of better accuracy for small timesteps.

- *Precise simulation systems*: Such systems usually use complex mechanical models on refined meshes. Continuum mechanics models would rather be suitable for these systems. Small timesteps are necessary not only for accurate simulation, but also as an example for all the collision phenomena that have to be reproduced accurately. When using particle systems, high-order explicit integration methods are usually suitable.

While the correct choice would actually depend on each particular context and situation that would allow a given method to be implemented in a particularly efficient way, the general rule is to consider implicit methods for robust simulation of stiff systems using large timestep, and explicit methods for accurate simulation of more complex systems and behavior.

3 Collision Detection

Garments characteristically do not exist in isolation, floating in the air. They interact with the objects in their environment – in most instances either with the body that wears them or with other garment pieces.

Modeling and simulating these interactions are essential to realistic simulation. A garment takes the shape of the body that wears it and follows its movements not only through its elastic behavior, but by its contact with the body.

The aim of collision detection procedures is to compute the geometrical interactions between objects and to perform this task efficiently whatever the number and complexity of the objects may be.

After introducing the problem of algorithmic complexity, we present the major algorithms that are used to perform collision detection. Finally, we discuss an efficient algorithm specially adapted for detecting self-collisions on animated polygonal meshes.

3.1 The Collision Detection Problem

3.1.1 Introduction

Virtual objects are determined only by a formal description in the computer's memory. They do not occupy any "real" volume in space. Nothing prevents several such objects from occupying the same volume in virtual space. However, if these objects were to represent solid objects simultaneously existing in a common scene, they would be unrealistically interpenetrating.

Collision management aims to produce, in the virtual world, what is "built in" to the real world: Objects should interact to prevent geometrical interference. The obvious mechanical interactions that occur during the contact of real objects, have to be completely remodeled in the computer world.

3.1.1.1 Collision Detection and Response

Collision effects are the consequences of the fact that two objects cannot share the same volume at the same time. When objects touch, interaction forces maintain this volume exclusion. The most important are the reaction forces which oppose geometrical intersection. The next important are the friction forces which prevent objects from sliding against each other.

From the point of mechanical simulation, dealing with collisions involves two types of problems:

- *Collision detection*: To find the geometrical contacts between the objects.
- *Collision response*: To integrate the resulting reaction and friction effects in the mechanical simulation.

These two problems are different in nature: the former is essentially geometrical whereas the latter is more relevant to the mechanical modeling. The collision detection is the subject of this chapter, and the collision response is the subject of the next.

3.1.1.2 Detection Problems

Various issues must be resolved in defining a good collision detection algorithm.

A. Complexity
The main problem in collision detection is to master the computational complexity due to the discretization. The cloth surface, as well as the surface of the body, is represented by polygonal meshes that can have several thousand polygons each. Testing each pair of polygons for

potential collisions is an unrealistic task. This *complexity problem* drives the development of advanced algorithms for collision detection.

The complexity of collision detection may arise in different ways. One is in the detection of collisions between numerous objects wandering in space. Another involves collisions between two complex objects consisting of a set of elementary primitives (Fig. 3.1). Cloth simulation, which deals with complex surfaces, is concerned with this second aspect.

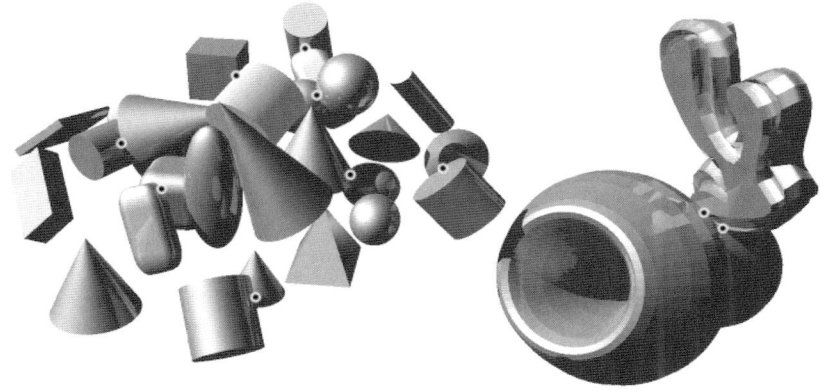

Fig. 3.1. Collisions between multiple objects, and between complex objects.

In the case of deformable objects such as cloth, collisions arise not only between different objects, but also possibly between two parts of the same object. The particular case of *self-collision detection* leads to specific questions about the algorithmic efficiency (Fig. 3.2).

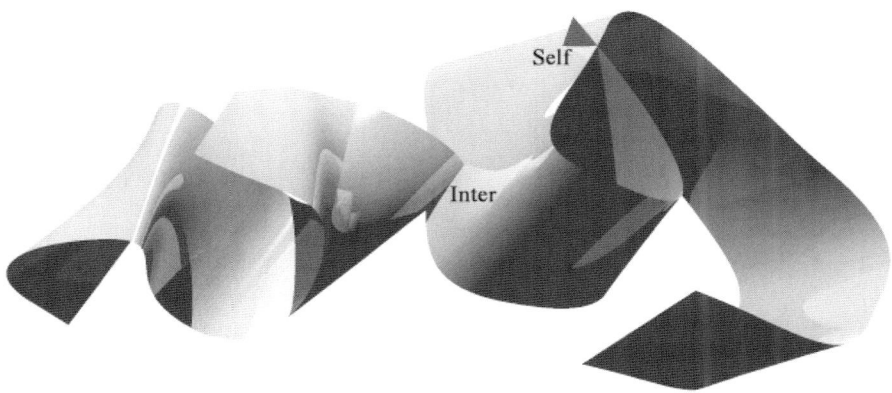

Fig. 3.2. Inter-collisions and self-collisions.

A detection algorithm should remain efficient in any situation that might arise during the simulation. Particular contexts may defeat the optimization mechanism of some algorithms. This *robustness* issue has to be considered when choosing an appropriate algorithm.

B. The Nature of Collisions

Geometrical collision detection can consist of detecting whether the objects interpenetrate (*interference detection*), or the objects come closer than a given threshold distance (*proximity detection*). The two problems are similar, but their interpretation for purposes of collision response may differ depending on the applications (Fig. 3.3).

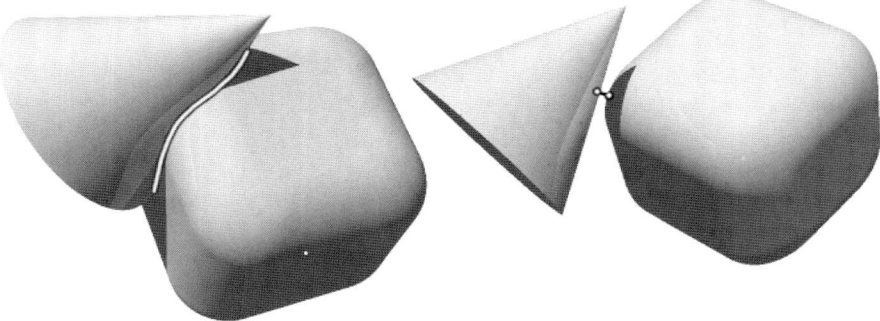

Fig. 3.3. Interference and proximity between two objects.

Collision detection relies on efficient geometrical tools for evaluating interference and proximity among the objects and their primitives. Whatever the choice of these tools, however, the most important problem is how the efficiency of the collision detection is hampered by the complexity.

3.1.2 Mastering Complexity

Detecting the object contacts and its proximity is, by itself, not very difficult. Depending on the kind of geometrical objects considered, it is always possible to subdivide them into simple primitives. Appropriate mathematical tools are available to determine the geometrical properties of the collisions.

3.1.2.1 Where Naive Methods Fail

One of the simplest collision detection algorithms is quite easy to implement: for all objects or geometrical primitives in the scene, we could test collisions between all the possible pairs, using the geometrical tools. Based on the procedure *ComputeObjCollision(objk,objl)* that uses these tools for computing collisions between two objects and on a set of **n** objects **obj1..objn**, we write the algorithm as follows:

```
for k from 1 to n-1
    for l from k+1 to n
        ComputeObjCollision(objk,objl)
```

When this algorithm is run, the number of calls to the procedure **ComputeObjCollision()** is $n(n-1)/2$. For large **n**, this is approximately proportional to n^2. Thus, this algorithm is said to have quadratic complexity, $O(n^2)$.

This means that if we apply this simple algorithm to a scene containing ten times as many objects, its execution time will increase roughly one hundred times. With one thousand times more objects, it will take about one million times longer. Even if the execution time of the procedure **ComputeObjCollision()** remains very low, this algorithm will suffer greatly from an increasing number of objects.

Thus the real problem the complexity. Given a large number of objects of various configurations, how can we determine *efficiently* the collisions between them? Efficiently means at a reasonable speed, even though the number of objects and primitives might become very large.

Solving this complexity problem is a major focus of research on collision detection, and different solutions have been proposed depending on the geometrical context and situation considered.

3.1.2.2 Principles of Complexity Reduction

Complexity is a function of the combinatorical nature of the problem. While a linear complexity can usually be achieved from the sequential processing of the primitives, quadratic complexity is inevitable if we must consider all possible the pairs of primitives.

Complexity reduction aims to reduce this quadratic behavior to a smaller function, such as logarithmic or linear. This is done in two ways:

- The use of tests between pertinent primitive groupings that might eliminate the need to perform tests between individual elements of these groups. This is usually done by taking advantage of some structural and geometrical consistencies between the primitives to be tested.

- Assuming the continuity in the structural or geometrical properties between successive frames in an animation, allow the incremental computation from frame to frame.

The extraction of relevant geometrical structures from the primitive arrangements to be tested and the consideration of their evolution is the basis of all the optimized algorithms for collision detection, as presented in the next section.

3.1.3 An Overview of Different Techniques

There are many variations of collision detection algorithms, adapted to different geometrical contexts, most of them relying on the geometrical attributes specific to the context in which they are implemented. Nevertheless, they can be classified into groups depending on the general idea which leads to the complexity reduction. The main groups are:

- *Bounding volumes*, where complex objects or object groups are enclosed within simpler volumes that can be easily tested for collisions.

- *Projection methods*, which evaluate possible collisions by considering separately the projections of the scene along several axes or surfaces.

- *Subdivision methods*, based either on the scene space or on the objects, which decompose the problem into smaller space volumes or object regions, usually evaluated through bounding volume techniques. Hierarchical subdivision schemes add efficiency.

- *Proximity methods*, which arrange the scene objects according to their geometrical neighborhood and detect collisions between these objects based on the neighborhood structure.

The following is a descriptive overview of these techniques.

3.1.3.1 Bounding Volumes

As a basic idea for reducing the collision detection complexity, preliminary collision tests can be performed using simplified *bounding volumes* that contain the complex objects to be tested.

A. Principles

A bounding volume is a geometric primitive that contains a group of objects, a complex object, or a group of primitives. Its construction should be simple and straightforward, as should the collision detection with points or other similar volumes. Hence, prior to performing collision detection with the individual objects contained by the volume, fast collision detection with the volume itself is performed. Full detection is carried out only if two volumes intersect. The collision detection algorithm is then:

```
TestCollision(obja,objb) is :
:       if BVolumeCollision(BVolume(obja),BVolume(objb)) then
:       :       TestElementaryCollision(obja,objb)

end
```

Bounding volumes is a general technique used in many collision detection schemes for optimizing the collision detection. It was described for computer graphics applications in [MOO 88]. Most of the collision detection algorithms to be discussed, uses it. It is a fundamental aspect of complexity reduction.

Different types of bounding volumes may be considered, each of them having their own strong points and weaknesses. Among them, the most common are the bounding boxes and bounding spheres. The bounding boxes are usually axis-oriented, described by two opposite corner vertices, and the bounding spheres are described by the center and the radius (Fig. 3.4).

Several criteria are considered in choosing the suitable bounding volumes:

- *Their geometrical or filling efficiency*: How well they contain the objects with minimum empty space.

- *Their compactness*: How many values are required for describing them.

- *Their building simplicity*: How efficiently can they be built from a set of objects, or by merging several other bounding volumes.

- *Their collision detection simplicity*: How efficiently can the collisions be detected between the two volumes, or between a volume and another given primitive.

- Their dependency on the environment: Axis-dependency, scaling,...

While the most common context of collision detection is dealing with objects in three-dimensional space, any of the volumes presented here can be extrapolated into spaces of any dimensionality.

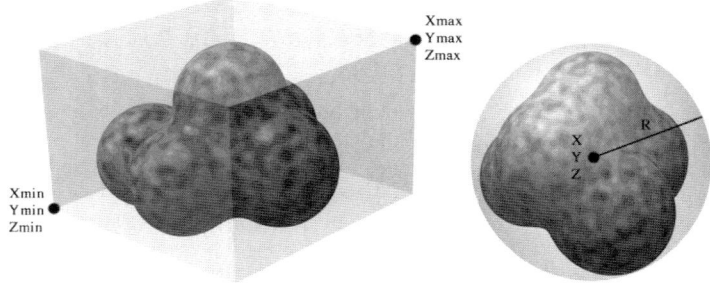

Fig. 3.4. Bounding boxes and spheres, and their characteristics.

B. Axis-Oriented Bounding Boxes

In a three dimensional space, an axis-oriented bounding box is characterized by six values describing the minimal and the maximal axis coordinates of the objects it contains. The axes of the box are aligned to those describing the workspace.

They are very easy to build, to merge, and to detect collisions. Building a box requires only finding its minimal and maximal coordinates which are respectively the minimal and maximal coordinates of the objects it contains. This also applies to merging several boxes together. Intersection tests are performed by simultaneously verifying the coordinate overlap along all the axes (Fig. 3.5).

3.1 The Collision Detection Problem

The advantages of axis-aligned bounding boxes are their fast processing (together with a rather compact representation). Their filling efficiency is however not very good, particularly for the objects elongated in diagonal directions.

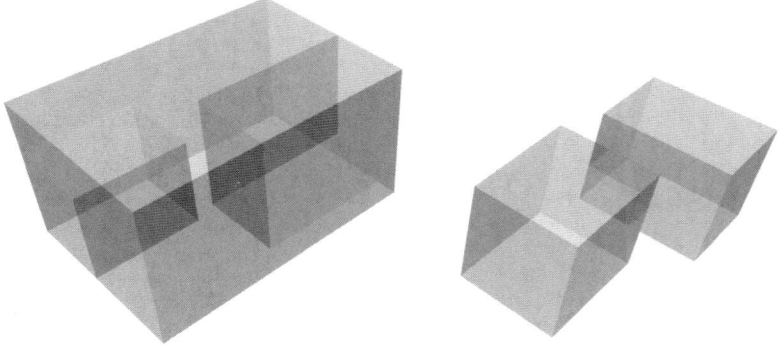

Fig. 3.5. Merging and testing intersection with aligned bounding boxes.

C. Bounding Spheres

A bounding sphere is described by four values: the coordinates of the center and the radius.

They are difficult to build and to merge, requiring complex, non-linear geometrical calculations to find the optimal position of the center. Furthermore, they are not geometrically efficient and do not bound elongated objects tightly. However, their description is very compact, and the collision detection is easily performed by comparing the distance between their centers to the sum of their radii (Fig. 3.6).

The main advantage of bounding spheres comes from the fact that they are not axis-dependent. Thus, they can be transformed by a rigid-body motion along with the transformation of the contained objects and do not need to be recomputed. While bounding boxes are the simplest and the most efficient choice for most of the applications involving deformable objects, bounding spheres can be advantageous in situations involving rigid body motion, such as in robotics. Both types can also be combined, as for example in bounding rigid objects by spheres and then grouping these objects by boxes.

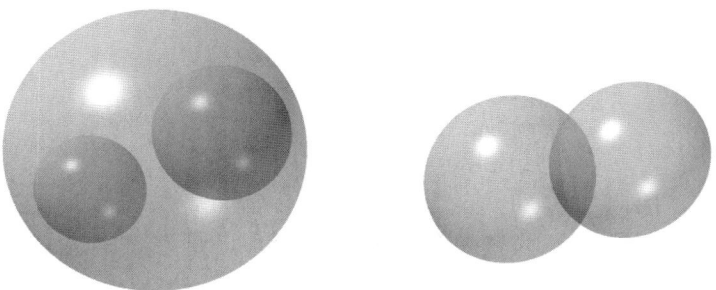

Fig. 3.6. Merging and testing intersection with bounding spheres.

D. Other Bounding Volumes

More complicated bounding volumes may be considered for efficient bounding when a small number of bounding primitives is required. Such volumes use more parameters in their description, allowing a wider range of shapes in optimizing their filling efficiency (reducing their "empty space" so their collisions become more representative of the collisions of the contained objects) and trading away some of their computational simplicity (more complicated shape description).

The choice is highly dependent of the shape of the objects to be bounded. For elongated objects, possible solutions include bounding ellipsoids and cylinders. For specific implementations related more to rendering than to collision detection, bounding metaball structures may also be considered.

Another efficient volume is the Discrete Orientation Polytopes (k-Dops), which are the volumes defined by truncature planes along fixed directions [KLO 97]. Hence, a bounding box is a 6-Dop truncated by planes orthogonal to the (1,0,0), (0,1,0), (0,0,1) directions and their opposites. Among the most common k-Dops, adding all the (1,1,1), (1,-1,1), (1,1,-1), (1,-1,-1) directions and their opposites would define a 14-Dop, which is a box with its corners truncated (Fig. 3.7). A 26-Dop is further truncated along its edges. A k-Dop is easily built by finding the extreme positions along all the relevant directions. Merging and detecting collisions between k-Dops of the same nature are simple, but become more costly as the orientation number k increases.

3.1 The Collision Detection Problem

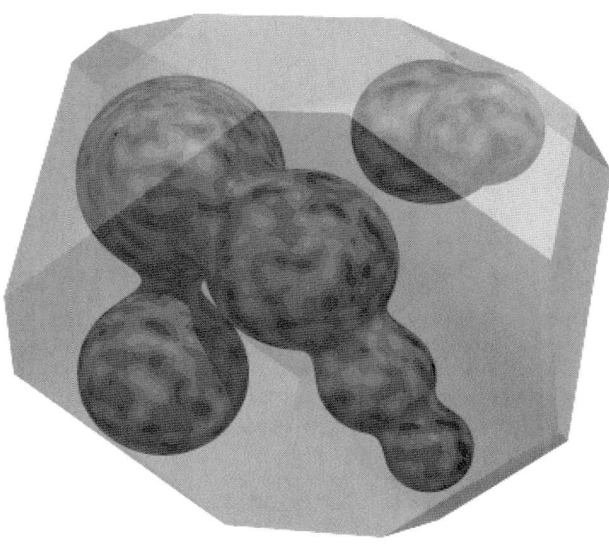

Fig. 3.7. A complex volume bounded by a 14-Dop.

E. Transformed Volumes

Some scene descriptions consist of an hierarchical structure with multilevel geometrical transformations, usually expressed as linear transformation matrices. An object group can then be moved and oriented by changing the corresponding matrix. To avoid recomputing of the bounding volume hierarchy for the whole group, the volumes can be expressed in the local coordinates defined by the current transformation (Fig. 3.8). This can lead to great economies in situations controlled by high-level definition of motion. Another use of transformed volumes is in optimizing the volume of an object, such as in bounding the polygons with "flat" boxes (for example the Oriented Bounding Boxes described in [GOT 96]).

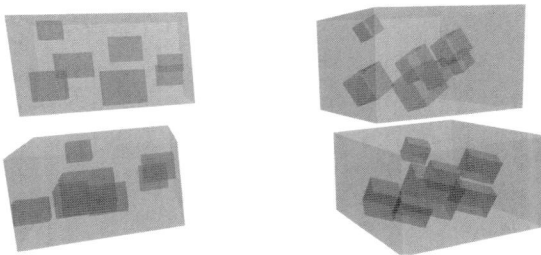

Fig. 3.8 Bounding box hierarchies without, and with transformations.

If the transformations are restricted to the rigid-body motion and the uniform scaling, bounding spheres work well, as translation components only affect their centers, scaling affects their radii and rotation has no effect. When only translation and scaling are considered, axis-oriented bounding boxes are a good solution. In any other cases, the operations of "converting" the volumes as the coordinate system changes are required at the expense of computation and bounding efficiency.

Only by considering the actual geometrical structure, the motion of the scene, and the particular shapes and possible deformations of the objects, we can hope to make an optimal choice of bounding volume structure and management.

F. Expanded Volumes

When proximity detection is based on a fixed threshold distance, bounding volumes are expanded by half of that distance in the detection test. Hence, the volumes will collide if the distance between the enclosed objects is less or equal to the threshold.

G. Bounded Volumes

In an approach similar to the complexity reduction by using simplified bounding volumes for precomputing collisions, *bounded volumes* can also be used for detecting collisions. Those are the elementary volumes which are fully included in the objects to be tested. Computational savings result from the fact that if bounded volumes collide, objects do collide. Full collision test need be performed only when the volumes do not collide. The aim of the bounded volumes is to detect non-collision rather than collision. While bounding volumes are preferable when object collisions are sparse, bounded volumes should be used when almost all the objects collide and interpenetrate to a large extent. While bounding and bounded volumes may combine efficiently in a general collision detection system, the contexts in which bounded volumes efficiently reduce collision detection complexity are rarely encountered.

3.1.3.2 Projection Methods

If objects are geometrically colliding, their projections also collide. This allows us to evaluate collisions quickly in spaces of reduced dimensions.

3.1 The Collision Detection Problem

The principal way to implement this technique is to project the objects onto the coordinate axes. Each object is then represented by an interval on the three axes, which are 1-dimensional spaces where simple interval interference algorithms can be implemented. Hence, the objects are likely to collide if their corresponding intervals on the three axes all collide (Fig. 3.9).

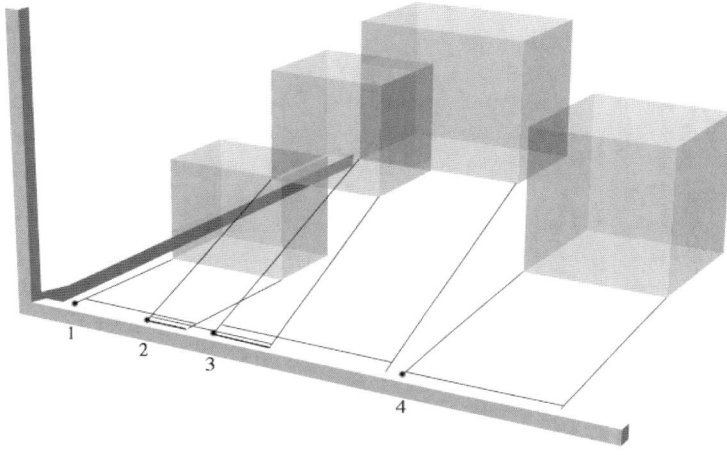

Fig. 3.9 Projecting objects onto axes.

As axes are 1-dimensional, efficient sorting methods for ordering and for sorting the intervals along the axes, and detecting the overlaps quickly can be implemented. Any simplified version of the other collision detection methods may also be implemented for detecting the collisions on the projection axis.

Bounding spheres and the axis-oriented bounding boxes trivially project intervals on the coordinate axes. This technique is particularly efficient when implemented with these kinds of bounding volumes. The main algorithmic difficulties are in building and updating efficiently the collision detection structure along the axes when objects are created and move.

A good example of such a technique is described in [COH 95].

3.1.3.3 Space Subdivision Methods

As numerous objects move in space, one obvious consideration is that collisions need only to be detected between objects that are geometrically close to each other. That is, the objects are in the same region of space. Space subdivision methods divide the space into regions and maintain a list of the objects contained in each region. Collision detection is necessary only between the objects that share a common region.

A. Grid Subdivision

The most straightforward subdivision of space is to divide it into a regular array of boxes called voxels. As the division is regular, it is easy to find the voxel at any point in space belongs to, and thus, the voxels that contain part of a given object (Fig. 3.10).

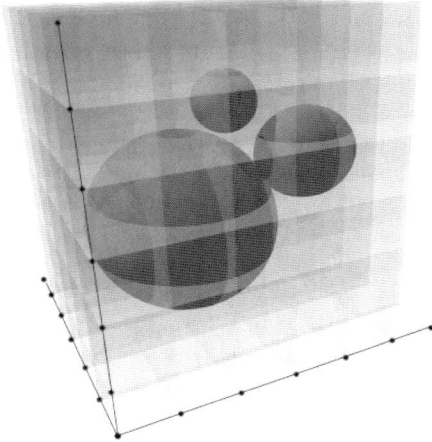

Fig. 3.10 Space voxelisation: Detection only takes place between objects sharing common voxels.

Building voxel-based collision detection algorithms is quite simple. The implementation difficulties arise from the way collisions between pairs of objects are characterized based on their contact in the voxel space, and how the related structures are efficiently updated as the objects move.

The main issue is to choose the optimal space discretization:

- Being too rough, too many objects will be contained in the same voxels.
- Being too refined, there will be too many voxels for efficient collision detection.

The optimal discretization depends on the choice of algorithm, the number of objects, their size and space-filling density, and their motion. More complicated techniques use progressive or dynamic voxel grids.

3.1 The Collision Detection Problem

Rasterisation techniques are related to the voxelisation techniques. They use special algorithms to "render" the objects in smooth voxel spaces. They are often combined with the axis-projection techniques. and use scanline rendering techniques.

B. Hierarchical Subdivision

Grid subdivision techniques suffer from their lack of adaptability to the shapes and geometrical distribution of the objects. The usual way to improve the space subdivision techniques is to implement a local refinement adapted to the context at particular locations in space. Hierarchization is also the best algorithmic technique for improving algorithmic efficiency, often allowing the replacement of a linear term by a logarithmic one in the expression for algorithm complexity.

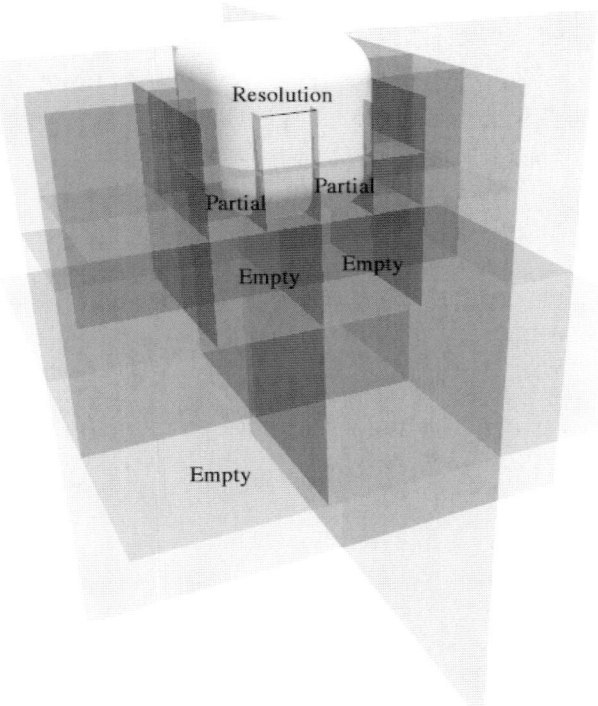

Fig. 3.11. Describing an object volume as an octree hierarchy.

Octree techniques use a hierarchical scheme for the space subdivision [MEA 82] [GRG 82] [FUJ 83] [YAM 84] [CHN 88]. Each space box is divided into eight, equal subboxes using the three, axis-aligned planes at the middle of the box (in 2D and 1D, the similar techniques are called quadtree and bintree). An octree can be defined to describe any volume contained in the space and a given resolution represented by the maximal depth of the octree structure. When dealing with volumes, the nodes of an octree structure have three states:

- *Full* if the corresponding space volume is contained in the object (Black node).

- *Empty* if there is no contact between the corresponding space volume and the object (White node)

- *Partial* if there is partial intersection (Grey node).

Only in the latter case, and only if the volume size is bigger than the desired resolution, the volume is further subdivided in the next step in the hierarchy (Fig. 3.11).

In the context of collision detection, the recursive subdivision should be carried out in any volume containing more than one object. The recursion stops either if no volumes containing two or more objects are found (no collision), or if volumes totally included in several objects are found (collision). Recursion should also stop when the size of the subdivided volumes becomes smaller than the required geometrical accuracy.

For the case in which the objects are described geometrically using octrees, it is simpler to directly test the overlaps between the octree structures. Considering the successive subdivisions of the scene space starting from the whole scene, the following cases are considered:

- If *Full-Full* or *Full-Partial* overlap: Object collision, the test can stop.

- Else if *Partial-Partial* overlap: Uncertain collision, the test should go deeper.

- Else: No collision, the test can stop on this level

The biggest algorithmic question of the octree method is how to update the octree structure efficiently as the objects move or deform. Several algorithmic variations store all the objects in a single octree structure or consider moving the structures for each object.

More general recursive subdivision methods are possible. One such method could adaptively cut a given volume into two halves according to variably cut-planes locally defined. A binary subdivision structure is thus obtained. Intersection tests between these structures, however, become more difficult.

Any subdivision technique can be combined with the projection methods along particular directions in order to speed up detection if there is anisotropy in the geometry of the scene or the motion of the objects.

3.1.3.4 Object Subdivision Methods

In order to overcome the update difficulties of hierarchical space subdivision algorithms as objects move, one approach is to build the hierarchical structure on the objects themselves and the bounding volumes for collision detection at each hierarchy level.

While the octree methods use hierarchies defined on the space they occupy at a given time, the object hierarchies are built on the objects themselves. Thus, the hierarchies are easily updated as the objects move. Hence, while the octree methods are efficient schemes when there is no constant geometrical structure of the problem (example: independent particles), object hierarchy methods are preferable when dealing with objects of constant local topology (example: deformable surfaces).

A. Object Hierarchies

The usual implementation of such hierarchical techniques groups the objects and performs successive tests using the bounding boxes of the groups. Recursively, if one group is colliding, collision tests will be performed for its daughter groups (Fig. 3.12).

The major difficulty of these algorithms is in building the hierarchical tree efficiently. A tree with minimum depth for which each tree node corresponds to a group of objects as close as possible to each other, so the bounding box test would be relevant. As the objects move around, it might be necessary to change the hierarchical organization using the incremental, tree-manipulation techniques, in order to reflect the changes in the proximity among the objects.

Various schemes derived from hierarchy trees have been implemented [HEL 95]. In [WEB 92] and [WEB 93], bounding box hierarchy trees are constructed on the objects and dynamically updated as the objects move. Bounding sphere hierarchies are considered in [PLM 95] and [HUB 96], object aligned bounding boxes are considered in [GOT 96], and k-

Dop trees in [KLO 97]. Specific implementation of these methods should be considered when dealing with polygonal meshes, as will be detailed in Part.3.2.

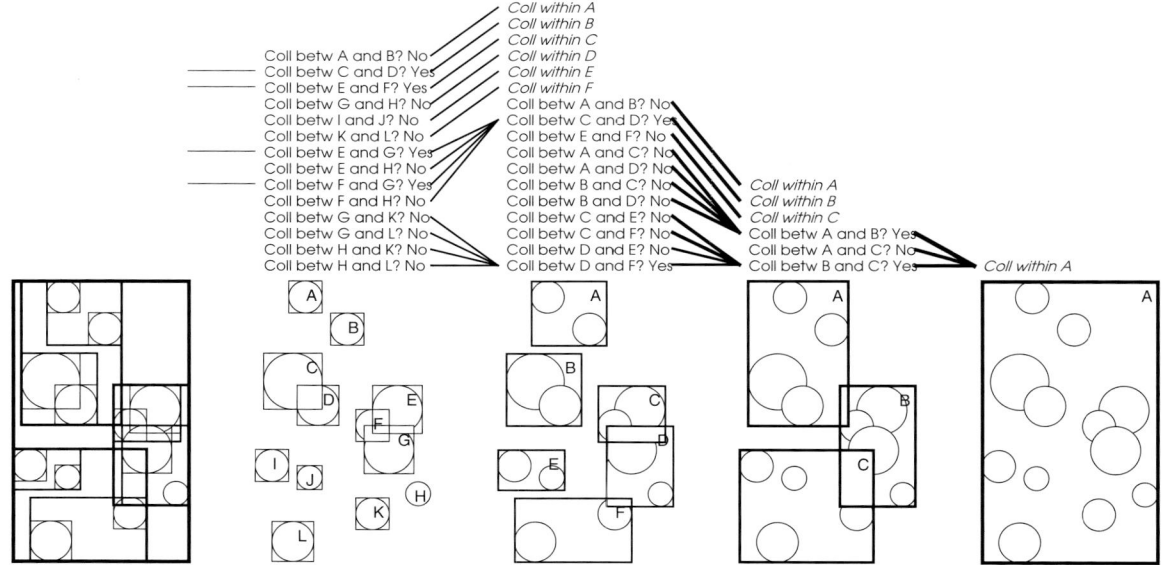

Fig. 3.12. Collision detection in a bounding box hierarchy.

B. Hybrid Hierarchies

The advantages of object hierarchies can be combined with the properties of space hierarchies, using the techniques detailed in [CRL 85] [CLR 87] [NAV 87] [BRU 90]. Most of these methods are based on the octree spatial subdivision or on the binary tree adaptive variants. However, instead of considering the tree as the only description of the object down to a given resolution, the tree is only a support defining a hierarchy on an actual polygonal representation of the mesh elements (usually the vertices, but possibly also the polygons and the edges). Hence, the tree subdivision carries on until the mesh elements are isolated.

These implementations are particularly useful for geometrical modeling and for including the fast boolean operations on complex volumes. However, they can also be used for collision detection, based on the interference between the hierarchichal trees of objects. A particular implementation is described in [GRB 94].

3.1.3.5 Proximity Tracking Techniques

An intuitive way of improving the efficiency of collision detection is to detect only those between the objects that are close to each other. Using computational geometry techniques, a "vicinity map" of the objects can be built and updated as the objects are displaced (Fig. 3.13).

Voronoi domains can be exploited for this purpose. A Voronoi domain, with for one object, contains the space points that are closer to this object than for other objects. There are techniques for building Voronoi domains for a set of objects with **O(n log n)** complexity. For simplification, bounding spheres may be considered as replacement of the objects themselves. Collision detection is only necessary between the objects in neighboring domains. The most difficult aspect of the algorithm is in updating the domains and their neighboring connectivity as the objects are moved around.

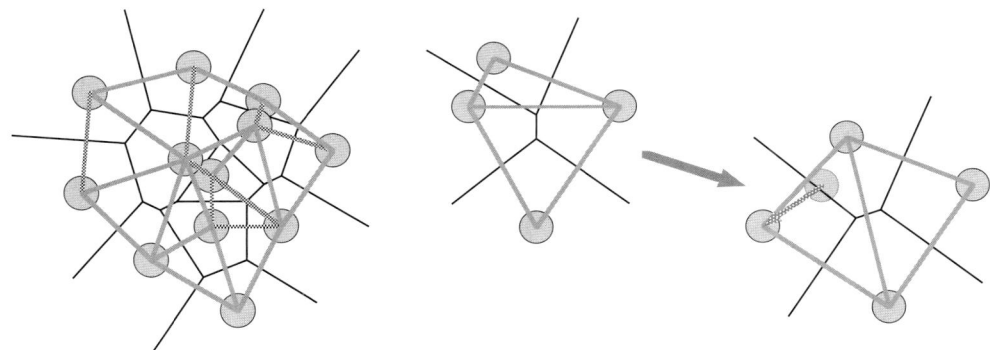

Fig. 3.13. Proximity tracking based on Voronoi domains, incrementally updated as the object moves.

One type of algorithmic variation tracks the closest distance between the sets of objects referring to their bounding spheres or, more efficiently to their convex hulls. The neighborhood may be determined roughly using, for example, a quick octree evaluation.

3.1.3.6 Incremental Techniques and Animated Sequences

In animation, full collision detection must be performed at least once for a given set of objects. The related data structures have to be built. The corresponding computation of **O(n^2)** complexity for simple and naive algorithms, can at best be reduced to **O(n log n)** using the techniques based on recursive binary subdivision. In the worst case, the whole process is repeated each time the collision detection has to be performed.

However, for most applications where collisions have to be detected for moving objects, the detections are carried out on successive configurations of the geometry of the scene where the objects slightly change position from one frame to another.

In many cases, **O(n)**, an incremental update of the collision detection structure, rather than a full **O(n log n)**, can ensure efficient collision detection when the objects have moved from frame to frame.

A. Constant Topologies

Some objects by nature, maintain a relatively consistent geometry. For instance, it would be a waste of time to test for the collisions between the two ears of a human head. While objects are deforming and moving, local deformations might also be quite small and slow. For instance, while a hand can move relatively quickly, all its fingers may have approximately the same relative motion. At a lower level, the neighboring polygons of a deforming mesh, keep approximately their relative positions. This consistency can be exploited, for example, by hierarchical structures built accordingly and which do not need to be updated with time.

B. Slow Evolution

Another consideration is that displacements are small between the two successive steps of an animation. This time-based continuity allows the simplification of collision detection by keeping constant detection structures between frames. A "tolerance region" around the objects has to be introduced in order to compensate for the expected movements (Fig. 3.14).

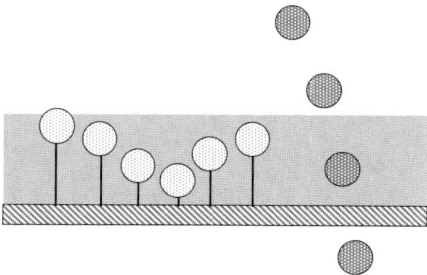

Fig. 3.14. A collision (here en a sphere and a surface) is tracked incrementally within an awareness distance.

This detection distance is also usually associated with a response domain, allowing correct collision effects on discretized motion. Tracking the evolution of the detected collisions incrementally within this awareness region is another way to decrease the computation time.

The description of collision detection for animated objects is found in [CUL 86].

C. Simplification Methods

In order to simplify the detection process, one economy is to sort the possible collisions by order of importance to the quality of the simulation and to truncate the processing at a given relevance threshold. This is possibly based on the kinematic or the dynamic factors (the degree of inaccuracy introduced by omitting the collision from the simulation), or on the perceptual factors obtained from the user. Such methods, usually quite complex, have to take advantage of the consistency of the model over time and are usually integrated into more general Level-of-Detail mechanisms.

3.1.3.7 Collisions on Polygonal Meshes

Deformable surfaces are often described in terms of polygonal meshes. This is usually the case, for example, in cloth simulation. Instead of addressing the difficulty of determining which surfaces collide when dealing with numerous surfaces, the main collision detection applications try to search efficiently for those surface polygons which are colliding, when considering highly refined meshes containing thousands of polygons.

A. Neighborhood Structure

The techniques previously described can be applied, considering each mesh polygon as an individual primitive. For efficiency, however, the algorithms should be adapted and tuned to the specific nature of polygonal meshes: numerous flat elements, connections between neighboring elements, a locally fixed topology, and a slightly deforming geometry during animations. This opposes to "polygon soups" where all the polygons are independent and evolving freely.

Fig. 3.15. A polygonal mesh and a polygon soup.

While collision detection has to find all the pairs of intersecting polygons, there are important differences. In polygon soups, each polygon is considered independently and tested for all the possible collisions. In polygonal meshes, on the other hand, the polygons are structured in neighborhood relations, and each polygon is naturally adjacent to a certain set of neighbors. Collision detection should not be triggered these adjacencies and collisions only tested for between polygons that are not structurally in contact through the definition of the mesh.

B. Collisions & Self-Collisions

The collision detections between two different objects and within a single object, might seem to be very similar problems. In both cases, groups of elements have to be tested for collisions. Indeed, self-collision detection may be affected using any standard collision detection algorithm, by detecting the collisions between an object and itself and by removing any irrelevant collisions such as an element colliding with itself.

In self-collision, and particularly on polygonal meshes, more disturbing categories of irrelevant collisions detected by this algorithm are caused by structural adjacencies of the elements in the mesh: neighboring elements are touching each other and therefore, "collide". Due to the numerous adjacencies occurring in a polygonal mesh (polygon pairs sharing at least a common vertex), the performance of traditional collision detection algorithms deteriorates seriously in self-collision detection, even on almost flat surfaces which contain very few or no self-collisions.

Specific algorithms have to be defined in order to deal with this problem, such as the one detailed in Part 3.2.

C. Discretization and Mesh Complexity

The mesh description accuracy of a curved surface depends directly on the refinement of the elements of that mesh (i.e. on the size and the number of mesh polygons). While the number of collisions involved in a curved surface only depends on the formal geometry of that surface, the complexity of detecting these collisions on the corresponding polygonal mesh increases with the number of elements. Collision detection on polygonal mesh surface representations thus should be able to handle a very large number of elements while detecting only a small number of collisions.

Complexity is thus an essential consideration in collision detection on polygonal meshes. For instance, a quadratic algorithm would have its computation time increased sixteen times as the mesh accuracy doubles, because the number of mesh elements increases four times. Hierarchical collision detection algorithms are best suited for this kind of problem.

On the positive side, the elements constituting a mesh always keep the same neighbors and therefore, maintain the similar relative positions. Collision detection techniques can take advantage of this consistency during animation by building the hierarchical description of the objects from those relative proximity which stay constant between all the detections in an animation sequence. Hence, hierarchies should be based on the shapes of the objects rather than on the occupied volume.

D. Object Proximity

In one particular type of collision detection, many algorithms have been defined for computing the distance between several objects. Quite easy to solve when dealing with convex objects, this problem becomes difficult in the more general case of complex, non-convex objects.

This topic has been extensively studied for polygonal objects [GIL 88] [GIL 90]. The Gilbert-Johnson-Keerthi algorithm (GJK) defines the distance between two objects to be the difference of the Minkowsky distances of the two objects from the origin. The closest point is then tracked making use of the convex hull. Several optimized implementations of this algorithm exist, as described in [CAM 97]. The Lin-Canny algorithm and its derivatives (V-Clip) are based on the construction of Voronoi domains which delimit, for each mesh element [MIR 98].

3.1.4 Robustness

While collision detection algorithms take advantage of the simplified geometrical assumptions in order to carry out their computation efficiently, particular geometrical situations may not satisfy these assumptions. This could lead to unreliable algorithms that "miss" some collisions or degrade the performance caused by the increased of computational complexity.

3.1.4.1 Degeneracies

The first type of problem arises from the lost efficiencies due to some particular, geometrical configuration of the objects. The algorithm is said to be degenerate in these cases, and its complexity, usually $O(n \log n)$ (average complexity), might increase to $O(n^2)$ (worst-case complexity).

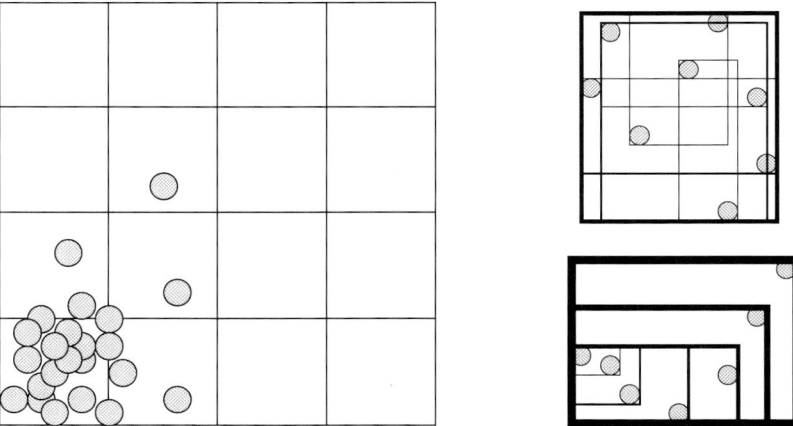

Fig. 3.16. Degenerate computations in voxel and hierarchical algorithms. Left: a voxel containing most of the objects of the scene. Top: A bad hierarchy where all the object groups collide. Bottom: A degenerate hierarchy with high hierarchy depth.

Some algorithms degenerate easily. For instance, if all the objects group themselves into a small number of voxels, a voxel-based collision detection algorithm would spend $O(n^2)$ time for computing collisions within these voxels. Hierarchical algorithms may degenerate if their hierarchy tree is degenerate (**O(n)** depth) due to an inappropriate tree construction algorithm, or if the tree does not reflect the actual proximity between the objects causing all the tree branches to collide with each other (Fig. 3.16).

In the hierarchical algorithm proposed in the next section, the tree construction method ensures that a balanced tree will be generated, where each node has a finite number of children. No degeneracy occurs from this, whatever the topology of the created mesh may be.

The major cause of degeneracy is inherent in the bounding-box method. If the surface is crumpled enough so that non-adjacent and non-colliding tree nodes frequently collide with their bounding boxes, the performance of the algorithm will suffer. This results from the irregular meshes and the hierarchical domains of irregular shapes. The adjacency problem would reappear despite the efficiencies based on curvature, and the algorithm would revert to the performance of a hierarchical algorithm without savings.

3.1.4.2 Coherence artifacts

Some algorithms rely on the assumptions of consistency between frames for optimizing the computation. Time coherence is most often used for computing collisions in animations. The assumption is that only small changes differentiate successive states where the collision detection is performed, and very small incremental updates suffice within the collision detection structures. Pathologically sudden transformations may result in sharp discontinuities between successive states so that the incremental-update algorithms may fail to perform their job efficiently. If the assumption of geometrical identity do not hold, the detection algorithm misses some collisions.

The most common assumption is that the displacements of the objects between successive frames remain small. While the detection-distance tolerance usually compensates for these displacements, fast-moving objects may go through the objects between two frames without any collision detection. Time-expanded bounding boxes may solve this particular problem (Fig. 3.17).

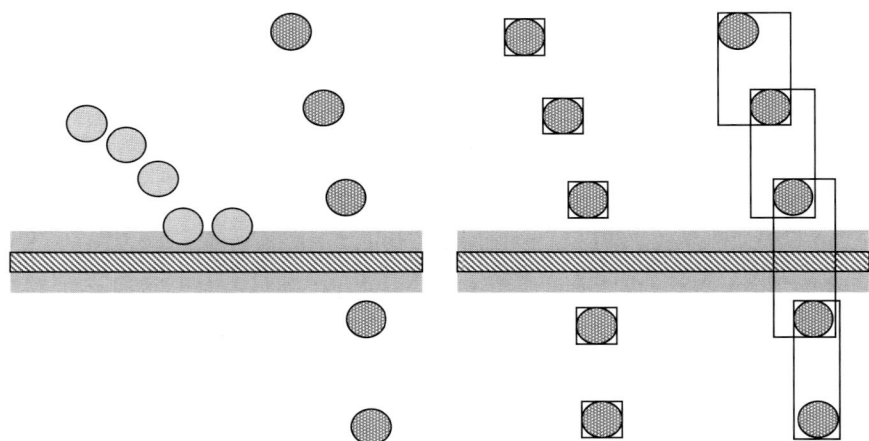

Fig. 3.17. The frame traversal problem (shown here with a sphere that should bounce on a surface), solved by time-extended bounding boxes.

3.2 A Hierarchical Scheme for Polygonal Meshes

Cloth objects and most of the objects in a scene are usually represented by animated polygonal meshes which are animated along time by move the positions of the mesh vertices in the space along time. This section details an algorithm optimized for collision detection of cloth surfaces in the context of animation and mechanical simulation, including efficient solutions for the fast detection of self-collisions.

The presented algorithm is based on a hierarchical bounding-box scheme constructed on the mesh elements. The algorithm is optimized for self-collision detection, by using the surface curvature evaluation within surface regions defined by the hierarchy.

3.2.1 Collision Detection on Hierarchical Meshes

One particularly efficient way to deal with the complexity problem is to use a hierarchical scheme, as presented in Part.3.1.3.4. Such a scheme would take an advantage of the structural continuity between the elements of the polygonal meshes during the animation.

3.2.1.1 Principle

The first step is to build a tree consisting of successive subdivisions of the entire scene, according to the proximity rules. Each tree leaf, being a surface element, is a polygon. Then, a bounding-volume hierarchical structure on the tree nodes is built. This is updated as the animation evolves. Collision detection is performed by testing the bounding-volume contact between the two nodes of the tree. If there is a contact, the test is resumed by recursively testing the daughter nodes. The algorithm yields the polygon elements for which the bounding boxes are colliding.

This algorithm is particularly efficient for detecting the collisions between two different objects, and if well implemented, the detection computation time can be proportional to the number of collisions multiplied by the logarithm of the total number of elements for the detection phase, preceded by a preprocessing step which is proportional to the number of elements for computing bounding volumes and propagating them up the hierarchy.

A node of the hierarchical tree is a surface region containing a certain number of polygonal elements. Considering a complete surface as being the root of the hierarchy, the daughter nodes are built recursively by successive subdivisions of the surface region of a parent node. The leaf nodes of the tree are the individual polygons of the surface.

To each tree node, a bounding volume is associated. Bounding boxes are adequate because of the processing speed. Each polygon is included in a bounding box of its corresponding leaf node. The bounding boxes of the other nodes are then computed by merging the bounding boxes of its daughters. The root bounding box is the bounding box of the whole surface.

3.2.1.2 Detecting Collisions

Collision detection is a fairly simple, recursive process.

For testing collisions between two surface regions represented by hierarchical nodes, a recursive scheme is used, implemented using two procedures **TestCollision()** and **TestSelf-Collision()**, for collisions between the elements of two nodes, or within the elements of one node, respectively.

```
TestCollision(obja,objb) is :
```

```
:       if not BBoxCollision(BBox(obja),BBox(objb)) then exit

:       if SizeAggregate(obja)>SizeAggregate(objb) then Swap(obja,objb)
:       if not Elementary(objb) then
:       :    for obj from FirstElement(objb) to EndOfList do
:       :    :    TestCollision(obja,obj)
:       else TestElementaryCollision(obja,objb)

end



TestSelfCollision(obj) is :

:       if not Elementary(obj) then
:       :    for obja from FirstElement(obj) to EndOfList do
:       :    :    TestSelfCollision(obja)
:       :    :    for objb from NextElement(obja) to EndOfList do
:       :    :    :    TestCollision(obja,objb)

end
```

For detecting collisions between two nodes, recursion can be limited by testing their corresponding bounding boxes in the function **BBoxCollision()**. No optimization is available for detecting the collisions within one node, and the collision testing will recurs down to the leaf elements. This is why such an algorithm is not efficient for self-collision detection.

3.2.1.3 Building an Efficient Hierarchy

The performance of the collision detection algorithm is highly dependent on the construction of the hierarchical tree is.

The tree should be well conditioned, meaning:

- Each node should have the maximum O(1) children.
- The tree should be balanced, so the tree should have O(log n) maximum depth.

The bounding-box-based algorithm defines that for each node of the bounding boxes to be minimal, all the regions of the child nodes should be located in the vicinity of each other.

One efficient solution is to build the hierarchical tree using an ascending process. First, the leaf nodes of the tree are constructed, corresponding to all the individual polygons of the surface. Then, an upper layer of the hierarchy is built by grouping two or three nodes in a common parent node. The tree is built level by level until only one element remains, which is the root node of the tree.

The grouping can be performed by the region-merging algorithm. Initially, each surface polygon is assigned a unique, region ID, which identifies a group of polygons. During the grouping process, candidate edges that separate the two different groups (two polygons having different ID) are considered. One of these edges is then selected, and all the polygons of one group (usually the smallest) are assigned the ID of the polygons of the other group. This algorithm generates groups of connected regions, within which all the polygons are connected by at least one edge. A counter should also be included in each group to keep track of the number of subgroups that have been merged in the group. It can be used to limit the number of children in a group. This algorithm is in fact very, close to the automatic, labyrinth-generation algorithms which are based on the same region-merging scheme.

It is important to efficiently determine which nodes to group in order to create the parent node. First, only the adjacent surface regions should be connected. Second, the generated regions should be as "well shaped" as possible (i.e. closer to a disk than a elongated or sprawling branched structure). The resulting bounding boxes will therefore, be as compact as possible, regardless of the result of the 3D deformation of the surface.

A good way to characterize "well-shaped" polygons is to compare its contour length to its surface area. The algorithm can construct groups by minimizing the "shape factor", **sqrt(SurfaceArea)/ContourLength**. At a given hierarchical level, this ratio is computed for any group that can be generated by the removal of an edge. The potential groups are sorted by this criteria, and the new groups are constructed wherever possible, according to this sorting. Between two hierarchical levels, the algorithm first tries to merge groups into pairs, and then merges the remaining groups into these new groups.

Though this proposed grouping process does not necessarily yield hierarchical regions that globally optimize the shape factors, the results obtained are however, quite acceptable for our application. More precisely, the self-collision detection algorithm remains efficient as long as the bounding boxes of the non-adjacent hierarchical groups (that do not share at least a common vertex) do not intersect. Using the proposed algorithm, this feature is verified almost everywhere in the usual polygonal meshes.

This algorithm to builds a hierarchy on any polygonal mesh that will be involved in collision detection. This computation should only be performed as a preprocess, and does not have to be performed for each collision detection when the surfaces have been moved.

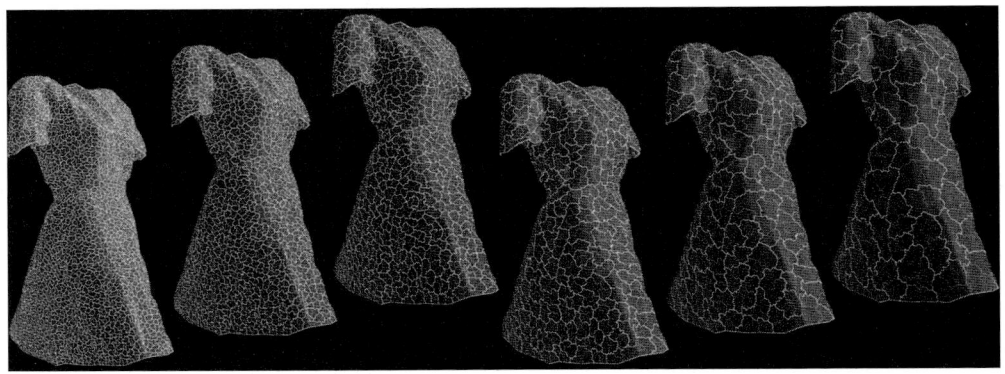

Fig. 3.18 Automatic hierarchisation of a 50000 triangle object. Shown levels: 5 to 10.

3.2.2 Optimizing for Self-Collision Detection

Detecting the self-collisions results in a drastic loss of efficiency for most collision detection algorithms. A good understanding of this problem will allow us to implement an efficient solution.

3.2.2.1 The Adjacency Problem

Self-collision detection pertains to the collisions between elements of the same surface. Of course, neighboring elements of the same surface are naturally in contact with each other. Any collision detection algorithm is designed to detect geometric contact between the elements, and thus will be misled by these adjacent elements as colliding elements (Fig. 3.19).

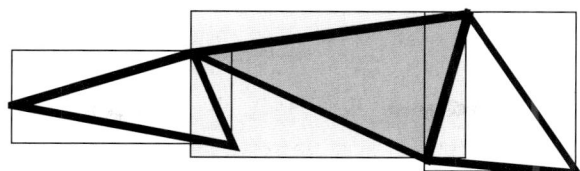

Fig. 3.19. According to bounding boxes, adjacent elements are seen as colliding.

The number of adjacencies is usually proportional to the total number of elements in one surface. In a triangular mesh, the adjacency number is roughly 1.5 times the total number of triangles for common-edge adjacencies and 6 times the total number of triangles for common-vertex adjacencies.

The time spent detecting the collisions is proportional to the number of colliding elements multiplied by the logarithm of the total number of elements. Typically, the number of self-colliding elements is very small compared to the total number of elements and often null if no collisions occur. Thus, "detecting" all the adjacencies as if they were collisions is a great waste of time, particularly in situations with very few collisions.

For efficiency, an algorithm should be designed to ignore all the collisions that are only the elemental adjacencies.

3.2.2.2 The Curvature Criteria

A flat surface cannot have self-collisions. On the other hand, if a surface has self-collisions, it must be bent enough to form a loop (Fig. 3.20).

Is there a way to formalize this intuition? Curvature appears to be the key for the achieving efficiency in self-collision detection.

When there are self-collisions on a surface, the surface appears twice at any geometrical intersection point. For obtaining such configuration, the surface has to be bent enough to form a loop.

This condition cannot be met if there exists a direction for which the orthogonal projection of the surface does not exhibit folds. If the surface is continuous, this means that all the normals of the surface have a dot product of constant sign with that direction vector.

Fig. 3.20. A self-colliding surface forms a loop.

We also have to consider the self-collisions that may occur because of the shape of the surface boundary. This may also exhibit loops even if the surface is almost flat, when the surface contour itself exhibits a loop causing self-intersection. An additional test has to be done on the surface contour. Having found the projection direction for the surface curvature, a sufficient criteria for non-intersection is that the projection of the surface contour along this direction should not self-intersect.

Thus, a surface does not have self-collisions if the following criteria are met (Fig. 3.12):

* Let **S** be a continuous surface in Euclidean space, delimited by one contour **C**.

if

- There exists a vector **V** for which **N.V > 0** at (almost) every point of **S** (**N** being the normal vector of the surface at the considered point)

and

- The projection of **C** on a plane orthogonal to **V** along the direction of **V** has no self-intersections

then

- There are no self-collisions on the surface **S**.

3.2 A Hierarchical Scheme for Polygonal Meshes

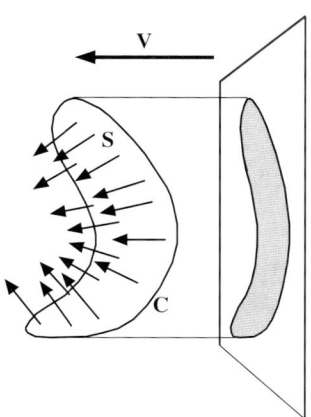

Fig. 3.21. Conditions for no self-collision of a curved surface.

Such criteria allow us to discard, from the detection process, "almost flat" surfaces that will not exhibit the internal self-collisions. The union of two adjacent surface regions may also be "almost flat", so we need not detect the collisions between these two regions. In particular, adjacent elements need not be checked for collisions. Implemented efficiently, this criterion will allow us to deal with the major cause of the inefficiency of self-collision detection.

3.2.2.3 Integration to the Hierarchical Algorithm

As discussed, the general hierarchical collision detection algorithm works with the bounding boxes. There are two main processes:

- For detecting collisions within a surface region, collisions are detected within and between all the children of its corresponding hierarchical tree node.

- For detecting the collisions between two surface regions, collisions are detected between the respective children nodes.

Collisions between two nodes may be efficiently detected using a bounding-box evaluation: if the bounding boxes do not intersect, there are no intersections. However, in the standard hierarchical algorithm, there are no bounding box techniques for self-collision detection within one node. Replacing the bounding box test by a curvature test can overcome this limitation.

A. Curvature Optimization

For the self-collision stage, the integration of the curvature is clear: Collisions should be detected within one node only if the corresponding surface does not match the curvature criteria.

When detecting the collisions between two nodes, we should consider two cases. Dealing with the two adjacent surfaces, collisions should be detected between the nodes only if the corresponding surface union does not verify the curvature criteria (obviously, the bounding boxes will always intersect, so the curvature criteria acts as a good replacement test). Dealing with non adjacent surfaces, the standard bounding box criteria should be used (Fig. 3.22).

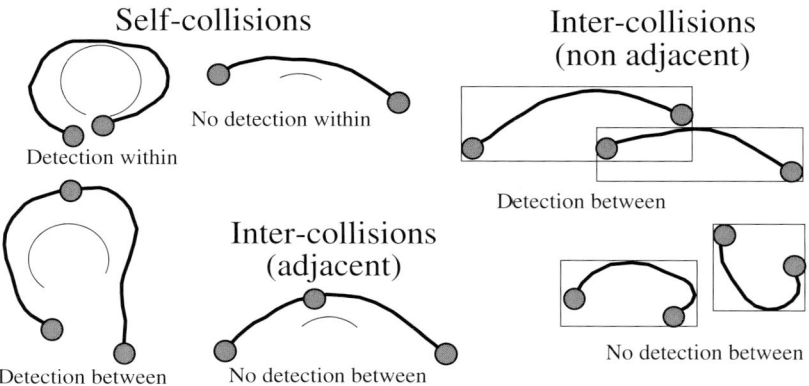

Fig. 3.22. Using curvature or bounding boxes: The different cases.

Thus, the curvature criteria is incorporated into the hierarchical algorithm by replacing the bounding box by a curvature test within the surface regions or between the adjacent surface regions (Fig. 3.23).

As we can see, two extra tests need to be implemented:

- How to determine if a surface region meets the curvature criteria
- How to determine if two surface regions of the hierarchy are adjacent.

3.2 A Hierarchical Scheme for Polygonal Meshes

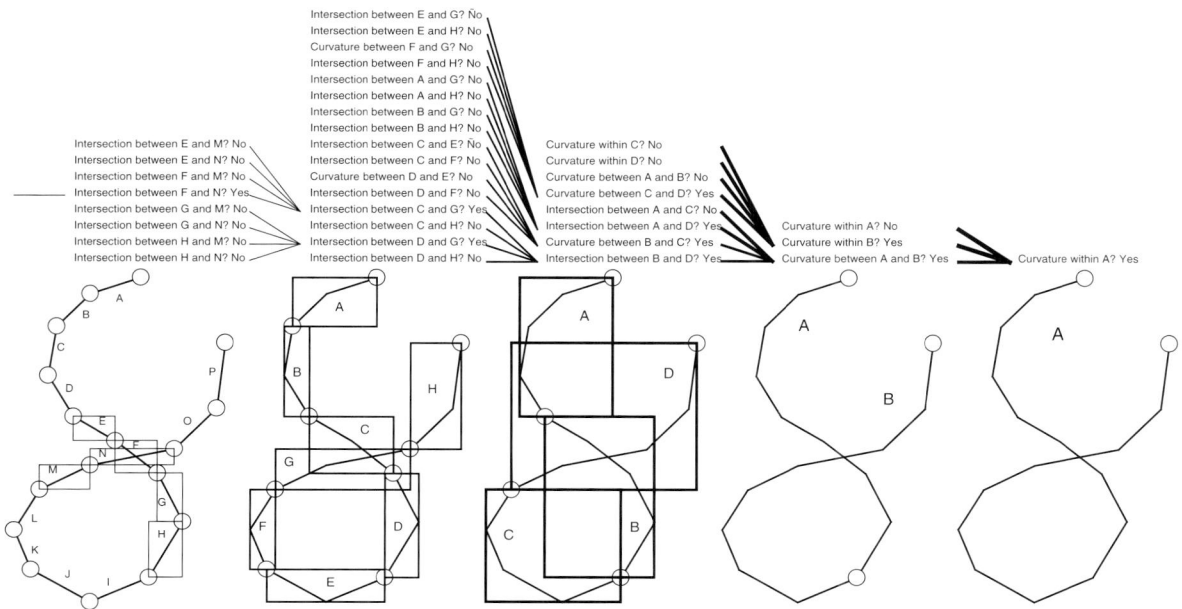

Fig. 3.23. Execution of the algorithm. For adjacent elements, bounding box intersection test is replaced by the curvature test.

B. Curvature Discretization

Given a curved surface, we need to determine and find the existence of a compatible direction vector that has a positive dot product with all the normal vectors of the surface. In our discrete model of the surface, that means that this vector should have a positive dot product with the normals of all the surface polygons.

Similar to what was done for the bounding boxes, "direction boxes" that contain the allowable directions, will be propagated up to the hierarchical parents.

Assimilating the direction space to a sphere, the allowable direction box of one elementary polygon is a half sphere. When we consider two polygons, the globally allowable direction is the common part of the corresponding two sphere halves. This gives us the mechanism that should be propagated upwards in the tree hierarchy. The resulting direction box at the root of the tree may be empty, and in this case no suitable direction can be found for the whole surface. If not empty, any vector within the direction box is suitable.

Unlike bounding boxes that can be represented efficiently using the space coordinates, there is no easy way to describe our direction boxes exactly. That difficulty can be addressed by building a discrete set of direction vectors that will represent our direction space.

There are several possibilities for choosing this set, depending on the required angle accuracy and the number of vectors we can afford to handle for each direction box computation. One way to define a "regular" set is to use the direction defined by the vertices, and the edge and the face middles of a regular polyhedron (a tetrahedron, a cube, a dodecahedron). For instance, a set of 34 sample vectors can be obtained by using the vertices and the face middles of an icosaedron. A simpler alternative to this is to use a set of 26 sample vectors using the vertices, and the edge and the polygon middles of a cube (Fig. 3.24). With this combination, the maximum angle between an arbitrary direction and the closest discrete direction is approximately 25°.

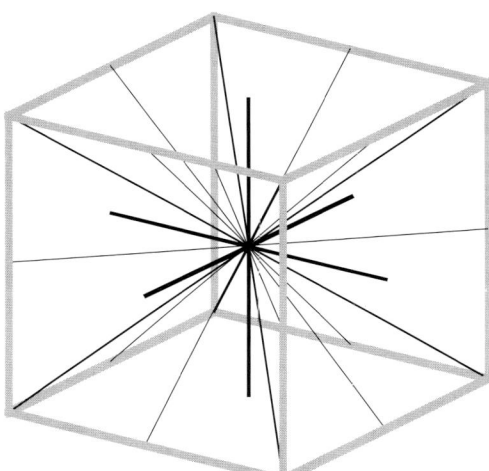

Fig. 3.24. A 26-vector direction sampling set using the vertices, edge and face middles of a cube.

For a given normal direction of a polygon, we then compute which of these vectors has a positive dot product. Using the symmetry of the sampling set, we only need to compute the dot product of the normal vector with half of the set, as opposite sample vectors yield opposite dot products. The result is stored into a boolean array that can, for instance, be the boolean representation of a 32 bit unsigned integer.

3.2 A Hierarchical Scheme for Polygonal Meshes

It is then easy to propagate the direction information upwards in the surface hierarchy, the direction box of a parent node being computed by logically AND-ing the boolean arrays of its children (Fig. 3.25).

For any surface node of the hierarchy, if the boolean array is completely null, the corresponding surface does not verify the curvature criteria. If not, any non-null array element corresponds to a suitable projection direction. For projection simplicity, it is preferable whenever possible, to choose an axis-aligned direction.

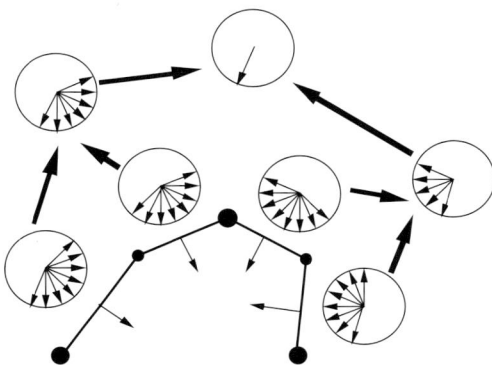

Fig. 3.25. Propagating the curvature criteria in the surface hierarchy.

In this way, we are able to test if a surface node verifies the curvature criteria and if so, obtain a suitable projection direction. Using the same technique, we can verify whether or not the two adjacent surface nodes globally match the curvature criteria.

C. Surface Contour Intersection

Having checked the surface internal curvature and the projection vector, we still need to verify if the projected surface contours intersect or not.

After projecting the contour-polygonal segments onto the orthogonal plane, it would be possible to define an algorithm which takes advantage of the existing hierarchy and to compute, using bounding rectangles, which boundary segments intersect. This solution is however, impractical as it is quite complex and noticeably slows down the computation. By implementing a simple, brute-force algorithm, we find that the boundary intersection criteria is never decisive in the final collision detection process. Our current algorithm does not use this test, and its implementation is removed from the final version.

D. Adjacency Detection

Another major problem is the adjacency test: given two arbitrary nodes in the hierarchy, are the corresponding surfaces adjacent? (Do they have at least one common vertex?)

This represents the major difficulty of our algorithm. This adjacency should be detected efficiently (the computation complexity should be O(log n)), and the extra storage in the tree data structure should be reasonable (the extra information for each node should be O(1)).

For each hierarchical node, a circular list of vertices surrounding the corresponding surface region should be defined. Several circular lists should be considered when dealing with non-connected surfaces with holes. Not all the boundary vertices should be stored, but only the vertices that separate the two different surface regions among those of the highest hierarchy level that also do not include the region being considered (Fig. 3.26). The term "outside" is considered as a particular surface region. Regardless of the node level and the total number of polygons surrounding this surface region, the number of stored vertices is approximately constant. For the usual cases, the meshes hardly exceed six vertices. As the adjacency information depends only on the mesh topology, this stage is usually performed once in the pre-processing stage.

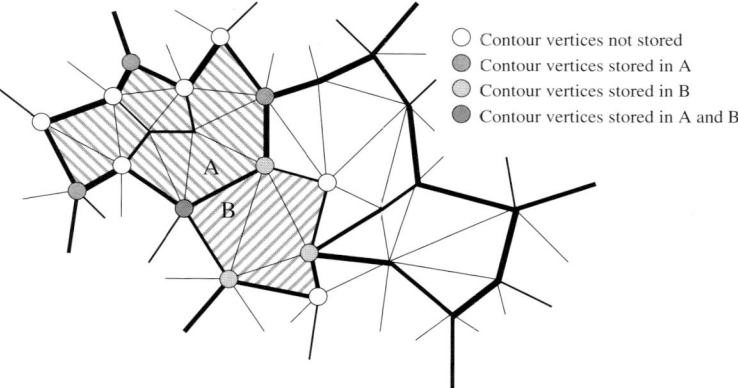

Fig. 3.26. Adjacency test: Two adjacent regions have at least one common stored vertex.

Adjacency testing is then performed easily: two hierarchy nodes are adjacent if and only if they have at least one common vertex among those stored. This test is performed in O(1).

E. Implementation

The implementation of the collision detection algorithm integrates the various points discussed above. It is divided into a preprocessing step, applied once to each object before detecting the collisions, and a processing step which detects the collisions, given a geometrical configuration of the objects.

The preprocessing step serves mainly to build the hierarchy from the polygonal mesh of the object surfaces. Each node of the hierarchy contains the information on the bounding box of the corresponding surface region. If self-collisions are to be detected for this object, the hierarchy node should also contain also the curvature information and the adjacency list. The hierarchy should be updated each time the object mesh topology changes.

The processing step itself detects the collision. First, it updates the bounding box of each node of the hierarchy using the standard, depth-first tree traversal: bounding boxes are computed for the elementary mesh polygons which are the leaves of the hierarchy, and then propagated to the parent nodes by merging the bounding boxes. If self-collisions are to be detected, the curvature criteria is updated in the same way. Detection is then performed using the recursive calls to the two procedures described as follows:

The procedure **TestCollision()** detects the collisions between two surface regions. It accepts a boolean parameter indicating the adjacencies of the regions. The procedure **TestSelfCollision()** detects the collisions within one surface region.

```
TestCollision(obja,objb,testadja) is :

:     if not BBoxCollision(BBox(obja),BBox(objb)) then exit

:     if testadja then
:     :     testadja <= Adjacent(obja,objb)
:     :     if testadja then
:     :     :     V <= FindCommonVector(obja,objb)
:     :     :     if Valid(V) then
:     :     :     :     if not ProjectedContoursIntersection(obja,objb,V)
      then exit

:     if SizeAggregate(obja)>SizeAggregate(objb) then Swap(obja,objb)
:     if not Elementary(objb) then
:     :     for obj from FirstElement(objb) to EndOfList do
:     :     :     TestCollision(obja,obj,testadja)
:     else TestElementaryCollision(obja,objb)
```

```
    end

    TestSelfCollision(obj) is :

    :     V <= FindCommonVector(obj)
    :     if Valid(V) then
    :     :     if not ProjectedContourSelfIntersection(obj,V) then exit
    :     if not Elementary(obj) then
    :     :     for obja from FirstElement(obj) to EndOfList do
    :     :     :     TestSelfCollision(obja)
    :     :     :     for objb from NextElement(obja) to EndOfList do
    :     :     :     :     TestCollision(obja,objb,TRUE)
    end
```

These procedures finally call, whenever necessary (that is, when two non-adjacent polygons are found to be colliding with their bounding-boxes), the procedure **TestElementaryCollision()** which geometrically evaluates the collisions between the two elementary polygons of the surface meshes.

As stated previously, there is no risk in skipping the projected contour intersection tests. This is done by assuming that the procedures, **ProjectedContoursIntersection()** and **ProjectedContourSelfntersection()**, always return the value *FALSE*. Therefore, there is no need to implement them.

3.2.3 Efficiency

The main interest of this algorithm is its efficiency in detecting self-collisions: hierarchy regions that are not curved enough to contain the self-collisions, are efficiently omitted from the detection process. The following figure shows the regions considered when performing the collision detection between the two objects within the objects themselves (Fig. 3.27). We clearly see that the algorithm efficiently focuses on the intersecting parts of the surfaces.

The efficiency of the algorithm can be demonstrated by comparing it to the traditional hierarchical algorithm which detects the self-collisions on simple objects, like a sphere (Fig. 3.28).

3.2 A Hierarchical Scheme for Polygonal Meshes

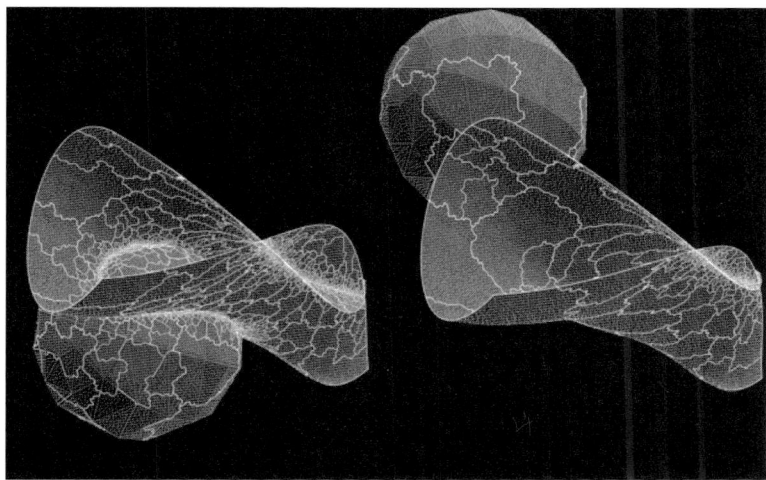

Fig. 3.27. Hierarchical collision detection at work, showing the hierarchy domains tested.

For the classical, hierarchical, bounding-box algorithm, the calculation charge of collision detection increases *linearly* with the total number of elements for the same basic shape using different levels of discretisation. For instance, the collision procedure for the spherical surface is called at an average of 20 times the total number of elementary polygons, and the elementary polygonal intersection procedure is called 6 times that number because of the "false" intersections caused by the adjacencies.

In contrast the algorithm we propose, performs the job with a *very little* and *constant*, calculations independent of the discretisation level. We get an average of 300 calls to the collision procedures, for instance, for the spherical surface, and the elementary polygon intersection procedure is *never* called. The number of hierarchical elements considered during the collision detection, does not increase with the smoothness of the discretisation.

We have also tested a regular surface with a self-intersecting a loop (Fig. 3.28), that's often encountered when simulating fabric deformations. This data set is used for checking the detection efficiency as a function of the number of colliding polygons. For a better comparison, we use the same discretisation rates as the ones for the spherical surface.

The classical, hierarchical, bounding-box algorithm is mainly affected by the total number of polygons, thus giving the performances close to those observed for the spherical surface. In contrast, with the proposed algorithm, the collision detection is now performed with the calculation *linear* to the number of *colliding* polygons. For instance, the collision procedures are called on an average 20 times the number of colliding polygons, and the polygon intersection procedure is called 3 times that number. High discretisation affects the search only on the regions close to the collision points.

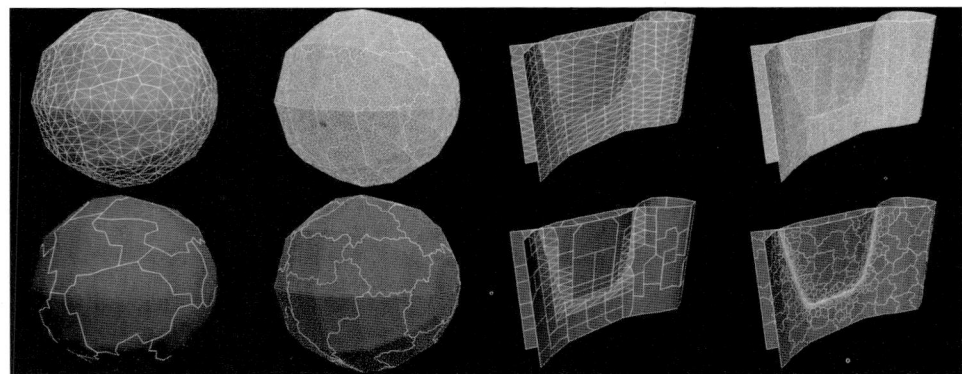

Fig. 3.28. Self-collision detection on a spherical and a self-intersecting surface, with different discretizations. The hierarchy group tested s are shown.

Thanks to the curvature criteria, the collision detection remains efficient in the case of self-collisions. The hierarchical algorithm is not fooled by false adjacency "collisions". The full power of the hierarchical scheme is thus maintained in this situation, and the computation time depends more on the number of colliding polygons than on the total number of polygons of the tested surfaces.

As for any hierarchical algorithms, the performance of this one relies greatly on how deep the hierarchy the collision check has to go to determine that collisions do not occur, either through the bounding box or curvature criteria. While simple and distant surfaces are quickly checked for collision, highly curved surface regions slow down the process. The performance is determined linearly by the number of collisions occurring or nearly occurring. For instance, the two large surfaces lying on each other, would produce a linear computation time roughly proportional to the number of mesh elements.

Plate A: "Flashback", 1990

Plate B: Various garment models made using the 1992 MIRALab software

Plate C: more garment models made using the 1992 MIRALab software

Plate D: "Family at the Museum", 1992

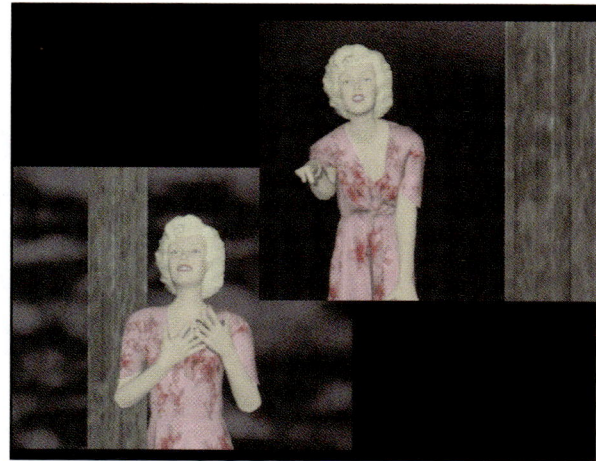

Plate E: "Computer Animation'92", 1992

Plate F: "Marilyn by the Geneva Lake", 1995

Plate G: "Golden Camera Award", 1996

Plate H: At the office, 1997

Plate I: "The Xian Terra-Cotta Army", 1997

Plate J: "Computer Animation'97", 1997

Plate K: "Marilyn at the United Nations", 1997

Plate L: "Cathy", 1998

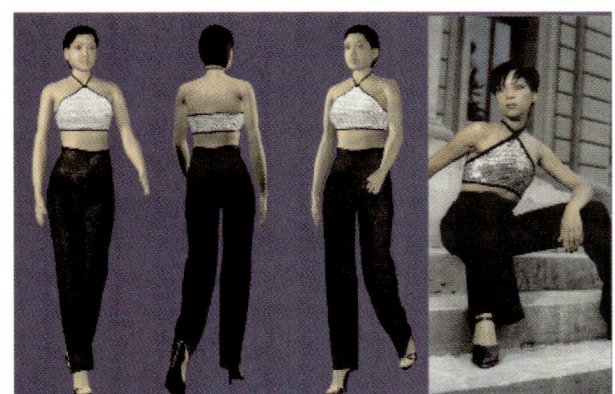

Plate M: Some virtual fashion models, 1998

Plate N: Some more virtual fashion models, 1998

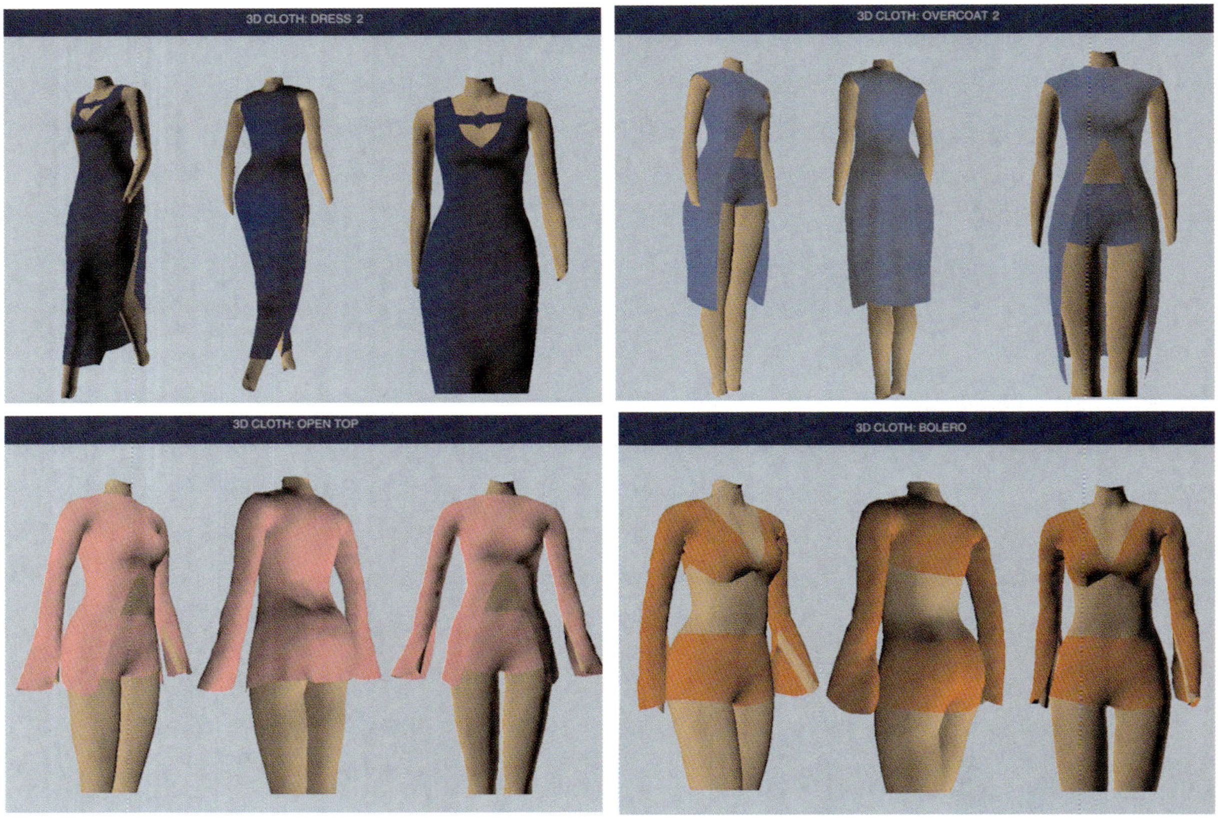

Plate O: Fashion models collection, 1998

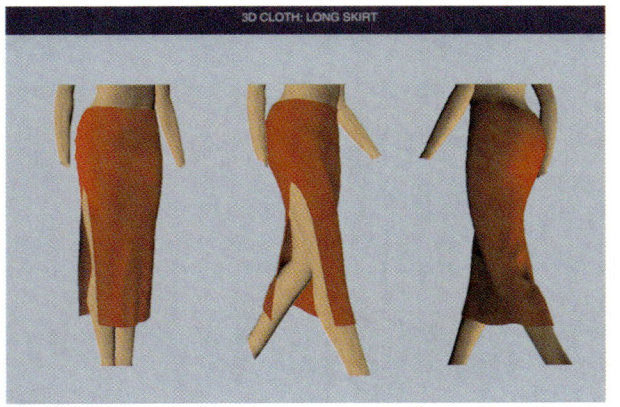
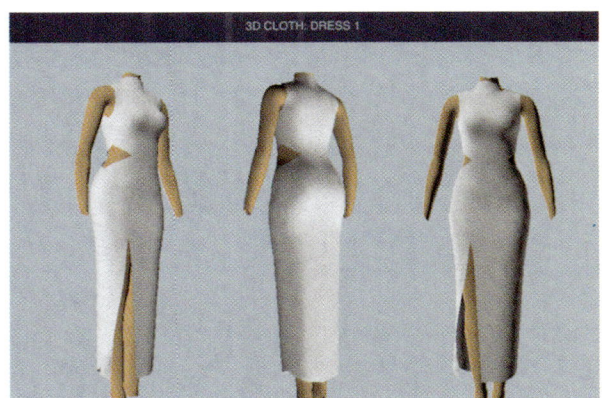
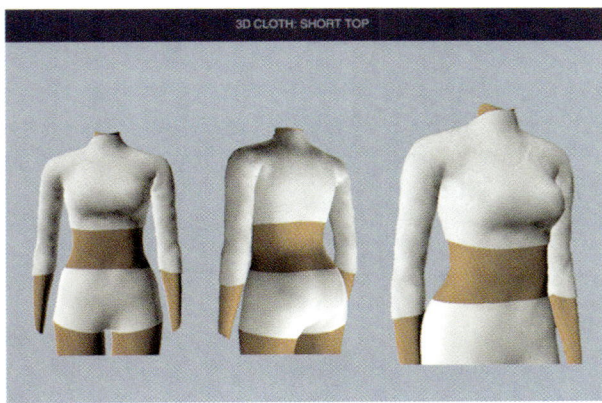

Plate P: More fashion models collection, 1998

Plate Q: "Fashion Dreams", 1998

Plate R: "MIRALab's Virtual Catwalk", 1998

Plate S: Christmas card, 1998

Plate T: "Charleston Party" and Models Style nouveau, 1999

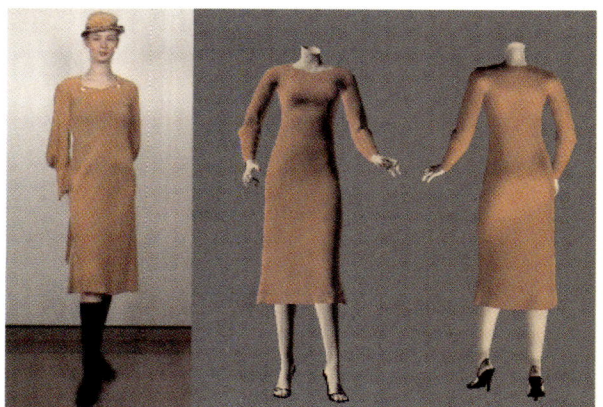 

Plate U: Models Style nouveau, 1999

Plate V: Models Style nouveau, 1999

Plate W: Evening dresses, 2000

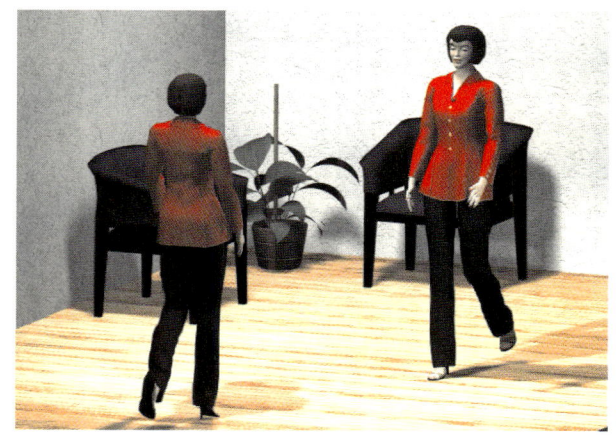

Plate X: Ladies suits variations, 2000

Plate Y: Men's suit, 2000

Plate Z: The couple of the year, 2000

4 Collision Response

As soon as the distance separating two objects is small enough to consider that they are interacting, a "feedback" should be performed on their behavior. The collision response aims to reproduce this interaction in an accurate way, primarily to avoid the unrealistic interpenetration of the objects, and secondarily to simulate the realistic bouncing and friction effects.

From the geometrical contacts computed from the collision detection, collision response should first consider in which way the surfaces of the colliding objects interact geometrically, and second, complete the effect on the object position, motion, or its underlying mechanical model from these geometrical parameters. Many difficulties related to the discrete mesh structure, geometrical surface orientation, and the integration in the process, have to be considered for obtaining a general scheme that is able to deal with any collision situation.

4.1 Characterizing Collisions Geometrically

Collisions may be thought of as geometrical constraints which can be enforced using either the mechanical or geometrical techniques. Whatever the considered solution may be, the collisions should be characterized by their geometrical properties essential for producing an accurate collision distance and orientation. Most of the collision detection algorithms return a bunch of polygon couples that are geometrically close enough to be considered interacting. However, a simulation process does not consider these polygons individually, but as a part of surface objects that have to be simulated as a whole. Some specific processing is required for obtaining "clean" geometrical data that will then directly be integrated into the collision response.

4.1.1 Intersections and Proximities

Depending on the application and the response type, two main kinds of collisions may be considered:

- *Intersections*: Objects are intersecting when they locally share a common space. For surfaces, it usually means that the two colliding surfaces are crossing each other.
- *Proximities*: Objects can be considered colliding when their closest distance becomes less than a given threshold distance. This distance represents an "influence region" around the objects.

These two kinds of collisions are identified differently, depending on the geometrical nature of the considered objects.

4.1.1.1 Sorting Out Collisions in a Polygonal Mesh

Polygonal meshes are considered when dealing with cloth simulation. They usually represent not only the deformable cloth surface, but also the other objects of the scene which can interact with the cloth objects.

A. Collision Types

When dealing with polygonal meshes, collisions may be considered on the vertices, edges or polygons of the mesh. Intersections are usually characterized by the point where the edge of one surface crosses the polygon of the other surface. The proximities are represented by the two "closest distance" points on the elements of the two surfaces, which can be vertices, edges, or polygons (Fig. 4.1).

Both the full interference and the proximity collisions may be detected on polygonal meshes. The proximities are mainly used for computing the collision response on the surfaces through an "influence zone" around each surface, while the intersections point out inconsistent situations where the surfaces cross each other.

4.1 Characterizing Collisions Geometrically

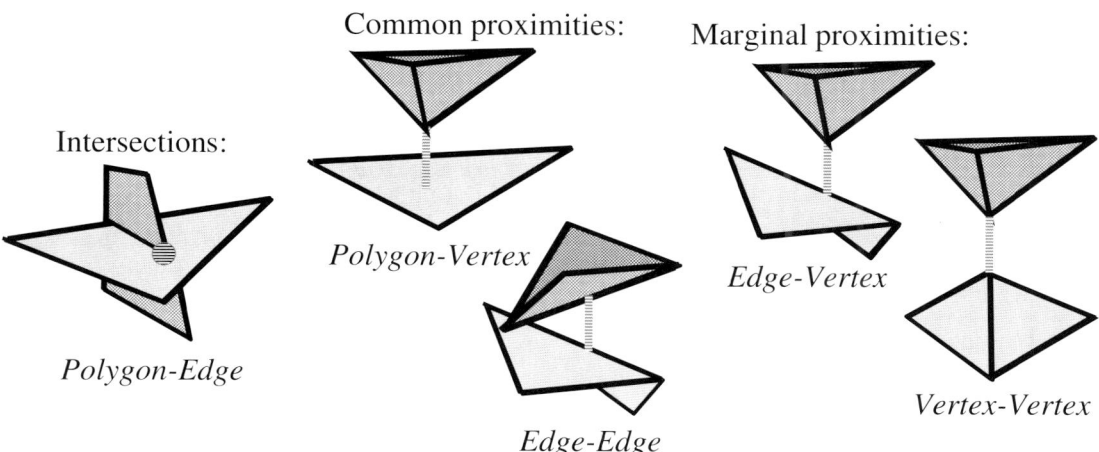

Fig. 4.1. Different collision types in a polygonal mesh.

B. Geometrical Continuity

The geometrical continuity of collisions is essential to good collision response. Basically, this means that a small change in the geometrical configurations of the objects should produce only a small change in the geometry of the collisions. Actually, the collisions should undergo "smooth transitions" from one kind to another and only appear or disappear if their distance becomes too big. Concerning the proximities on a mesh, the collision points may slide along the polygon surface and reach an edge. It may then slide along the edge direction to reach a vertex. The "marginal" proximities are the "filling" collision states ensuring that a collision will not disappear in a gap created by some curvature between two polygons or at the meeting point of several edges (Fig. 4.2).

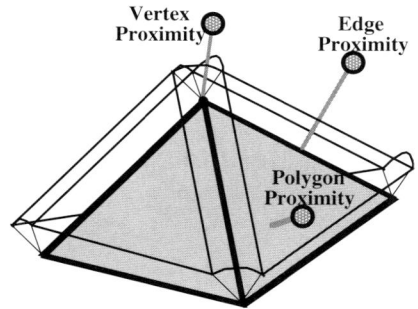

Fig. 4.2. Proximity domains for polygon, edge and vertex.

4.1.1.2 Proximity Extremality

Proximities are defined by the distance separating two colliding elements. These elements can be vertices, edges or polygons. They can be classified as the extremal proximities if they locally represent the closest distance between the two colliding objects.

Among the combinations of possible elements involved in the proximities, a collision is extremal if both of its contact points are in the extremal positions on the mesh, relative to the proximity direction. A non-extremal position may occur on a vertex or an edge, and the property can be evaluated using simple geometrical tools (Fig. 4.3).

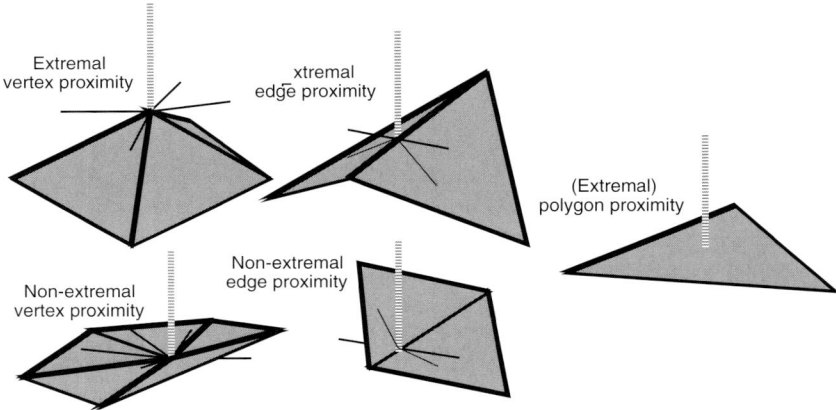

Fig 4.3. Extremal and non-extremal proximities on mesh elements.

Extremality may be a factor used to consider or to discard a collision from being processed for the collision response. Three combinable choices should be decided:

- (A) Proximities for all the vertices, or only for the extremal vertices.
- (B) Proximities for all the edges, or only for the extremal edges.
- (C) Proximities for the polygons.

For the usual cloth simulation where the animation deals with "full" surfaces, proximities for polygons (C) are always to be considered. The choice is then to be made for the vertices (A) and the edges (B). The following four cases are then considered:

- With full proximity detection on the vertices and the edges, a dense network of Edge-Edge and Polygon-Vertex proximities are detected. Other collisions result from the marginal closest-distance extremas.

- With only full detection on the edges, only the Edge-Edge proximities are detected, along with the marginal closest-distance extremas.

- With only full detection on the vertices, only the Polygon-Vertex proximities are detected, along with the marginal closest-distance extremas.

- With detection on extremal elements only, a very sparse network of collisions is detected, containing the marginal, closest-distance extremas.

Each type of detection has its advantages and disadvantages. Full proximity detection on all the elements generates a very dense collision network that can be appreciable for a precise response. No extrema computation is required, and the collisions do not "disappear" because of the slight angle variations that ensured good collision-response continuity. Considering only Edge-Edge or Polygon-Vertex proximities, yields lighter collision networks adapted for quicker processing. The Edge-Edge network is approximately twice as dense as the Polygon-Vertex network. While the latter provides a relatively steady response because the collisions mainly "follow" the vertices of the object, the collisions of the former may move greatly along the edges. With only the extrema, proximity detection, very sparse and highly time-limited collisions are detected, suitable only for rigid object simulation.

For cloth simulation, the best choice is either the full proximity detection for precise simulation, or the full detection on vertices for quicker processing. When dealing with highly deformed objects, full detection on the edges may be considered.

When removing the proximity detection on the polygons of the meshes, the detection behaves as if only the web defined by the edges exists, rather than the plain surface. Four additional cases can be considered, which detect the proximities between all the vertices and the edges, or between all the edges with only the extremal vertices, between the vertices only, or no detection at all.

4.1.1.3 Collisions with Other Surface Representations

Instead of using polygonal meshes, some models build the objects of the scene using higher order surface representations, such as Bezier patches. These surfaces are curved, and therefore it is important to identify the collisions accurately within the patch surface. Furthermore, a reduced number of patches are used for modeling complex objects. The identification of collisions based on vertices and edges may lead to only the sparse and inaccurate collision representations. Specific methods have to be developed for such situations, possibly involving local rediscretization of the surfaces into polygonal meshes.

When there is no explicit representation of the surface (for example, with metaball modeling), the mathematical nature of the model should be used directly for computing the surface orientation. Iterative mathematical methods could then converge to the local minimal distance between the two surfaces.

4.1.2 Collisions and Surface Orientation

Ideally, mechanical surfaces should never cross each other. This is a condition of consistency with the "real world" situations where such a configuration obviously never happens. Unfortunately, in numerical simulations where objects are modeled through approximate geometrical entities such as polygonal meshes, where the animation process itself is based on discrete and approximate algorithms such as numerical integration on discrete time points, full consistency cannot be ensured all along the simulation. Thus, surfaces might erroneously cross each other, and the collision response algorithms must be able to cope with these situations.

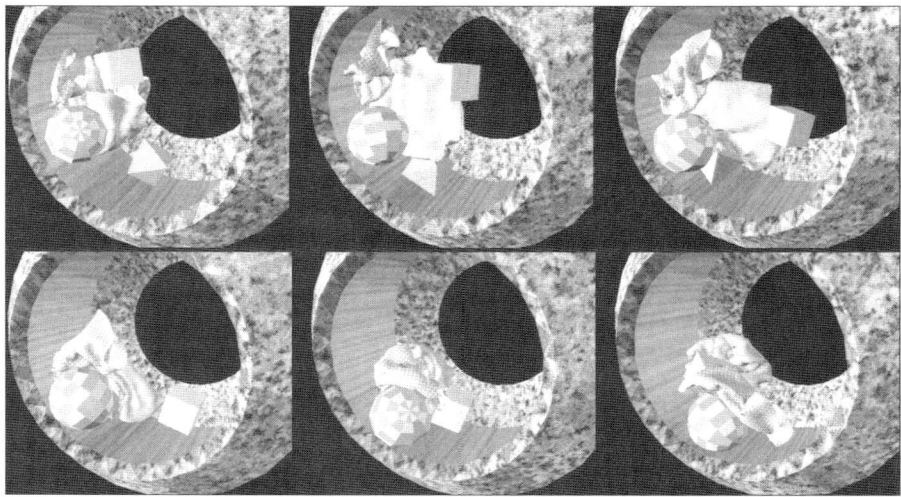

Fig. 4.4. A very general simulation context: Garments crumpling in a rotating dryer.

Such situations are very important for simulations involving cloth that are free from any "standard" geometrical context, and are allowed to crumple in any possible shape. The orientation problem arises from the fact that any cloth surface region may collide with any other region of whatever side and orientation.

4.1.2.1 The Orientation Problem

When two surface regions are located in proximity to each other, the "usual" way is to consider whether they are in contact through their current relative positions . However if, for any reason, the surfaces cross each other, this relative position will be wrong compared to the global geometrical context. Thus, any detected proximity should be classified into two categories: non-crossed proximities (noted "+") reflecting the correct relative position, and crossed-proximities (noted "-") reflecting the inversion of relative positions. While a non-crossed proximity refers to a "normal" situation where the surface should repulse each other to simulate mechanical reaction, a crossed proximity refers to an "abnormal" situation caused by simulation errors and should make the surfaces attract in order to re-cross each other and bring the relative position back to normal (Fig. 4.5). The difficulty is in classifying the detected collisions in a consistent way.

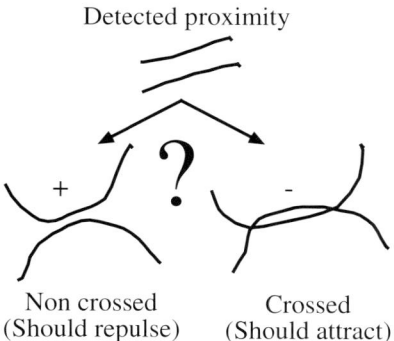

Fig. 4.5. Orientation ambiguity: Choosing the right collision side.

Usually, as the surfaces collide, more than one punctual collision is detected. Significant surface regions come in contact with each other, and they are represented by several collisions involving adjacent elements of the colliding regions. The proximity orientation problem described above should be considered in a consistent way for all the collisions.

While an erroneously oriented and independent collision would only cause the two concerned objects to cross with no further consequences, non consistent orientations between interacting proximities would cause the surfaces to cross in some regions, while being maintained in some others and the global result would be a definitive and unrealistic mangling of the surfaces. Therefore, the collision orientation consistency between the interacting collisions in a region is more important than the collision orientation itself.

Within a region, the consistency rules can be defined between the neighboring proximity collisions, depending on the relative positions of the surfaces at the collision points (Fig. 4.6).

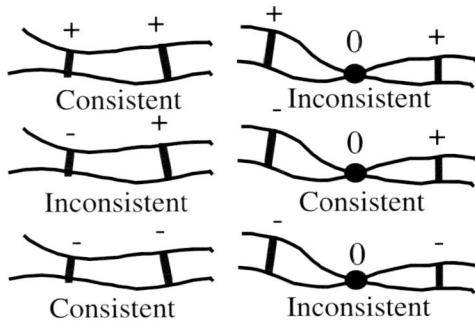

Fig. 4.6. Orientation consistency between neighbor collisions.

Similar rules can be defined between the collision proximity orientations of interacting collision regions, ensuring the global positioning of the multiple surfaces (Fig. 4.7).

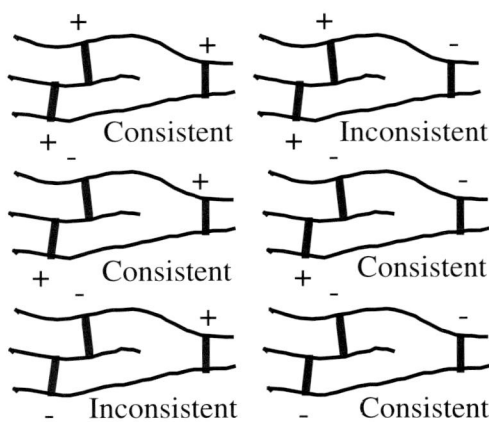

Fig. 4.7. Orientation consistency between several collision regions.

4.1 Characterizing Collisions Geometrically

A robust collision response system should maintain the global consistency on all the detected proximities in order to produce a consistent and realistic response and to cope efficiently with the simulation errors and the approximations of the numerical models.

4.1.2.2 Correcting the Collision Orientation

There is no simple and efficient way for individually determining the orientation of each detected proximity. One method could be to track the displacement of the colliding elements and to deduce the orientation through their history. The colliding surfaces could have crossed each other if a surface crossing occurred in the past. Unfortunately, such detection cannot be ensured, and there are always numerous and complex geometrical situations which have to be considered separately. Furthermore, involving the history of the animation, which is not always available, introduces extra storage and expensive data management.

Instead of trying to compute the collision orientations exactly, it would be better to implement a method which deduces the "most probable" orientation compatible with all the orientation-consistency considerations from the current geometrical states.

To implement this solution, an algorithm could use a statistical approach, where initially all the proximities of one collision region would be considered as non-crossed. Then, for each surface side, the proximities oriented towards that side are counted. Consistency would require that the proximities of the opposite surface sides to be of a different type. Depending on which side holds the majority of the collisions, the collisions of the minority side are inverted, and ensures the global consistency within the collision region (Fig. 4.8).

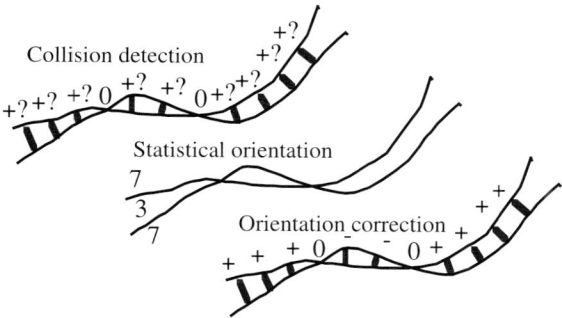

Fig. 4.8. The collision orientation correction process. Counting and orientation correction for the minority side.

The implementation of this algorithm requires the grouping of collisions within collision regions. This can be carried out with a linear algorithm according to the number of collisions, that "walks" along the adjacent proximities on the surface meshes.

Although this process is linear, it requires some extra computation mainly resulting from the walk on the mesh structure for identifying the adjacent collisions belonging to the same group. Optimization will require this algorithm to be involved only when the geometrical situation will obviously imply the surface crossings. One simple way to characterize such a situation is the detection of the surface intersections. This implies crossings involving the concerned mesh elements.

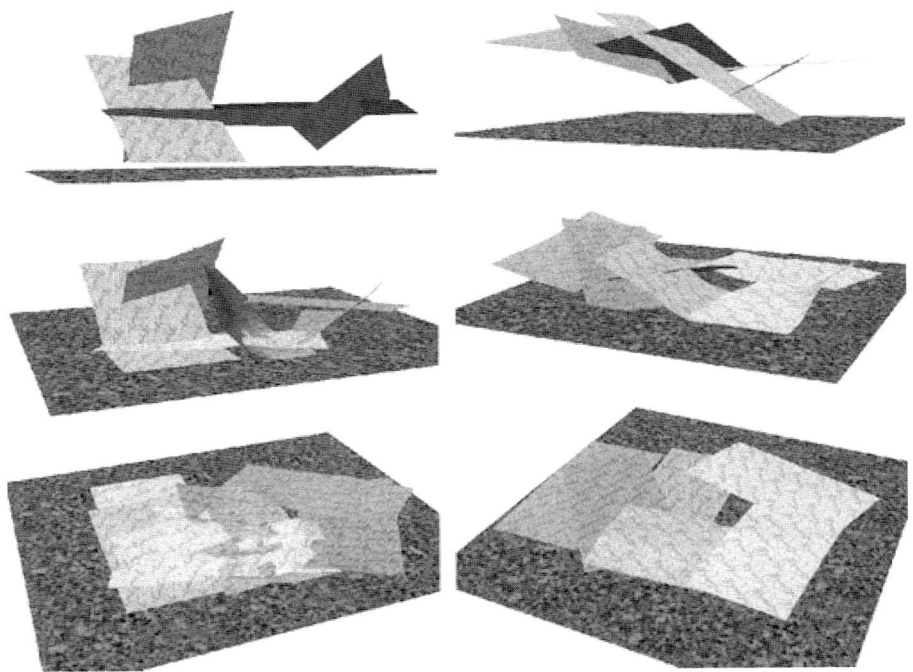

Fig. 4.9. Orientation consistency correction at work: Intersecting cloth surfaces falling on the ground, without (left) and with (right) orientation correction.

This algorithm efficiently corrects small collision errors resulting from simulation artifacts for cloth simulation. More complicated situations (such as initially crossing cloth rectangles falling on the ground) can be efficiently solved by this method. However, it may fail in very complex situations such as high crumpling of very soft surfaces, where collision zones can hardly be individualized and each one only contains a few collisions, making a statistical orientation determination irrelevant. A more advanced and complex surface shape analysis is required to ensure geometrical consistency in such situations.

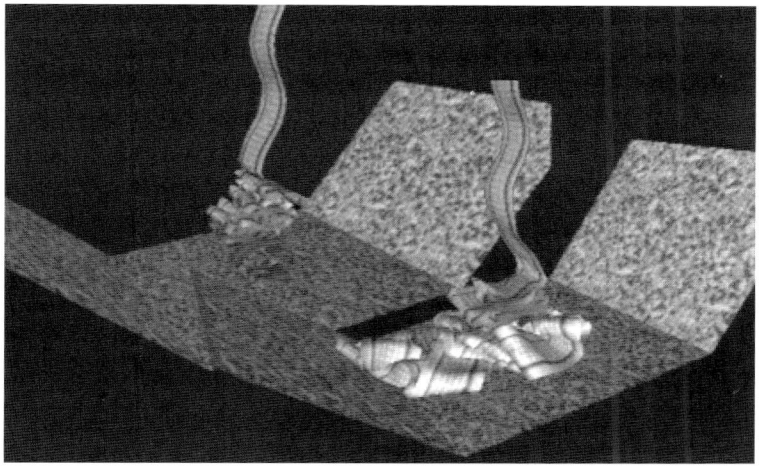

Fig. 4.10. Surface orientation consistency maintained during an animation containing complex collision patterns.

4.2 Implementing Collision Response

Collision response is an interaction between two objects (or between two object regions) relating the effect of the collision by altering the course of the simulation.

This response, whatever its nature (force, displacement, acceleration, impulse), has to be distributed on the object according to the basic, impulse conservation laws which will ensure the realism of the response.

As polygonal meshes are the most common structures used for cloth simulation, a detailed repartition model will be studied for distributing the effects of geometric collisions described in Part 4.1.1. Such a response scheme is particularly useful for the particle systems models, where the mesh vertices explicitly support the geometrical state and the evolution of the system.

4.2.1 Collision Response on Polygonal Meshes

On polygonal meshes, the colliding mesh elements may be vertices, edges, or polygons. A collision means an interaction between two mesh elements, each element being one of the previously mentioned types. Collisions are usually identified by both a *contact point* on each element and a *collision distance* separating the two contact points of a collision.

As the mesh vertices carry the state of the object position and velocity, collision effects are distributed on the vertices supporting the colliding elements (Fig. 4.11), depending on the mass of the mesh elements. The global result of this repartition should produce an adequate effect on the collision point thus ensuring an adequate response.

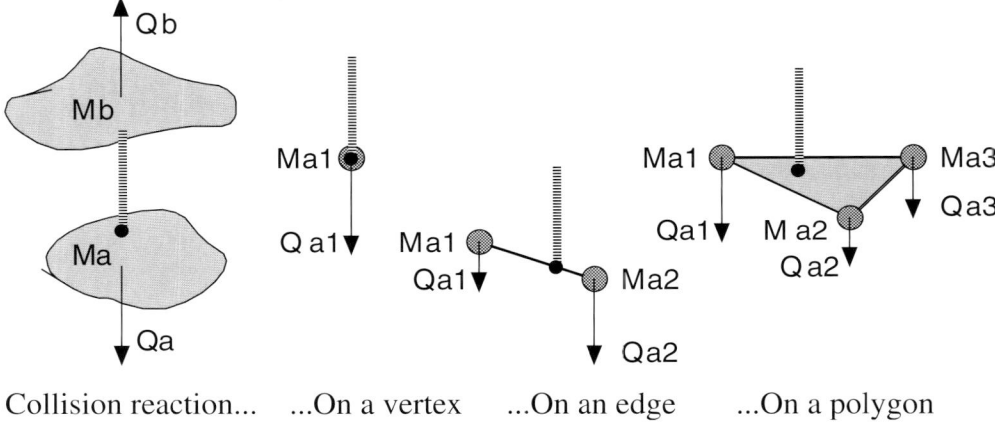

Fig. 4.11. Distributing collision reaction on the vertices of mesh elements.

4.2.1.1 Distributing Collision Effects

In a polygonal mesh, collisions are interactions taking place between the elements **A** and **B**, which can be vertices, edges or polygons. The collision itself is applied on specific geometrical locations of these elements, **Pa** and **Pb**. These locations can be described by their barycentric coordinates from the vertices defining the concerned mesh vertices, **Pai** and **Pbi**. Once the position of the contact points are computed, these barycentric coordinates, **rai** and **rbi**, can be computed using simple geometry. They verify the following relation:

$$Pa = \sum_i rai\,Pai \quad Pb = \sum_i rbi\,Pbi \tag{1}$$

If needed, the same relation would compute other cinematic parameters of the collision points (speed of acceleration) with the same interpolation, using the values of the vertices weighted by their respective barycentric coordinates. From these values, a mechanical collision model would compute the adequate collision response between the two objects **A** and **B**.

In most mechanical systems, two kind of responses are generally used:

- *Dynamic response*, which acts as forces or pressures exerted on the objects.
- *Geometric response*, which acts directly on the object positions, velocities, and accelerations.

As for any mechanical interaction, collision interactions fulfill some mechanical conservation laws. The major law is the action-reaction equality, which states that the forces exerted on the two objects are exactly opposite. As a result of Newton's law, the collision does not change the total mechanical momentum of the two objects in translational and rotational motion. Hence, the motion of the mass center of the two objects, as well as the rotation around it, is not altered by the collision. These effects have to be expressed locally when considering the collision between two mesh elements.

Translation of a dynamic response into a geometric effect goes through the division by the object mass, according to Newton's second law. This implies different ways of expressing the conservation laws of these quantities.

A. Dynamic Collision Response

When the collision response acts as a force **Fab** or a form of pressure between two objects, the effective force or pressure, **Fa** and **Fb**, on each object are of the same intensity and with the opposed orientations (law of action-reaction). This means:

$$Fa = -Fab \quad Fb = Fab \qquad (2)$$

The response exerted on one object is obviously the sum of the responses exerted on its vertices:

$$Fa = \sum_i rai\, Fai \quad Fb = \sum_i rbi\, Fbi \qquad (3)$$

A suitable way to perform the response repartition between the vertices is to use a linear interpolation with the barycentric coordinates:

$$Fai = raiFa \quad Fbi = rbiFb \qquad (4)$$

This yields a response which is continuous as the collision points move on the object surfaces and jump from one mesh element to another.

B. Geometric Collision Response

When the collision response is a geometric value **Qab**, such as distance, speed or acceleration, the conservation laws have to consider the mass of the different objects, and the response distribution becomes more complex.

Generally, the geometrical collision response is considered to be the difference between the responses of the two objects, **Qa** and **Qb**:

$$Qab = Qb - Qa \qquad (5)$$

The response should be distributed between the concerned vertices according to all impulse conservation laws. Again, it can be more convenient to perform the computation using the *inverse* mass values. This formulation allows us to represent fixed and constrained objects (non mechanically animated) as having a null inverse mass rather than an infinite mass, and also allows suppression of the problems of dealing with singularities and particular cases. The reaction distribution computation needs the masses of the two objects **Ma** and **Mb** for which the computation will be detailed later (11).

According to the conservation laws, the distribution collision reaction between the two objects is as follows:

$$Qa = \frac{-Ma^{-1}}{Ma^{-1} + Mb^{-1}} Qab \quad Qb = \frac{Mb^{-1}}{Ma^{-1} + Mb^{-1}} Qab \qquad (6)$$

The object masses cannot simply be considered as the sum of the masses of the vertices defining the concerned mesh elements (vertex, edge or polygon). First, such a solution would lead to mass and therefore response discontinuities when a collision jumps from one element to another while the objects are moving in an animation, which is unacceptable. Second, the response needs to be distributed between the element vertices in an appropriate way to generate adequate correction on the collision point while ensuring the mechanical conservation laws taking effect within the elements.

4.2 Implementing Collision Response

Working with the response on the object **A**, the correction on the object **Qa** is the weighted sum of all the corrections on its vertices:

$$Qa = \sum_i rai\, Qai \qquad (7)$$

It can be assumed that the response **Qai** on the vertex **i** is an impulse which results from a force **Fai**, and is therefore proportional to this force and to the inverse particle weight **Mai^{-1}**. Thus we introduce a γ coefficient, and using equation (4) we get:

$$Qai = Mai^{-1}\gamma \quad Fai = Mai^{-1} rai\, \gamma\, Fa \qquad (8)$$

Using relation (7), the total desired correction **Qa** resulting from the collision force **Fa** is then expressed as follows:

$$Qa = \sum_i rai\, Mai^{-1} \gamma\, Fa \qquad (9)$$

Substituting γ **Fa** from relation (8) into the relation (9), we can finally express the correction exerted on each particle as follows:

$$Qai = \frac{Mai^{-1} rai}{\sum_i Mai^{-1} rai^2} Qa \qquad (10)$$

The result is a collision response which is continuous as the collision points move on the object surfaces and jump from one mesh element to another.

The computation of the resulting object masses **Ma** and **Mb** of the objects **A** and **B** are still needed in formula (3). For this, it is considered that the impulsion on the objects is equal to the sum of the impulsions on their vertices:

$$Ma\, Qa = \sum_i Mai\, Qai = \frac{\sum_i rai\, Qa}{\sum_i Mai^{-1} rai^2} \qquad (11)$$

With the sum of the barycentric coordinates being unity, we finally express the relation (10) for both the objects as follows:

$$Qai = Ma\, Mai^{-1} rai\, Qa \quad Qbi = Mb\, Mbi^{-1} rbi\, Qb \qquad (12)$$

The equivalent object masses are expressed as follows:

$$Ma^{-1} = \sum_i rai^2\, Mai^{-1} \quad Mb^{-1} = \sum_i rbi^2\, Mbi^{-1} \tag{13}$$

Practically, the object mass computation (13) is first performed, and these results are used as the intermediate variables for computing the vertex response contributions from each object (6) and then on each vertex (12).

4.2.2 Collision Models

The previous part has dealt on how to distribute the collision effect on the elements of a geometrical representation of the simulated surfaces. The mechanical collision model which computes the effect from the collision geometry, has to be studied now.

The interaction between two objects is described by the resulting mechanical interactions between them, which can then be simulated using several schemes in a collision response model.

4.2.2.1 Reaction and Friction

When two objects make contact, a mechanical interaction occurs, which will mainly prevent the two objects from interpenetrating each other. This *reaction force* is often associated with a *friction force* which acts against the sliding effect between the objects.

Assuming that the contact point between the two objects is well located in the space, a contact surface is defined parallel to the two object surfaces at the contact points. The reaction force is orthogonal to the contact surface, while the friction force is parallel and oriented along the relative speed between the two object contact points (Fig. 4.12).

4.2 Implementing Collision Response

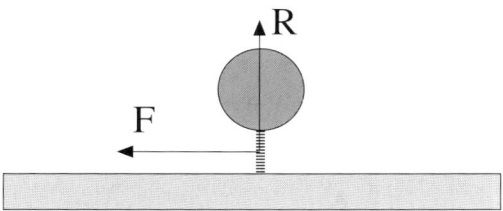

Fig. 4.12. Reaction and friction forces during a collision.

The collision interactions may exhibit some energy dissipation effects. Concerning the reaction forces, a purely elastic shock does not dissipate any energy and the objects bounce perfectly during the shock, whereas a perfectly damped shock absorbs all the energy and leaves the two contact points without relative normal speed. Such dissipation usually results from viscosity or plasticity effects from the material deformation during the shock. Usually, the mechanical energy is mostly converted into heat.

Frictional forces result from another dissipative behavior generated by the relative sliding of the object contact points. The frictional force usually opposes the relative motion of the contact points by contributing parallel to the contact surface. Friction models vary from the collisions without friction to totally dissipative collisions which immediately cancel the relative speed tangent relative speed to the contact points. The most known model for frictional forces is the Coulombian model which considers a friction force proportional to the normal reaction force and with the direction opposed to the relative sliding speed. Particularly when there is no sliding speed (static friction), the proportionality coefficient may vary with the sliding speed.

4.2.2.2 Collision Response Models

Collision response has to reproduce reaction and friction effects through adequate action in the ongoing mechanical simulation. Its integration in the mechanical simulation system goes through an alteration of the mechanical quantities from the value they would have without the collision effects. Different schemes are available for performing this integration.

A. Collisions as Mechanical or Geometrical Effects

There are two main ways for handling collision response:

- *Mechanical response*: The collision reaction is simulated by the forces or by the force adjustments which reproduce the contact effect.

- *Geometrical response*: The collision reaction is simulated by the direct corrections on the positions and velocities of the objects.

Each of these methods have positive and negative points related to their accuracy and efficiency. Many different collision models can be derived from each of them, possibly combining the two aspects in one hybrid model. These two schemes will be detailed in Part 4.2.2.3 and Part 4.2.2.4.

B. Analytic Collision Response

Another solution is to integrate the collision response in terms of analytical constraints in the motion between the two objects, directly into the equations of motion of the two objects in the mechanical model.

The motion of an object is described as an evolution along given degrees of freedom, these constraints are integrated as additional equations between these variables. In this case, the resolution is often carried out using the technique of the *Lagrange multipliers*.

This technique has been very successfully implemented in systems dealing with the simulation of rigid objects, which can be described using a reduced number of degrees of freedom (six for a free moving volumic object) and for which the constraints remain in a constant configuration (articulated objects and constant collisions). However, when considering deformable surfaces for which the motion is described using a huge number of degrees of freedom (usually three for each mesh vertex), and for which the collisions are numerous and constantly evolve between the mesh elements (no constant analytic formulation of the constraints is possible), this technique is quite inapplicable. Such techniques are therefore, rather suited for robotic applications than for cloth simulation.

Some implementations of these techniques for rigid mechanics are detailed in [BAR 89] and [BAR 90].

4.2.2.3 Collisions as Mechanical Response

The mechanical approach is the most formal way of dealing with the problem. The forces or energetic contributions generated from the response can directly be integrated into the mechanical model and simulated. As all the effects are taken into account in the same computation step, the resulting simulation produces an animation where collision response and other mechanical forces add their effects in a compatible way.

A. Collision Penalty Forces

Designing a suitable, collision-penalty force depends more on the context and the expected collision behavior than on the mechanical nature of the collision. Several factors account for this:

- The expected collision distance, which is the distance kept between the colliding objects.

- Average motion impulsion with respect to the objects that are likely to collide with, related to their speed and the simulation timestep.

- The behavior of the objects if interpenetration occurs.

- The possible external forces.

The repulsion force function is usually designed as a continuous function of the collision distance and as a piecewise function using simple linear or polynomial intervals. The major parameters should be the following:

- The threshold distance for which the collision has an effect. It is sometimes related to the collision distance in consideration. The larger it is, the more robust the response is, but also the less is the realistic contact.

- The force amplitude during contact. The higher it is, the less likely the objects would interpenetrate, but the numerical resolution becomes stiffer, causing collision stability problems.

- The function behavior after interpenetration. It may reach higher values, forcing repulsion and separation, at the expense of stability and robustness for complicated shapes.

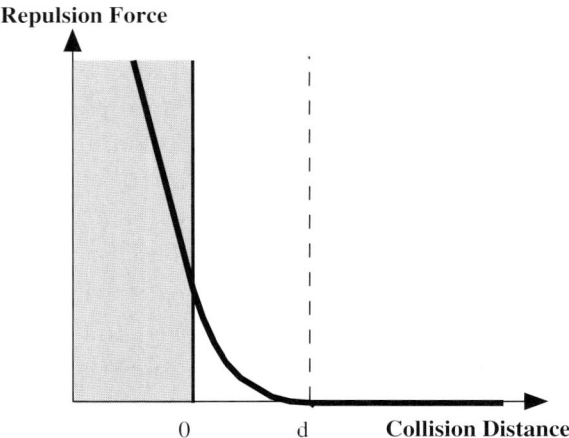

Fig. 4.13. Collision penalty force vs. Collision distance.

Designing the optimal shape is difficult, because all these compromises depend on the actual mechanical context of the simulation. The biggest issue is to model, in a robust way, the geometrical contact (very small collision distance) in which the collision response forces only act in a very small range when considered at the macroscopic scale. This implies the use of a very strong and rapidly evolving reaction forces which are difficult to simulate numerically, since a suitable numerical process should discretize the collision contact duration into timesteps. These timesteps must be numerous enough for an accurate reproduction of the collision effects which can cause a problem with large simulation timesteps.

B. Friction

Modeling the traditional Coulombian friction is quite easy when using a force-based collision response. It is done simply by considering the tangential force proportional to the reaction force and oriented against the relative tangential speed of the colliding objects. Non-sliding objects are however, quite difficult to maintain together in purely mechanical collision forces without using additional geometrical constraints.

4.2.2.4 Collisions as Geometrical Constraints

The geometrical approach aims to directly reproduce the effects of collision response on the geometrical state of the objects without making the use of mechanical forces, and thus in a process separated from the mechanical simulation. The advantages are obvious: geometrical constraints are directly enforced by a geometrical algorithm, and the simulation process is relieved from high intensity and highly discontinuous forces or other mechanical parameters, making it faster and more efficient. The drawback however results from this separation: as collision response changes separately the geometrical state of the objects from the mechanical process, nothing ensures the compatibility of this deformation to a correct variation of the mechanical state that would normally result from it. Furthermore, there is no compatible "additivity" of geometrical variations as there is for forces and energy contributions. The resulting collision effects may be incompatible with the mechanics, but also between several interacting collisions. All these issues have to be addressed for providing a collision response model that provides acceptable and steady responses between all the frames of an animation.

A. A Geometrical Correction Scheme

As an example of collision response implementation, here is described a complete scheme for collision response on polygonal meshes using corrections on the cinematic properties of the colliding elements.

The proposed hybrid approach performs collision response on position, speed and acceleration simultaneously, ensuring the response as accurate as possible, depending on the geometrical context of the collision:

- *Position correction* is used to displace the colliding elements to a relative position reflecting the contact between the two objects, possibly with a given "contact distance". It controls the geometrical constraints resulting from collisions without the use of dynamical effects.

- *Speed correction* ensures that the objects will not continue moving toward each other and controls the "bouncing effect" of collisions as well as friction effects. It controls the simulation of the mechanical behavior of the collision.

- *Acceleration correction* ensures that the desired speeds are maintained along with time. It controls the stability of the collision response along with time.

B. Collision Geometrical Properties

A collision between two objects **A** and **B** is described by the following geometrical values:

- The collision point positions **Pa** and **Pb**, which are the "contact locations" of the collision on the objects **A** and **B**.

- The collision point speeds **P'a** and **P'b**, which are the speeds of the points **Pa** and **Pb** at the moment of the collision.

- The collision point accelerations **P"a** and **P"b**, which are the accelerations of the points **Pa** and **Pb**.

When working with polygonal meshes, the positions of the collision points **Pa** and **Pb** can be defined by the barycentric coordinates **rai** and **rbi** corresponding to the vertices of the mesh elements. Their speeds **P'a** and **P'b** and accelerations **P"a** and **P"b** can also be computed by the linear combinations of these values for the vertices using the barycentric coordinate weightings:

$$Pa = \sum_i rai\, Pai \quad Pb = \sum_i rbi\, Pbi$$
$$P'a = \sum_i rai\, P'ai \quad P'b = \sum_i rbi\, P'bi \tag{14}$$
$$P"a = \sum_i rai\, P"ai \quad P"b = \sum_i rbi\, P"bi$$

From these values, we compute the collision distance **Pab**, the collision speed **P'ab** and the collision acceleration **P"ab** by substracting between the objects as follows:

$$Pab = Pb - Pa$$
$$P'ab = P'b - P'a \tag{15}$$
$$P"ab = P"b - P"a$$

The collision-response model then computes the desired collision distance P_0ab, speed $P_0'ab$ and acceleration $P_0"ab$ derived from the reaction and friction mechanical collision model. The collision response **Qab** acts as a correction to be performed on the current geometrical state of the collision (as considered in the formulas (5-13)). For position, speed and acceleration correction, the position difference $P_0ab-Pab$, the speed difference $P_0'ab-P'ab$ and the acceleration difference $P_0"ab-P"ab$ respectively, or any combination of these.

C. A Progressive Reaction and Friction Model

Reaction and friction are respectively modeled as a normal and tangent effect along the collision surface. The first task is to decompose the actual collision speed and acceleration into normal and tangential components by projecting along the collision direction **Pab**:

4.2 Implementing Collision Response

$$P^N ab = Pab \qquad P^T ab = 0$$
$$P'^N ab = \frac{P'ab \bullet Pab}{Pab^2} Pab \qquad P'^T ab = P'ab - P'^N ab \qquad (16)$$
$$P''^N ab = \frac{P''ab \bullet Pab}{Pab^2} Pab \qquad P''^T ab = P''ab - P''^N ab$$

- * The *position correction* alters the position **P** of the colliding vertices so that the collision distance is maintained at the current frame. Given the desired collision position **P₀** (collision "thickness") at the current frame, the correction should be:

$$P_0^N ab = P_0 \qquad (17)$$

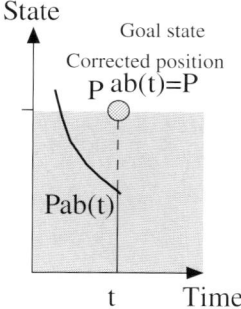

Fig. 4.14. Position correction for collision reaction response.

- The *speed correction* alters the speed **P'** of the colliding vertices so that the collision distance is obtained at the next frame. Given the desired position **P₀** (collision "thickness") at the next frame, the speed correction should be:

$$P_0'^N ab = \frac{P_0 - P^N ab}{dt} \qquad (18)$$

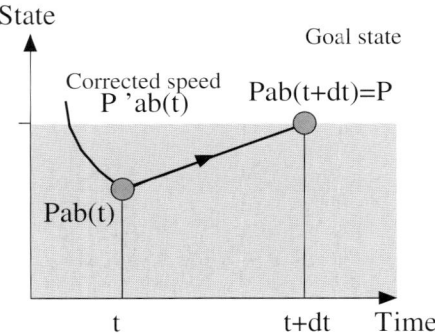

Fig. 4.15. Speed correction for collision reaction response.

- The *acceleration correction* alters the acceleration **P"** of the colliding vertices so that the collision distance is obtained two frames thereafter, with a null distance evolution. Given the wanted position **P₀** and speed **P₀'** (speed after bounce, null in the case of perfectly inelastic contact) at the second next frame, the acceleration correction should be:

$$P_0''^N(t) = \frac{P_0 - P^N ab}{dt^2} - \frac{0.5 P_0' + 1.5 P'^N ab}{dt} \qquad (19)$$

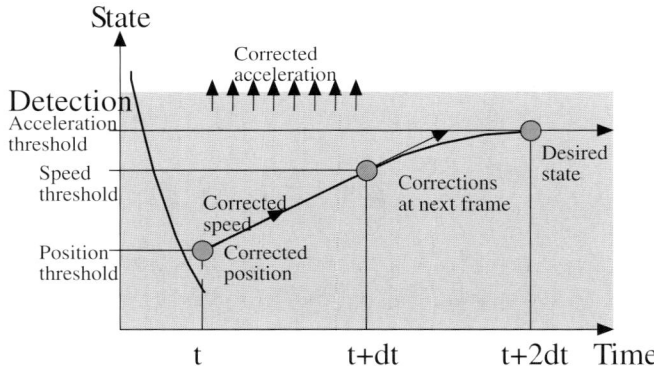

Fig. 4.16. Acceleration correction for collision reaction response.

Depending on the simulation context, the use of these three successive schemes appears to be the most robust solution, using specific collision distances for each one. In practice, the position correction is first applied in order to replace the particles in "reasonable" configurations, the speed correction then orients the particle evolution toward a better configuration, and the acceleration correction finally ensures smooth evolution toward the desired configu-

4.2 Implementing Collision Response

ration. Collision response should rely mostly on the latter, whereas the two others act depending on the collision severity, typically during the initial shock.

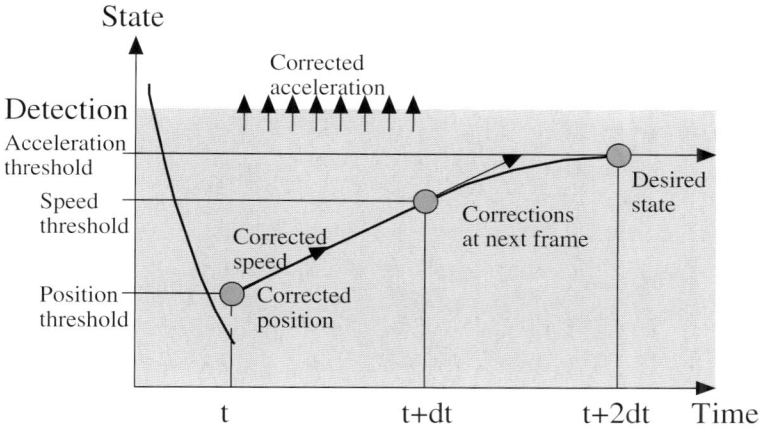

Fig. 4.17. Combined corrections of position, speed and acceleration.

For usual collision response, these corrections should only be applied in situations where the state and the evolution of the objects are against the constraint of the collision (repulsion). That is, in the cases where $P_0^N ab > P^N ab$, $P_0^{N'} ab > P^{N'} ab$, $P_0^{N''} ab > P^{N''} ab$ along the collision orientation **Pab**, bidirectional constraints (stitching) would be simulated without these restrictions.

Coulombian friction is defined by a friction parameter, and the tangential collision friction force is a force opposed to the sliding of the colliding objects, and its norm is the norm of the normal collision reaction force. This friction model can be integrated into the correction scheme, in terms of position, speed and acceleration corrections, using the same correction scheme. For simplification, correction on position, speed and acceleration can be performed independently, assuming a direct relation between the friction force and the collision position and speed related to the corresponding collision acceleration. The tangential friction corrections related to a Coulombian-friction coefficient **f** are computed from the normal reaction corrections as follows:

$$P_0^T ab = \max\left(1 - f\frac{|P_0^N ab - P^N ab|}{|P'^T ab|}, 0\right) P^T ab$$

$$P_0'^T ab = \max\left(1 - f\frac{|P_0'^N ab - P'^N ab|}{|P'^T ab|}, 0\right) P'^T ab \qquad (20)$$

$$P_0''^T ab = \max\left(1 - f\frac{|P_0''^N ab - P''^N ab|}{|P''^T ab|}, 0\right) P''^T ab$$

The final step is to recombine the normal and desired tangential collision positions, speeds and accelerations, to obtain the correction values to be used in the mesh state correction scheme:

$$P_0 ab = P_0^N ab + P_0^T ab$$
$$P_0' ab = P_0'^N ab + P_0'^T ab \qquad (21)$$
$$P_0'' ab = P_0''^N ab + P_0''^T ab$$

It is important to note that an acceleration-based collision response can be indeed considered as a "mechanical" collision response, as there is equivalence between force and acceleration, through Newton's second law. The collision force **Fab** is expressed as follows:

$$(Ma^{-1} + Mb^{-1}) Fab = P_0'' ab - P'' ab \qquad (22)$$

The biggest interest of this equivalence is the integration of geometrical collision response in a force-based mechanical model. For instance, when considering implicit integration schemes, the "force derivatives" of an acceleration-based collision response correction can be computed using the correction model, here corresponding to the expression (19) and the related friction model.

The difference between an acceleration-based correction model and a "real" force-based mechanical collision model is that the correction model computes the adequate "force" according to the geometrical context and the time step size in order to reach the desired state at the next time steps, whereas a mechanical model only relies on a mechanical modeling of the collision, regardless to any parameter depending on the simulation conditions.

D. Handling Interacting Collisions

In typical cloth collision situations, individual collisions are not independent from each other. They may interact in the following ways:

- Several collisions may constitute a single "collision zone", which is an extended surface region where two sheets are in contact with each other. Adjacent elements collide within the zone, and the effect of neighboring collisions adds up usually in the same direction.

- In a multi-layer collision pattern, three sheets or more may pile up, and the intermediate sheets collide with other sheets on both sides. The elements of these sheets are involved in two collisions that usually have opposite effects.

Combining the effects of interacting collisions in a force-based response scheme is straightforward, as the only thing to do is to add up the resulting contact forces to obtain the global response. However, in a collision response model based on corrections to fulfill constraints based on the state of the system, it is difficult to find a general scheme that can deal efficiently with interacting collisions and give a global correction for enforcing all the collision constraints simultaneously. Two kinds of schemes are usually implemented:

- *A simultaneous correction scheme* will compute the collision response independently for each collision from the uncorrected system geometry. The collision effects are then added together, using a possible weighted factor based on the collision priority.

- *A successive correction scheme* will compute the collision response and apply its effect on the system successively for each detected collision. The effect on one computed collision thus takes into account the state resulting from the former collision effects. The order in which the collisions are taken into account is important, and adequate sorting algorithms are usually implemented.

While the simultaneous scheme has the advantage of simplicity due to the independent handling of the collisions, the way collision effects are added up sometimes does not give satisfactory global solutions. For instance, simply adding independently the collision corrections would lead to an over-correction of mesh elements involved in several complementary collisions, whereas mesh elements involved in several antagonist collisions would be under-corrected. The best way to perform this combination is to build a linear system which considers the geometric evolution of a given collision as a linear combination of the corrections exerted on all interacting collisions. Solving this system would yield the corrections on all collisions and that would lead to the desired, global geometric evolution.

An algorithm using the successive corrections on the collisions is less accurate than a well-resolved global method, but is much simpler to implement. Additional accuracy can be obtained by iterating the corrections on all the collisions several times. The method is also more efficient when the collision list is sorted, so that the collisions requiring the largest corrections are processed first.

Fig. 4.18. Several cloth layers with interacting collisions. Stability should be ensured in such configurations.

E. Limits of Collision Response Model

Modeling friction as a geometrical constraint is of course, an approximate model which, being suited for simulating Coulombian friction, shows its limits not because of the model formulation itself, but rather because of the geometric nature of collisions between polygonal meshes.

A precise, mechanical collision response model would require an accurate characterization of the contact region between the objects, as well as a precise map of the contact forces. However, curved polygonal meshes cannot adjust to each other to form a well-defined contact region, and the contacts are roughly described by discrete collision events on the elements of the meshes, which furthermore evolve rapidly as the surfaces slide against each other. The measured "collision distances" are only a very rough evaluation of a supposed surface distance between colliding objects.

Building a collision response model on these discrete collisions therefore, can only be a rough approximation of the "real" collision effect which would require another curved surface description scheme for more accurate results. Such limitations are present regardless of the considered collision response scheme and can only be solved by an improved geometrical description of curved surfaces

4.2 Implementing Collision Response

Fig. 4.19. A crumpling dress, illustrating a complex collision situation.

For geometrical correction response models, the main issues still derive from the interactions between the collision response effects and the mechanical model. The major consideration for dealing with this issue is to ensure collision-response effects is as continuous as possible with respect to the small changes in the collision geometry. This would contribute to the existence of stability configurations between colliding elements which is essential to the animation quality of tight cloth (Fig. 4.20). The main difficulty is to minimize the cost of geometrical evaluations for evaluating sufficiently accurate, collision geometries.

Fig. 4.20. MIRALab "Golden Camera Awards" 1996: Collision response stability is particularly important for tight garments.

4.3 Constraints & Seaming

Among different interactions a cloth object can be subjected to, by other objects or entities, collisions are the main contributors. However, collisions are not sufficient to reflect a wide range of other miscellaneous interaction types, such as user interaction, attach points, or other tools that help bring objects together and position them in space.

Such interactions can be identified as kinds of generalized "collision" effects, which are not triggered by a geometrical contact nor defined by the geometrical properties of this contact, but defined in a more general way between distant object regions that enforce a certain kind of motion constraint.

For instance, "elastics" are tools created for helping the construction of a garment by assembling several patterns together. Using the adapted-constraint scheme rather than mechanical-force scheme, the elastics become more efficient for bringing objects together and can also be used as attaching tools, whilst also being easier for the user to parametrize.

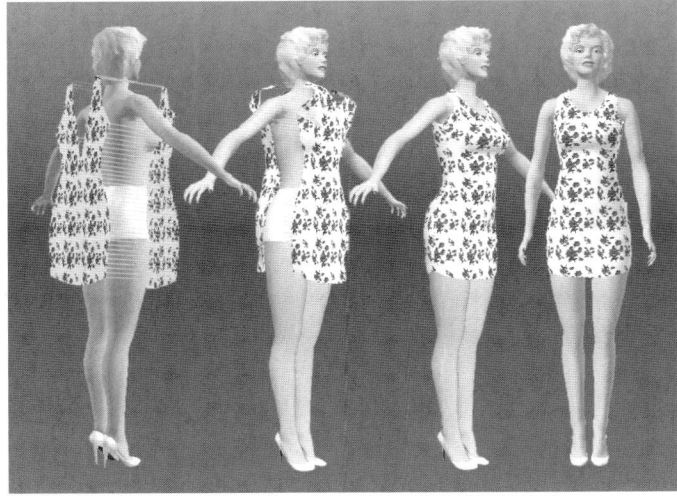

Fig. 4.21. Seaming garment patterns around a virtual body.

4.3.1 Elastics to Bring Objects Together

While many different kinds of interactions may be defined, one of the most important tools are those used to bring and maintain objects together.

For the field of garment simulation, interaction is needed in the simulation of the virtual cloth in order to provide a way to control the animations in a given way, to move them through an additional action or constraint, or simply to keep objects stitched together. Elastics are defined as additional interaction tools to fulfill these tasks.

Basically, the effect of elastics can be one of the two types:

- To bring two object's attach points progressively together.
- To maintain the attach points together during motion.

For the seaming process, one idea could be to geometrically bring the attached points together in a single step through a very simple geometrical displacement. This solution is however, not acceptable in most cases as, since initial distance between the attached points is initially high compared to the mesh element size, and the resulting deformations would be excessively high after the correction. Furthermore, the resulting shape often has to satisfy some constraints related to deformations or to the environment, such as some colliding objects in between the points to be attached. Only a progressive evolution, in conjunction with the mechanical model and collision constraints, would provide a satisfactory result.

Attaching and maintaining several objects together can involve similar issues. In particular, if the objects are already subject to constraints incompatible with the attachment, a geometrical solution cannot be defined. Elastics give the most satisfactory result by maintaining the attached objects at the closest distance between them. This is also true for any kind of user interaction for which the generated displacements are not governed by mechanical laws and constraints. Attaching an object by the user-defined elastics will exhibit the closest motion that is compatible with its mechanical laws.

Elastics an be thought of as ordinary rubber bands that attract their extremities together. Bsides just modeling such simple interactions, defining additional geometrical properties would help them to fulfill their task more efficiently with a minimum of user tuning and interaction.

There is quite a strong analogy between the effects of these elastic constraints and collision response, and these can both be carried out either by using mechanical forces or geometrical constraints.

4.3.2 Controlling the Elastic Effect

The major difficulty in using elastics is to tune their effect accurately so that they pull the objects together in a suitably short time, without producing too large a number of constraints and deformations on the objects.

Obviously, heavy rigid objects would require very strong elastics, whereas light, deformable objects would require very weak elastics. Unfortunately, it is difficult to quantitatively evaluate the adequate strength, which also depends on the current object geometries and other constraints (i.e. collisions and other attaching points).

The problem of having elastics producing efficient effects without a manual tuning of their force parameters can be solved using the adaptive algorithms applied on either the elastics producing mechanical forces or the elastics that use geometrical constraints.

4.3.2.1 Adaptive Elastics

The most intuitive approach is to use the force-driven elastics directly integrated in the mechanical model. An adaptive scheme would then modify the elastic strength force depending on the actual motion and deformation of the concerned objects.

The scheme basically monitors the evolution of the distance separating the two attach points of the elastics during time. The elastic force is increased if the objects are not quickly brought together, and reduced if the approaching speed or object deformation is too high.

While this scheme would produce satisfactory results in most situations, several limitations and problems are present:

- A very general adaptive algorithm is very difficult to design because of the high variety of object shapes and constraints which each require different effects.

- In particular, the effect of geometrical constraints (blocked points, collisions and other elastics) in the vicinity of the attach points highly alters their speed and perturbs the adaptive scheme.

- User interaction, such as object displacements, furthermore alters the response of the adaptive algorithm.

- The actual elastic force does not depend only on the geometrical situation (the positions and velocities of the attach points), but also on their history. A simulation containing elastics cannot be reproduced in a deterministic way using the knowledge of only the starting position.

While the integration of the elastics in the mechanical model provides an efficient response, particularly in the situations containing numerous elastics interacting by common attach points, these problems however, generate artifacts degrading the global simulation motion and reproducibility. While its application in the model described in [VOL 95] yields satisfactory results for the garment pattern seaming purpose, a new model is required to avoid problems in very general situations.

4.3.2.2 Elastics as Constraints

The second idea is to produce the effect of the elastics not by a mechanical force, but directly by a geometrical constraint. This is apart from the mechanical model which alters the position and speed of the objects in a more deterministic way. Constraint-based interaction is a general scheme that may be implemented in the particular case of collision response effects.

A. Elastic Parameters

The user should be given a very simple way to characterize the effect of the elastics and to describe its "strength", using as few parameters as possible.

The mechanical force exerted by an elastic is obviously not a suitable parameter. It has to be adapted according to the geometry and mechanical parameters of the objects to produce similar visual results. The best parameter seems to be the measure of the *time* the elastic needs to bring the objects together, regardless of any other factor. This time only needs to be adapted to the simulation timescale context, which often does not vary with different simulations.

In a similar way, other minor factors for improving the elastic effects, such as damping, can be defined using parameters that scale only on time and which basically remain constant.

B. An Acceleration Correction Scheme

As elastics are not used to enforce geometrical constraints on position and speed, such as for collisions, this is certainly not the solution for producing the elastic effect. Such corrections may also raise lots of problems concerning the combination of interacting elastics and interaction with collisions.

A better choice is to perform the correction on the acceleration of the attach points of the elastics, as these are initially computed by the mechanical model. Hence, given the current positions **Pa**, **Pb**, speeds **P'a**, **P'b** and accelerations **P"a** and **P"b** of the attach points of the elastics on the two objects **A** and **B**, the elastic models compute the acceleration corrections Δ**P"a** and Δ**P"b** (Fig. 4.22).

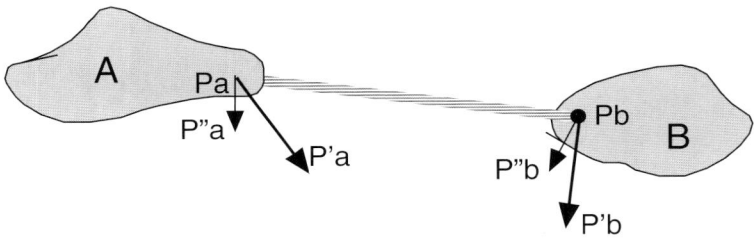

Fig. 4.22. An elastic between the attach points of two objects.

Many different solutions can be proposed to define the behavior of an elastic. In order to provide an extensive versatility, the elastic should be controlled by the time it needs to bring the objects together, the damping of initial motion, and anisotropic behavior. As an example, such a general model is described in the following section.

A general and versatile model for the elastic effect can be represented by five parameters:

- An actuation parameter *force* which represents the approximate inverse time for the elastic to bring the objects together.

4.3 Constraints & Seaming

- A damping parameter *relax* which represents the approximate inverse time for the elastic to damp the elongation speed.

- A damping parameter *damp* which represents the approximate inverse time for the elastic to damp the transversal speed.

- An attenuation parameter *atten* which represents the attenuation factor of the elongation acceleration resulting from mechanical forces.

- An attenuation parameter *attet* which represents the attenuation factor of the transversal acceleration resulting from mechanical forces.

The parameter *force* is mainly used for the control of the amplitude of elastic effect. Combined with the parameter *relax* which takes into account the current elongation speed between the attach points, a smooth and damped approach is obtained.

The parameter *damp* is used to reduce the transversal speed of the elastic, which will avoid the objects swinging around each other if their motion does not converge to the same point. It should be noted that since the rotation momentum is not conserved in the whole system, this parameter cannot be representative of a "real" mechanical elastic. This parameter is however very important to help attach points to converge directly with each other without any rotation and bouncing artifacts.

Finally, the parameters *atten* and *attet* attenuate respectively the existing elongation and transversal accelerations, originally resulting from the mechanical model. By setting them to 1, these initial accelerations are totally cancelled and the attach points move through the effect of the elastic interaction only. While having the elongation acceleration suppressed in order to get the full attraction power of the elastic, the transversal acceleration should however be kept to allow relative rotation of the attach points and reflect the global motion of the objects.

A set of values suitable for garment attachment and seaming simulations at a frame rate of 25 frames per second may result in the following:

```
force = 20
relax = 5
damp  = 25
atten = 1
attet = 0
```

In order to compute the correction, the first step is to compute the relative position **Pab**, speed **P'ab** and acceleration **P"ab** between the attach points of an elastic:

$$Pab = Pb - Pa$$
$$P'ab = P'b - P'a \qquad (23)$$
$$P"ab = P"b - P"a$$

The elongation and transversal components of the relative speed and acceleration are then separated:

$$P^{N}{}'ab = \frac{P'ab \bullet Pab}{Pab^2} Pab \qquad P^{T}{}'ab = P'ab - P^{N}{}'ab$$
$$P^{N}{}"ab = \frac{P"ab \bullet Pab}{Pab^2} Pab \qquad P^{T}{}"ab = P"ab - P^{N}{}"ab \qquad (24)$$

The acceleration correction should be computed from the elastic parameters as follows:

$$\Delta P"ab = (force\,relax)Pab + (force + relax)P^{N}{}'ab + damp\,P^{T}{}'ab + atten\,P^{N}{}"ab + attet\,P^{T}{}"ab \qquad (25)$$

The correction should finally be distributed to the attach points using their masses **Ma** and **Mb**:

$$\Delta P"a = \frac{Ma^{-1}}{Ma^{-1} + Mb^{-1}} \Delta P"ab \qquad \Delta P"b = \frac{-Mb^{-1}}{Ma^{-1} + Mb^{-1}} \Delta P"ab \qquad (26)$$

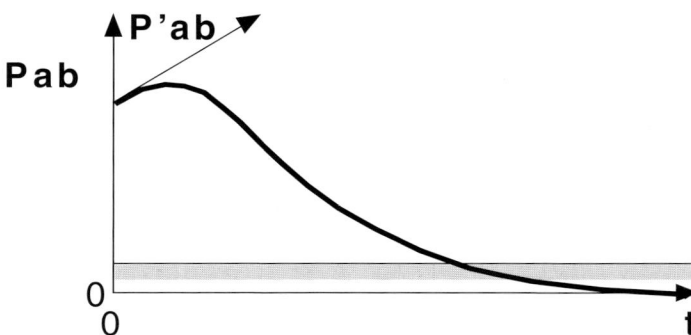

Fig. 4.23. Typical evolution of an elastic length along time.

If an attach point is shared by several elastics, all the corrections are always computed simultaneously with the uncorrected acceleration of the attach point and then added together.

C. Combining Elastics and Collision Response

Both elastic interactions and collision response are handled as geometrical corrections, and their interaction cannot be a simple addition of the effects.

Since elastics only simulate some force contributions, whereas collisions enforce geometrical constraints, the elastic effects should be considered as mechanical effects with regard to collisions. Therefore they should be computed directly after, and as a correction of the mechanical model, for obtaining the accelerations, before any collision correction.

As collisions are enforced after the effect of the elastics, there is no risk of seeing an elastic pull an object through another. In particular, the final result is that the two attach points are steadily maintained together by the elastic separated by the collision distance. Friction effects may interfere with the correct elastic action. In order to prevent this from happening, a solution is to disable friction forces on attach points.

D. Results

The properties of the implemented elastics indeed differ from real-life rubber bands: First, they attract their attach points to an ideally null distance. In practice, this is limited by the collision distance between the objects. They also have damping properties that help the objects come together very quickly, regardless of their shape and mechanical parameters.

Basically, the user only controls the approximate time needed to bring the objects together, whatever any mechanical parameters or even the size scaling of the scene may be. In practice, this time corresponds to the number of animation frames.

Unlike what happens with real-world rubber bands, damping is applied on the elongation speed. The effect is to slow down objects approaching too rapidly and to avoid shock effects during collision. Damping is also applied on the transversal motion of the elastic. While not corresponding to any kind of physical phenomenon as the rotation momentum of the system is not kept constant, this property really helps the attach points to move towards each other whatever their initial position and speed, and discardings the situation where the objects keep rotating around each other slowing down convergence.

Practical tests have demonstrated the insensitivity of the elastic effects to the mechanical parameters and even the scaling size of the scene. Hence, the elastic parameters do not have to be modified for most simulation contexts.

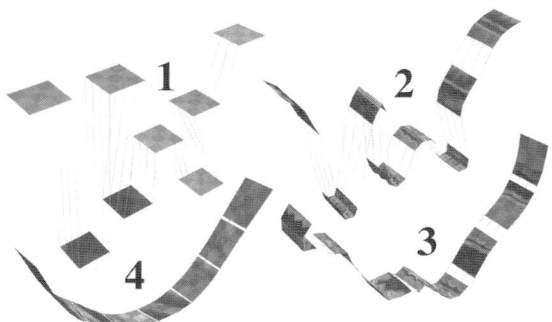

Fig. 4.24. Elastics pull together surfaces quickly and in an approximately constant time, whatever the scaling, constraints and mechanical parameters of the individual objects.

The main limitations of this scheme involves deformations that might be generated on the objects. As generated speed on the attach points does not vary with the geometry and mechanical parameters on the attached objects, the local mesh deformations around the attached points may become high. The mechanical model governing the object deformations should be able to support high deformations in order to prevent instability problems experienced using elastics that only need a few frames to bring the attach points together.

4.3.3 Applications

Elastics are very suitable tools to help the construction and seaming of virtual garments. From initial positioning of garment patterns around a virtual body, such elastics can be used to bring together the seaming lines of the patterns by a mechanical simulation process that uses mechanical parameters suited for such kind of "virtual" seaming.

However, performant elastics may also be used in interactive design systems as a particular kind of manipulation tools for attracting object points together. Interactive seaming and attachments allow intuitive garment manipulation through interactions that reflect the actions of real-world tools.

4.3 Constraints & Seaming

Fig. 4.25. Using elastics for assembling garment patterns around a virtual body.

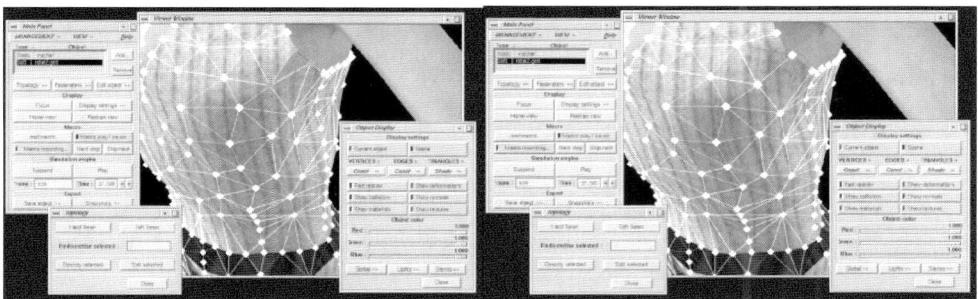

Fig. 4.26. Interactive garment seaming using elastics.

5 Smoothing & Wrinkles

Computation can be accelerated by using coarser surface meshes. Not only do rough or coarse meshes reduce the amount of data for computation, but they also allow larger simulation steps, due to improved numerical stability. Using a standard, flat triangle mesh representation, the range of deformations possible is limited by the maximum curvature allowed by the discretization, which cannot be smaller than the size of an element.

In cloth simulation, the realism results mainly from the appearance of wrinkling and buckling of the surface. The purpose of this chapter is to describe some techniques which enhance the rough meshes of simple cloth models, by smoothing the surface and adding geometrically controlled wrinkles. Practical details are given for implementation which can be adapted to more general situations involving the animation of rough meshes.

5.1 Multilayer Models

It is possible to define a three-layer model for simulating a wrinkled cloth. The layers are:

- *The mechanical layer*, which geometrically deforms a triangular mesh according to mechanical laws
- *The smoothing layer*, which replaces each triangle by an interpolation patch ensuring a smooth surface using the vertex normals.
- *The wrinkling layer*, which draws a wrinkle on the surface modulated by geometrical deformation data extracted from the mechanical layer. This can be geometrically rendered either by altering the surface geometry to reflect the actual wrinkle height, or through texture bump-mapping with controlled amplitude.

The interpolation process smoothes of the whole surface, replacing the flat triangles of the mesh by curved patches and using vertex positions and surface normals as control points, as done in [BAJ 92]. In contrast to the approximation schemes, this approach is local to individual triangles, each of which can be smoothed independently. Our main objective is, however, to develop a very simple and flexible algorithm for to fast rendering. By dropping some continuity requirements that do not usually affect the perceived smoothness of the surface, we can drastically simplify the process, reducing computation and limiting it to simple vector operations on triangle positions and normals.

The wrinkling process simulates geometrical deformation the wrinkles on the triangles. The wrinkles are stored in a "texture" heightfield, and can be defined by the color channels of any regular texture. Using the current triangle-deformation state, easily computed from the length variation of its edges, the heightfield is modulated in order to simulate the wrinkle height variation according to surface deformation. This method successfully simulates the wrinkles having significant depth as if they were "real" deformation and is suitable for macroscopic wrinkling, such as that occurring with cloth. A proposed extension to this method is to modulate the bump-mapped wrinkles using the same technique, allowing thinner details to be rendered.

Considering different aspects of the speed versus realism, these techniques can be combined efficiently for rendering realistic surfaces based on triangle mesh, the vertex normals (as are usually used for shading), the deformation state (initial length of the edges), as well as the texture maps defining the wrinkle patterns.

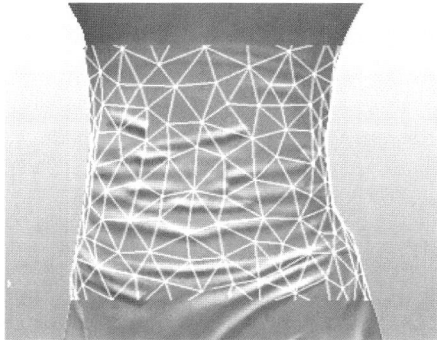

Fig. 5.1. Small wrinkles on a rough mesh used for mechanical simulation.

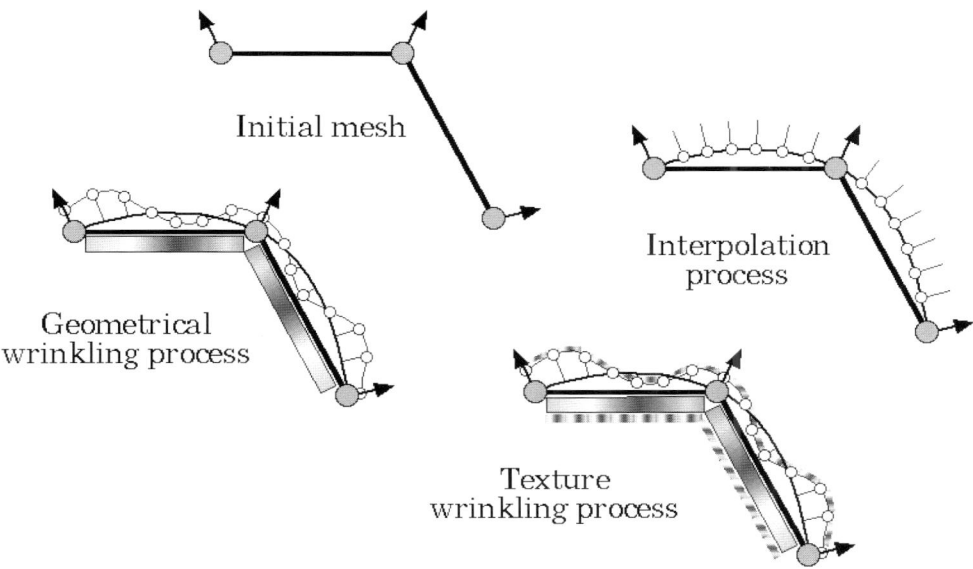

Fig. 5.2. Processes in the multilayer wrinkling approach.

5.2 A Simple Geometrical Interpolation Algorithm

Interpolating a polygonal mesh into a smooth surface is the first step in improving the visual quality of cloth described by rough meshes [VOL 98].

5.2.1 The Problem

In a way similar to [BAJ 92], we compute a triangular smoothing patch that interpolates the vertices of a triangle by a surface that is orthogonal to given vertex normals (Fig. 5.3).

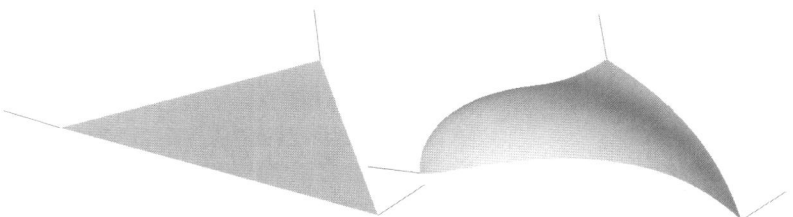

Fig. 5.3. The initial triangle and the interpolation surface orthogonal to the vertex normals.

Phong normals are a good approximation to the "ideal" smooth surface orientation. The main idea of our technique is to build the smooth surface out of these normals from any point of a triangle using a very simple geometric construction.

Unlike the requirements of most techniques in the literature, we wish to avoid complex preprocessing such as setting up local coordinates, computing curve parameters, or constraining recursive subdivision scheme. In order to reach this level of simplification, we drop strict requirements for curvature continuity between triangle edges in our smoothing model. This results in curvature discontinuities that usually are not visually apparent, as shown in the examples at the end of this chapter.

5.2.2 Constructing the Surface

Given the triangle defined by the vertices **Pa,Pb,Pc** and their respective normals **Na,Nb,Nc**, the goal is to compute an interpolated point **Q** expressed by the triangle barycentric coordinates **ra,rb,rc**.

We first compute the corresponding point **P** on the flat triangle surface and then compute the Phong normal **N** at this point by linear interpolation using the barycentric coordinates (Fig. 5.4). These Phong normals represent the normals of an approximate curved patch surface over the triangle.

$$P = (ra\,Pa + rb\,Pb + rc\,Pc)$$
$$N = (ra\,Na + rb\,Nb + rc\,Nc)_{Normalized}$$
(1)

5.2 A Simple Geometrical Interpolation Algorithm

For each vertex of the triangle, we then compute the corresponding displacement contributions (Fig. 5.5). For the vertex **Pa**, we compute the contribution **Qa** associated with the triangle point **P** as follows:

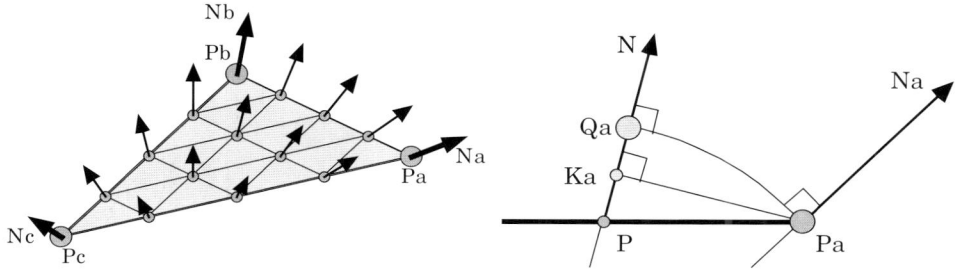

Fig. 5.4. Interpolating positions and normals on the triangle. Fig. 5.5. The construction of the vertex contribution for a given point.

We want to position **Qa** on the line defined by **P** and in the direction **N** by constructing a circular arc linking **Pa** to **Qa**, orthogonal to **Na** at **Pa** and orthogonal to **N** at **Qa**.

The first step is to orthogonally project **Pa** into **Ka** following the direction **N** from the point **P**:

$$Ka = P + ((Pa - P) \bullet N)N \qquad (2)$$

Then we find **Qa** from **Ka** by describing the circular arc, as shown in Fig. 5.5. Skipping geometrical detail and introducing the parameter $\mu = 1$, we finally obtain:

$$Qa = Ka + \frac{(Pa - Ka) \bullet Na}{2 + \mu((N \bullet Na) - 1)} N \qquad (3)$$

For any point **P** defined on the triangles adjacent to **Pa**, **Qa** describes a continuous curved surface passing through **Pa**. We now have to blend the three surfaces generated by **Pa,Pb,Pc** over the triangle surface. Calculations (2) and (3) for the three vertices **Pa,Pb,Pc** give us three points **Qa,Qb,Qc** aligned on the line defined by the point **P** and in the direction **N** (Fig. 5.7). We now blend these three points into one point **Q** using a shape function **f** constructed on the barycentric coordinates and normalized:

$$Q = \frac{f(ra)Qa + f(rb)Qb + f(rc)Qc}{f(ra) + f(rb) + f(rc)} \qquad (4)$$

The choice of the blending function **f** is critical to the final shape of the surface. It should be regularly increasing along the **[0,1]** interval and have null value and the derivative at **0**. A low order polynomial, such as **f(x) = x^2**, does the job perfectly (Fig. 5.6).

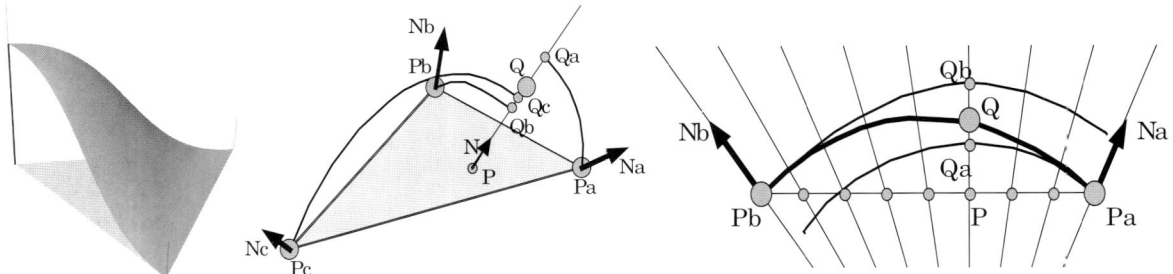

Fig. 5.6. The vertex blending function. Fig. 5.7. Interpolating the vertex contributions. Fig. 5.8. Building the interpolation surface.

Using this algorithm, the interpolated point of any point on the barycentric triangle can be computed. We integrate this algorithm in our system by a rediscretizating of the surface triangles: each triangle is subdivided into smaller ones by interpolating extra vertices.

5.2.2.1 Interpolated surface normals

For some applications, such as shaded rendering, the surface normals are required. Rather than carrying out a complex derivation of the resulting parametric surface, it is considerably more efficient to compute them directly from the rediscretized surface triangles obtained after interpolation.

But do they really need to be recomputed? We have already computed the approximate Phong normals. For shading purposes, where real orthogonality is not strongly required, these normals will suffice. Furthermore, they suppress the shading of the extra blending beveling and inflections inherent to interpolation techniques near the curvature inflections and also, hide away shading discontinuities due to non-perfect curvature continuity along the edges. To further improve the quality, developments from [OVE 97] which providing better normal orientation models on polygonal meshes, may be considered.

5.2.2.2 Extension for N-Sided Polygons

While the interpolation algorithm has been illustrated here for triangular polygons, it can be easily extended for polygons having an arbitrary number of sides (Fig. 5.9). The only question is how to work with barycentric coordinates in such polygons, which involves various optimizations related to this problem.

Fig. 5.9. An N-sided polygon surface deformed to be orthogonal to its given vertex normals.

A. Generalized Barycentric Coordinates

When working with polygons that have more than three sides, the main difficulty in applying the algorithm presented above is how to define an efficient way to build a local coordinate system with the same, desirable properties as the barycentric coordinates of a triangle. A good solution is described in [LOD 93] and [KUR 93], where the barycentric coordinates $\mathbf{r} = (\mathbf{r1..rn})$ of a point $\mathbf{P}$ in a polygon is computed by building a surface partition of that polygon and calculating the contributions from the surface areas $\mathbf{Amn}$ in the following way:

$$ri = \left\{ \prod_{mn \neq i} Amn \right\}_{(i)} \quad Amn = \|(Pm - P) \wedge (Pn - P)\| \tag{5}$$

B. Building a Polygon Rediscretization Set

The above results are directly useful for building our interpolation surface. However, for the majority of applications the polygons will have to be rediscretized into a given subdivision pattern and hence into a set of barycentric coordinate vectors that represent all the intermediate subdivision vertices. However, computing the barycentric coordinates of a set of interpolation vertices using the generalized version of formula (5) is time-consuming, if it has to be performed for all the polygons each time they are rendered. It is better to precompute the generic sets of coordinates, each corresponding to a given **n**-sided polygon and a discretization pattern.

In our system, an **n**-sided polygon is regularly divided by locating its center and then joining it to its **n** vertices, thus constructing **n** triangles. These triangles are then divided regularly by defining intermediate vertices and computing their barycentric coordinates in the full polygon. For a given discretization rate, this operation is done for the usual triangle, square, pentagon, hexagon, or any regular **n**-sided polygon inscribed in the unit circle (Fig. 5.10). During the interpolation process, the barycentric coordinates are read directly from the corresponding precomputed table.

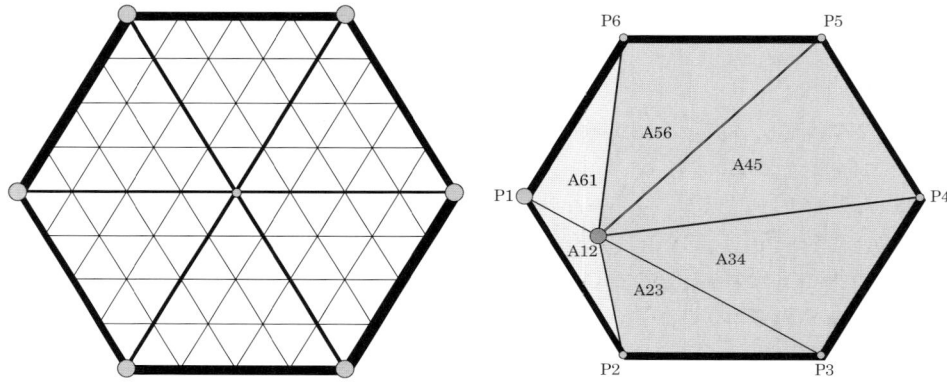

Fig. 5.10. Building a discretization mesh on a regular polygon using the triangular subdivision determined by the center.

Fig. 5.11. Computing the barycentric coordinates of a discretized vertex, here the contribution of the vertex **P1**.

Computing the barycentric coordinates based on generic regular polygons instead of the actual polygons also ensures discretization continuity along the edges. The interpolation vertices along an edge will have the same barycentric coordinates when computed from any adjacent polygon if the initial discretization pattern is the same.

Integrated into our rendering application, this improved greatly speeds up the computation, since, for each interpolation performed, the computation for each interpolated vertex is reduced to the formulas described for interpolation.

5.2 A Simple Geometrical Interpolation Algorithm

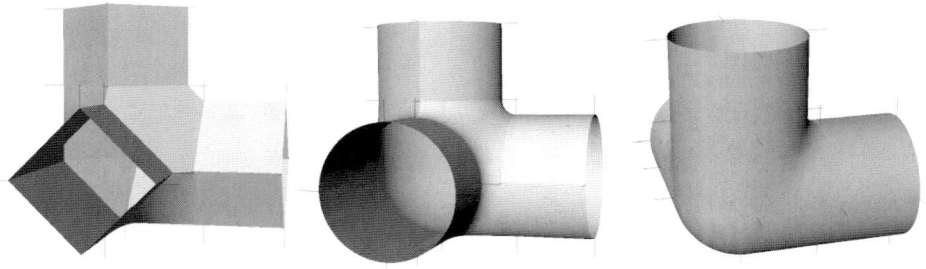

Fig. 5.12. Pipe blending, using 3, 4, 5 (non planar) and 6 sided interpolation patches.

5.2.3 Results

The interpolation method described above combines simplicity and efficiency, since interpolation points are computed directly from the triangle vertices and normals using simple vector operations, without complex spline parametrization [BAJ 92] or mesh subdivision [SAB 86] [HAL 93] [ZOR 96]. It can be implemented in a straightforward way into any system since it does not require a particular data structure or subdivision scheme, nor does it entail heavy processing or preprocessing. Furthermore, each triangle is interpolated individually and independently from its neighbors, allowing a great deal of flexibility in the context of applications where object topologies vary over time.

Though mathematical-curvature continuity is not formally ensured, excellent results are obtained, especially when the surface curvature is fairly regular. For example, almost perfect spheres or cylinders result from the discretizations containing very few polygons (Fig. 5.9).

All the examples shown demonstrate the visual quality of the interpolation. The curvature continuity appears perfect everywhere, despite high curvature. The interpolation patch we have described is a good compromise between speed and visual quality, especially adapted for computer graphics applications with fast rendering.

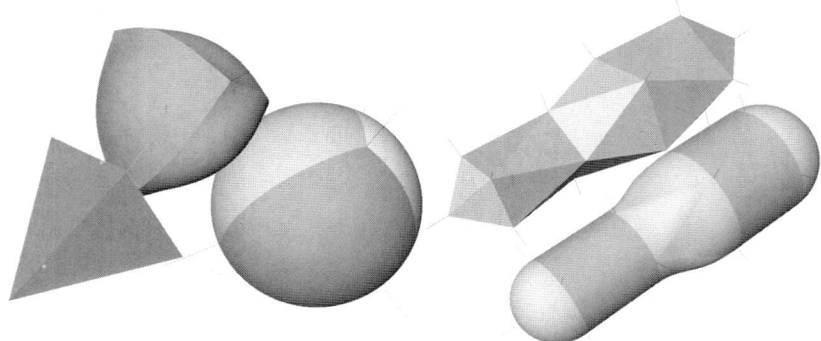

Fig. 5.13. Turning the crudest sphere discretization -a tetrahedron- into an almost perfect sphere. Shown here with 0%, 50% and 100% deformation.

Fig. 5.14. A 32-sided polygonal object turned into a cylinder-like volume. Discontinuities are barely apparent.

Fig. 5.15. A hanging cloth defined by a very rough mesh. Shown with its initial mesh, Gouraud shaded, interpolated.

Modeling is really simplified, as rough meshes can be used for object definition. The interpolation is performed "on the fly" at display time, without explicit storage of the rediscretization. Quality rendering is obtained while the data storage is kept very small.

Interpolation allows us to produce good quality representations of cloth using very rough triangle meshes which undergo mechanical simulation. As the interpolation can be performed at rendering time, mechanical computation time is not affected. It is important to note, however, that the main advantage of the interpolation is the possibility of using very rough meshes, as in cloth simulation. An efficient processing time can be obtained in the mechanical simulation and the collision detection. This is a definite step towards simulation interactivity.

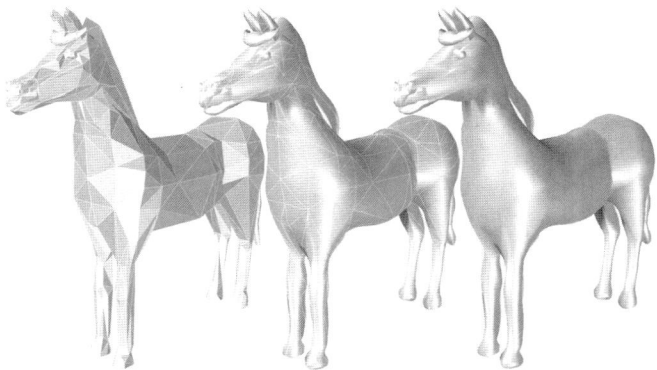

Fig. 5.16. Smoothing a rough horse.

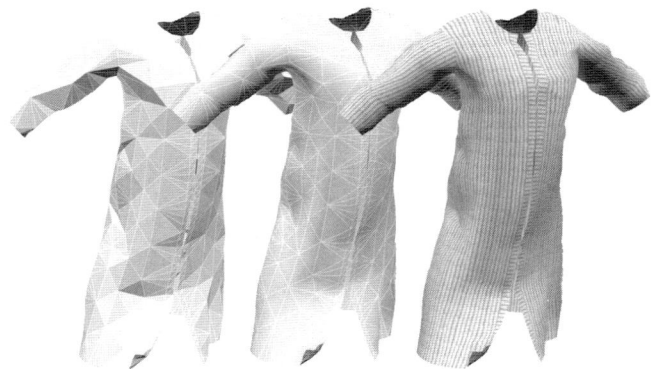

Fig. 5.17. Smoothing a coat, with texture mapping.

5.2.4 Texture as a Height Field

Using a rediscretized triangle polygon, it is easy to move the rediscretization vertices along the surface normal direction to a height that is computed from the current texture color. This can be naturally combined with the smoothing process, using the same triangle discretization and moving the smoothed surface along the computed Phong normals.

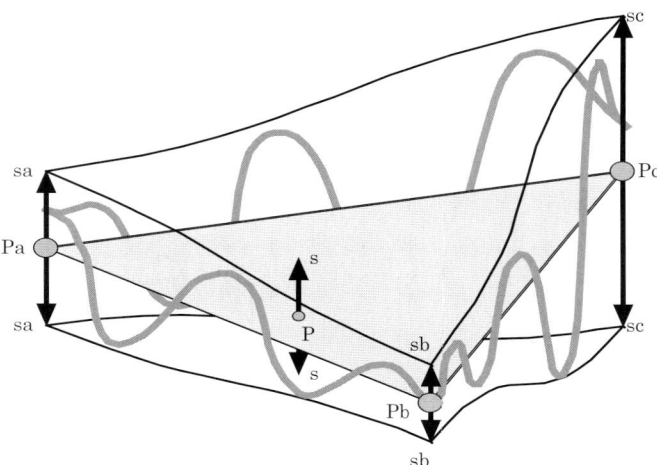

Fig. 5.18. Wrinkle amplitude interpolation between the vertices of a triangle.

In order to control the wrinkling amplitude, the coefficients **sa,sb,sc** can be defined on the mesh vertices. For any point **P** on the triangle surface defined by its barycentric coordinates **ra,rb,rc**, the amplitude coefficients are smoothly interpolated to a value **s** using the blending function defined in formula (4), using the shape function $f(x) = x^2$ (Fig. 5.18):

$$s = \frac{f(ra)sa + f(rb)sb + f(rc)sc}{f(ra) + f(rb) + f(rc)} \tag{6}$$

The remaining key issue is to compute appropriate wrinkle amplitude coefficients at the mesh vertices, given the mesh deformation.

5.2.5 Modulating Wrinkle Amplitude

The wrinkling model needs a function that computes the wrinkle amplitude as the surface is deformed. This function should be derived from the area conservation of the deformed surface, which bends and wrinkles as compresses.

Two models are presented here. The first, from [VOL 99], is a simple, fast approach to model directly the wrinkle amplitude from the elongation of the edges of the mesh. The second, from [HAD 99], is a more accurate model based on the area conservation on the mesh triangles.

5.2.5.1 Simple Geometric Approach

The most direct measure of the deformation of a mesh is found by comparing the current length of the edges to their initial or rest length. An edge contribution, **ti**, is computed for each edge **i** of the mesh (initial length **Li**) as a function of the current length **li** of this edge. The wrinkle amplitude **sa** of the mesh vertex **Pa**, is an average of the contributions of all the edges around the vertex. The edge contribution **ti** is scaled by the product **Li mi**, roughly representing the wrinkle's maximum amplitude when the edge is compressed to a very small length. Negative values of **sa** are truncated to zero.

$$sa = \sum_{I \supset Pa} Li\, mi\, ti \Big/ \sum_{I \supset Pa} 1 \tag{7}$$

The edge contribution **ti** is a normalized function defined by the current edge length variation. We model it by the expression:

$$ti = 2\lambda \left(\frac{1}{1+(li/Li)^2} - 1 \right) + 1 \tag{8}$$

The **ti** curve depicted in Fig. 5.19 illustrates how wrinkling amplitude evolves with surface elongation. Multiplied by the initial length **Li** of the edge and the shape coefficient **mi**, it captures the effect of surface length conservation along an edge as its current mesh length changes. From a maximum amplitude of **1** corresponding to maximum compression, it decreases to **0** and then to negative values, which has the effect of eliminating wrinkles when the surface is highly stretched. The λ parameter controls the degree of edge elongation that is required for the surface to produce wrinkles (Fig. 5.20). For the value greater than **1**, some compression is required to produce wrinkles, whereas for the values less than **1**, the undeformed surface is already wrinkled.

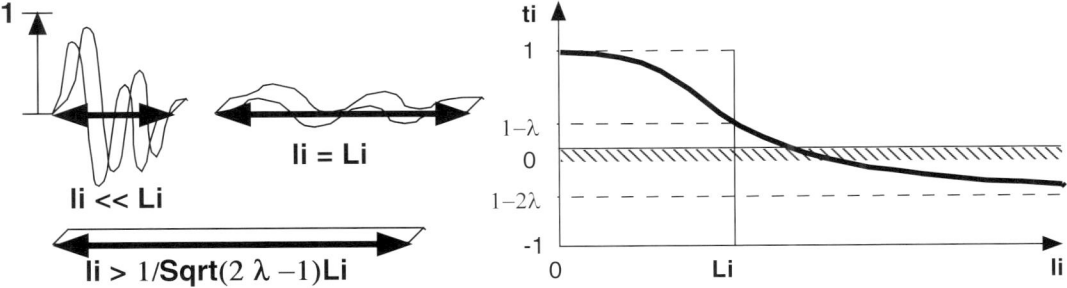

Fig. 5.19. The evolution of wrinkles and edge contribution according to the current edge length.

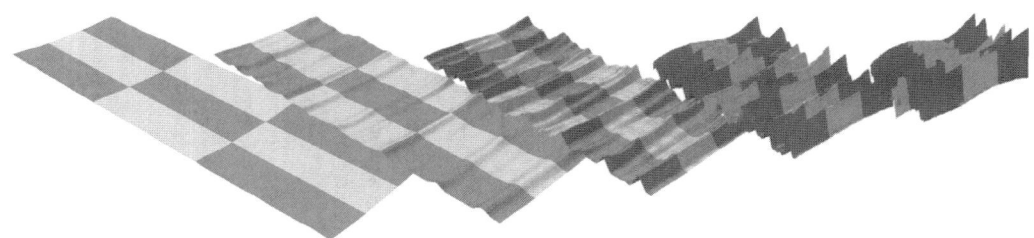

Fig. 5.20. Wrinkling amplitude variation for 120%, 100%, 80%, 50%, 20% elongation of the original length.

Wrinkles do not all react in the same way to deformations, since they vary their shape and their alignment according to the directions of elongation. The wrinkle shape coefficient **mi** controls how the wrinkle pattern reacts to the elongation of edge **i**. The closer the wrinkle deformation runs orthogonal to the direction of an edge, the more it will react to variation of that edge's length. We model the shape coefficient **mi** by the simple expression:

$$mi = 1 - \frac{1}{1 + v Ai} \tag{9}$$

Ai of the wrinkle evolution along an edge direction is the integral of the texture map gradient over the mesh triangles adjacent to the edge. A simple 1-dimensional discrete integration along the edge, however, can suffice for this evaluation. Given a discretization of the edge into **n** segments, **Ai** is **n** times the square of the wrinkle texture map height differences at the segment extremities, summed over all segments. The v parameter is introduced to control the evolution of the shape coefficient with respect to wrinkle complexity (Fig. 5.21).

The shape coefficient depends on the mesh topology and on the wrinkle texture application to the mesh. There is **no** need to recompute it if the wrinkle texture definition does not change or move on the mesh surface.

5.2 A Simple Geometrical Interpolation Algorithm

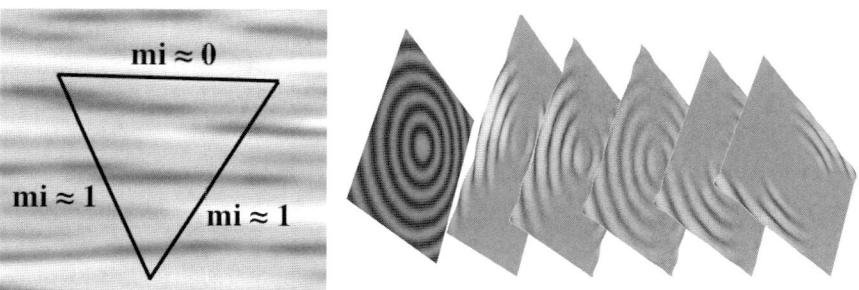

Fig. 5.21. Shape coefficients for triangle edges with respect to a given texture map. Fig. 5.22. Wrinkle amplitude depends on wrinkling orientation and deformation direction.

5.2.5.2 More Accurate Approach

An accurate approach to wrinkle amplitude should consider area conservation in the deformed surfaces. The accurate model modifies the wrinkle amplitude to obtain a wrinkled surface similar to the flat undeformed surface.

The computation proposed in [HAD 99] first considers the area of the undeformed mesh triangles. Then, using a local coordinate system for each triangle, the current deformation of the triangles is expressed, and the area of the wrinkled triangles is expressed depending on the wrinkling amplitude. This computation is carried out numerically by sampling the triangle surface. The model is simplified using a first-order development, yielding four coefficients that express the change in area with the deformation expression in local coordinates. These coefficients depend only on the initial triangle shape and the wrinkling pattern and are precomputed prior to the animation. During the animation, the wrinkling amplitude for each frame is obtained directly from the current deformation of the triangle using these coefficients.

The wrinkling amplitude is computed for each mesh triangle using this method, and an interpolation is needed to obtain a smooth wrinkling over the entire surface.

5.2.6 Multilayer Wrinkle Textures

Complex wrinkle patterns are often a combination of wrinkles in different directions, each reacting differently to the current deformation state. In order to reproduce such patterns accurately, several wrinkle structures have to be computed concurrently and combined to obtain the final deformation. Our wrinkle texture has several channels, each of them containing a wrinkle structure.

Typically, we use the RGB channels of a 24-bit color image to define three wrinkle structures. The shape factor **mi** of equation (9) has a different value for each channel and these values are computed separately. Thus, for a surface point, the wrinkle amplitude **s** of equation (6) has a different value for each wrinkle channel. These different wrinkle contributions all contribute to the global surface deformation (Fig. 5.23).

Using this multichannel approach, it is possible to design different wrinkle patterns, each of them appearing or disappearing as the surface is stretches in different directions.

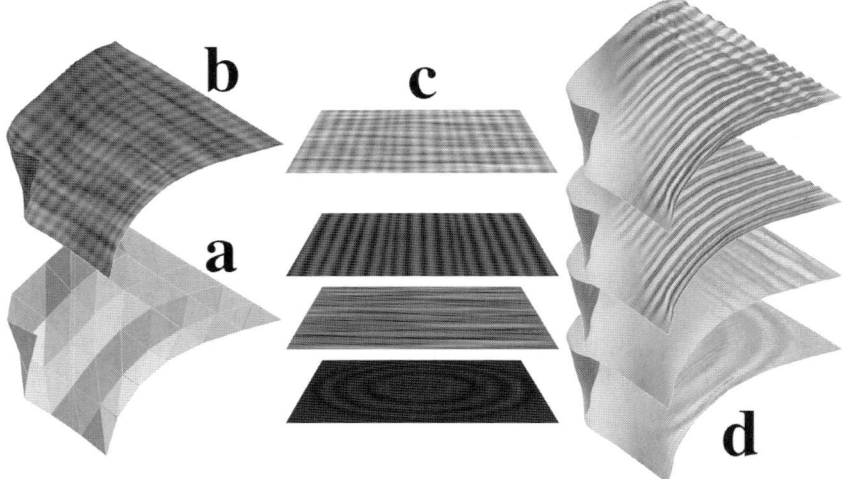

Fig. 5.23. Multichannel wrinkle generation: (a) The initial mesh with edge deformations and (b) the interpolated and textured mesh. (c) Three wrinkle patterns as texture RGB channels, (d) wrinkle computation for each channel and their combination.

The blending of the wrinkle patterns can be performed in an additive way. However, orthogonal wrinkles are usually exclusive so that only one pattern shows up locally in a given region. The wrinkling coefficient can be computed using an appropriate formula that enhances the dominating wrinkle pattern (which has the biggest amplitude) while reducing the others. There should however be a smooth transition of the amplitude between the situations where the dominant wrinkles change. Denoting by **si** the amplitude computed for pattern **i** and **Si** the corresponding final amplitude after combination, a suitable formula, proposed in [HAD 99], is:

$$Si = si \frac{si^k}{\sum_i si^k} \qquad (10)$$

The higher the **k** exponent is, the sharper the transition between the dominant wrinkle patterns.

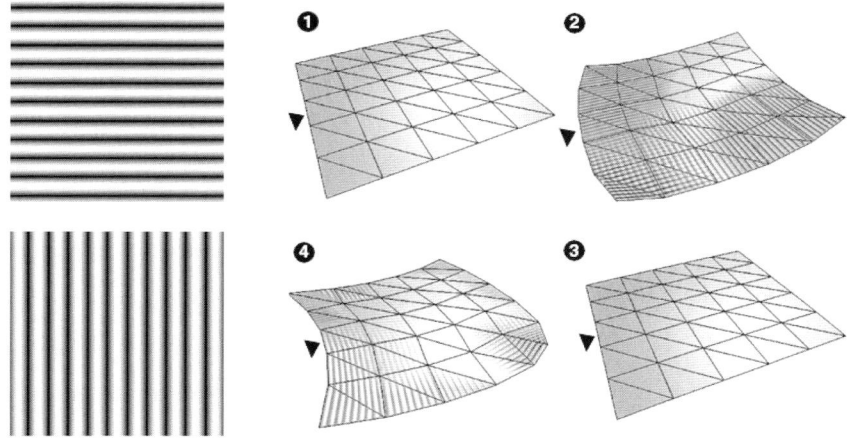

Fig. 5.24. Blending orthogonal wrinkle patterns on a deformed surface square. (From [HAD 99]).

While this formula is purely geometric and violates the area conservation considerations, it does produce visually realistic results.

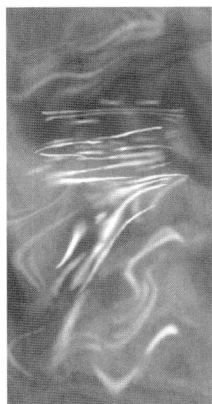 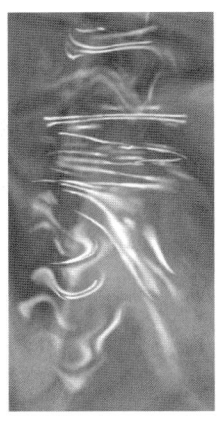 

Fig. 5.25. Two layers of wrinkle patterns, and the deformation stress on the mesh triangles of a dress. (From [HAD 99]).

5.2.7 Rendering Wrinkles

The algorithm described allows for the efficient rendering of wrinkles through a surface re-discretization. Although it is effective for high amplitude wrinkles that are rendered as real volumetric deformations, this technique does require rendering elements that are quite smaller than the wrinkle size. To overcome this limitation, the wrinkle modulation technique can be extended to the modulation of texture shading. We preview here the future developments in integrating texture wrinkles efficiently into a simulation framework.

For example, the amplitude coefficient computed in equation (7) can be used directly for modulating the texture contrast on the individual interpolated triangles. Depending on the rendering architecture and its capabilities for modulating texture rendering, different possibilities can be considered: If texture interpolation is available, either using high-end texturing hardware or bitmap rendering techniques such as ray tracing, the texture intensity should be computed on the triangle vertices and interpolated. The interpolation can take place on the mesh triangles (linear interpolation), or the amplitude can be computed directly on the rediscretized triangles. In this case, intensity discontinuity problems may arise between adjacent triangles if the elements are too big.

Bump-mapping rendering is essential to wrinkle realism. Trivially handled in the case of ray-tracing, advanced techniques may be required for fast polygon-based rendering, either

5.2 A Simple Geometrical Interpolation Algorithm

through hardware solutions [PEE 97] or by modulating precomputed gradient textures to simulate bump shading.

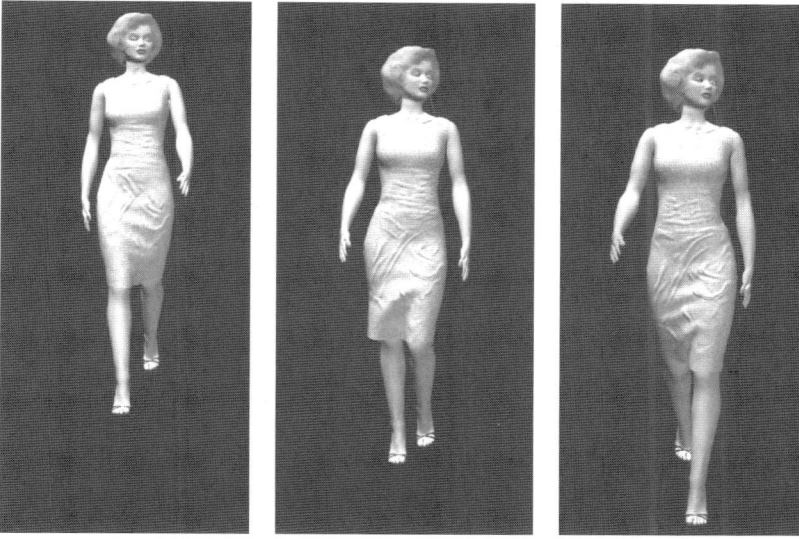

Fig. 5.26. Geometrical wrinkles rendered as bump mapping.

5.2.8 Applications

The considerable potential of these smoothing and wrinkling algorithms lies in their generality. In addition to cloth simulation, they can be integrated into many different applications in computer graphics. We describe here some of these developments.

5.2.8.1 Cloth Simulation

Integrating the interpolation algorithm into cloth simulation and animation software allows us to generate cloth with considerably enhanced realism. Rough garment models suited for fast cloth generation can be displayed with a greater degree of realism.

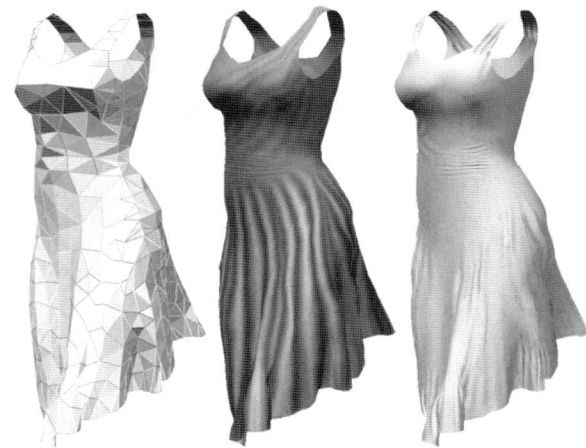

Fig. 5.27. Wrinkling a garment: From left to right, original mesh from mechanical computation with edge elongation shown, the dress shown with multichannel wrinkle texture map, and the wrinkled dress.

Moreover, like the interpolation, the generation of wrinkles is carried out "on the fly" on the deforming polygonal mesh at display time, without the need for explicit storage of the interpolated and wrinkled structure. The wrinkles are modulated dynamically as display "postprocessing". Hence no fundamental adaptation of any existing cloth simulation software is required. Some changes in the mechanical properties of the fabric material containing wrinkles and a significant decrease of the compression rigidity parameter, are required in order to take into account the equivalent surface rigidity after wrinkling.

Fig. 5.28. An animated dress, dynamically wrinkled according to the mesh deformation.

5.2 A Simple Geometrical Interpolation Algorithm

Fig. 5.29. A garment on an animated character, without and with geometrical wrinkles (From [HAD 99]) (see also color section, plate T).

Such wrinkling techniques can dramatically improve the consequences of the realism-speed compromise in our clothing system. For instance, it is possible to use very rough triangular meshes for generating realistic and attractive garments.

5.2.8.2 Other Applications

Another application of dynamical wrinkles is in skin deformation. Since skin wrinkle pattern shapes are usually constant and do not move on the skin surface. Skin extension or compression simply modifies the depth of constant wrinkle patterns defined on the skin.

In a polygonal mesh model of the human face, facial expressions are simulated through mesh deformation. The pattern of facial wrinkles is defined on the facial texture to create the volumetric and shading features. The animation of the face elongates or compresses some regions of the mesh, automatically varying the wrinkles through the algorithm presented above. Again, interpolation improves the quality of the rendering. Skin aging is also simulated by simply increasing the metric rest length at certain locations.

6 Rendering Garments

While they are not directly related to cloth simulation, good rendering techniques are required for visual realism of the garment output.

This chapter helps to understand the basics of rendering by a short overview of the problems and related technologies. The particular case of fabric material is also considered.

6.1 Rendering Techniques

Rendering techniques are needed for the realistic display of 3D models on a surface, which could be a computer screen, a video projector or printed material. Rendering is basically a collection of methods aimed at drawing the objects accurately and realistically on a 2D surface to be viewed (Part..6.1.1). These methods are implemented by rendering systems of different algorithms, each of them having various degrees of realism and rendering speed (Part.6.1.2).

Some basic principles of rendering techniques are presented here. A more detailed references about rendering and computer graphics in general can be found in [FOL 93] and [GLA 95].

6.1.1 Visualization Principles

Rendering is accomplished through a collection of techniques which solve a number of problems:

- *Projection techniques*, for reproducing the shape of the 3D objects on the viewing surface.

- *Shading and illumination techniques*, for reproducing the color of the objects to be displayed according to their material and the lighting of the scene.

- *Mapping techniques*, for reproducing small details of the surface, such as textures and bumps not described by the geometrical model.

- Additional techniques designed to improve the quality of the display, such as antialiasing techniques.

The following sections describe the basic principles of these techniques.

6.1.1.1 3D Visualization

The display of three dimensional objects is basically a projection transformation, where the 3D world and its objects are projected onto a 2D screen surface. This projection is computed as a geometrical transformation which converts 3D object coordinates into 2D screen coordinates, possibly with additional depth information.

A. Perspective Display

The projection parameters are usually defined in terms of the camera position in 3D scene. The traditional viewing parameters are:

- *Eye point*, which corresponds to the position of the camera.

- *Look point*, which corresponds to a point centered in the camera image and defines the camera azimutal direction. This may be expressed using orientation and elevation angles.

- *Up vector*, which is a direction seen as vertical in the camera image and defines the camera dolly angle.

- *Field of view*, which is the visibility angle and defines the camera zooming (magnification). It should approximately correspond to the angle the screen subtends to the viewer.

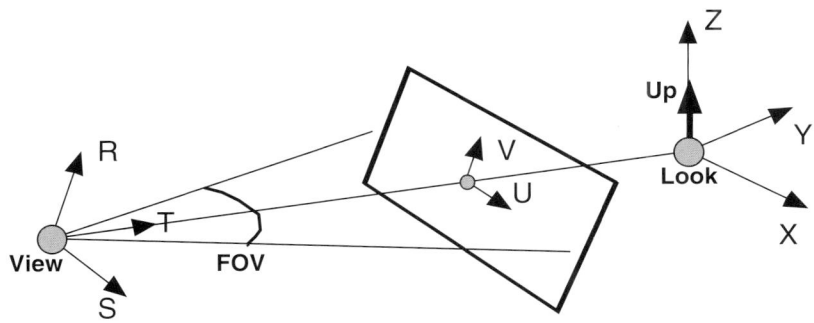

Fig. 6.1. Viewing parameters.

Transformations are expressed in homogeneous 4x4 transformation matrix form, which is actually a 3x3 linear 3D transformation matrix with an additional translation column and an additional projection row. The 3D coordinates are expressed in vectors of size 4, containing the actual 3 coordinates and an additional normalization value initially set to **1**. Matrices and vectors are combined in the standard way. To obtain the final 3D coordinates, the 3 position coordinates of a vector are divided by the final normalization value.

The transformation from the 3D world coordinates into the 2D screen coordinates is usually computed in two transformations. The first transforms the world coordinates **(X,Y,Z)** into an eye-centered and screen-oriented, 3D coordinate system **(R,S,T)**. The transformation taking into account the eye and look points, and the up vector. The second performs the projection on the screen surface **(U,V)** and takes into account the perspective, the field of view, and the screen-display coordinate system.

B. 3D Stereo Visualization

The physiological perception of depth is possible because (human beings take advantage of the two eyes separated by a distance). As the two eyes are in different positions, the perceived images are not equal. The alignment difference between the two perceived images hint the human brain to "reconstruct" the depth perception.

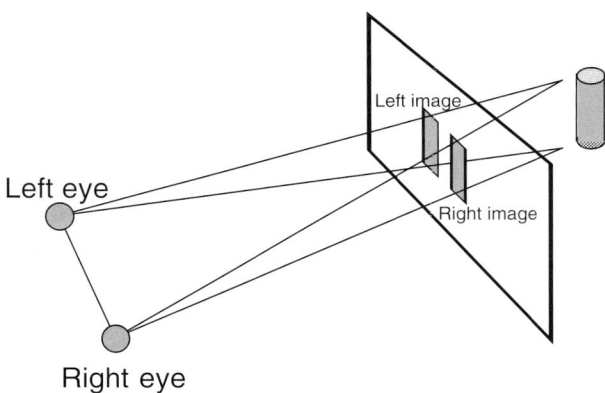

Fig. 6.2. Stereo 3D visualization.

The stereo-visualization devices are designed to recreate the two different images simultaneously, one for each eye. The projection methods described above are used for each image, each of them using the same viewing direction, but with different points of views to simulate the separation between the two eyes. Different methods are available:

- *Dual display devices*: Two separate displays are used, and their images are directed only to the corresponding eye. This is obtained through the use of miniaturized screens (such as small LCDs in head-mounted devices) or through mirror arrangements directing the screen images to each eye.

- *Single display devices*: Both images are mixed on the same display, and a head-mounted image separation system (glasses) separates the images to their respective eyes. The advantage is the possibility of collective visualization using a single display device.

3D stereo vision is the most convenient of the single display devices since it allows the freedom to move independently around a fixed display. The major image separation techniques are the following:

- *Color filtering* (red-blue images and glasses). This is an inexpensive and easy method suited to any kind of media, but produces low quality results without color perception.

- *Polarized filtering* (images with different polarization). This produces good results, but requires dual projection techniques on a metallic screen. It is usually implemented for 3D cinema.

- *Switch imaging systems* (images are separated using the synchronized LCS glasses and are switched alternatively between its transparent and opaque states, at a very fast frame rate). This is a rather complex method which can be adapted to any dynamic displays standard computer.

Though 3D stereo displays produce impressive results, the accuracy of depth perception remains very poor. 3D displays are quite common in perception-based applications such as video games and simulation frameworks, but are rarely used in systems that require quantitative appreciation of geometry, such as CAD applications.

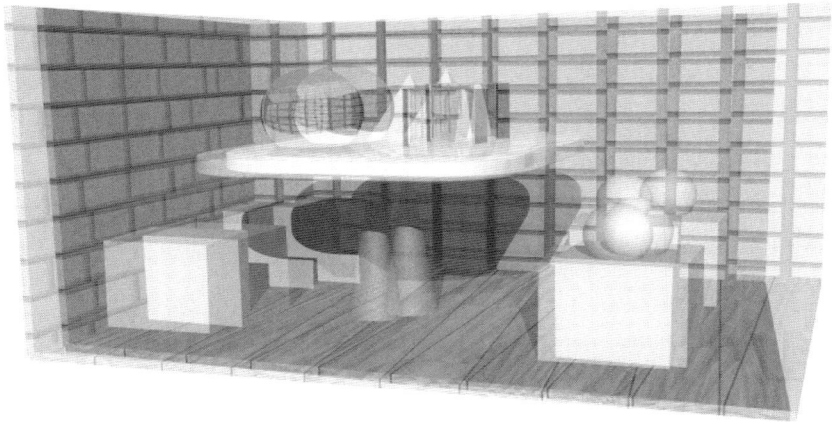

Fig. 6.3. Stereo 3D view with superposition of left and right images.

6.1.1.2 Illumination and Shading

Once the location of the objects on the screen is computed, they can be displayed by filling in the pixels of the screen with adequate colors.

These colors depends on several factors:

- *The object material*, which defines the base color of the object and the effect of light on it.

- *The lighting of the scene*, which is usually defined by the ambient light and a set of light sources.

- *Shadowing*, which is light occlusion between the objects.

- *Reflection* and *refraction*, which are light propagation effects between the objects.

While the physical phenomena of illumination is very complex, simplified models allow effective rendering with varying degrees of realism. More details on illumination can be found in [HLL 89].

A. Lighting Models

Lighting models determine the apparent color a surface region, depending on its material, the light sources, and the position of the observer. The main components of a lighting model are the following:

- *Emission lighting*, where the surface produces its own light. Usually, emission lighting is isotropic and does not depend on the surface orientation.

- *Ambient lighting*, when computing the color of an object that is not lit by any source. In simple lighting models, it is considered as isotropic (it does not depend on the orientation of the surface) and represents the average, indirect light present in the scene.

- *Diffuse lighting*, the additional color generated by a given light source. Among existing models, the *Lambertian lighting model* defines its intensity as being proportional to the cosine of the angle formed by the surface normal and the light source direction (if this value is negative, shadowing occurs).

- *Specular lighting* models the "reflection dot" of the source on the object. It renders the surface shininess of the material. Among the existing models, the *Phong illumination model* considers the intensity proportional to a given power of the cosine of the camera direction to the theoretical reflection direction of the light source. The power parameter defines the apparent size of the reflection dot. This lighting also varies as the observer moves.

Depending on the object material, each of these lighting components has various intensities and is usually defined by the material color.

6.1 Rendering Techniques

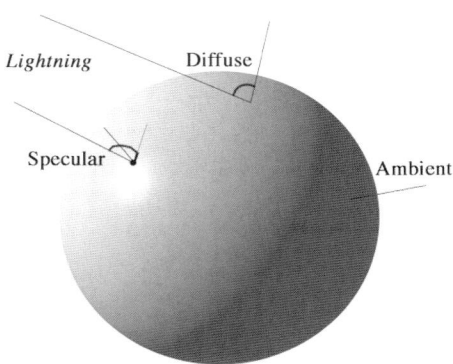

Fig. 6.4. Ambient, diffuse and specular lighting on a sphere.

Advanced models, such as the Blinn lighting model [BLI 77], are more accurate in modeling the light reflected by a surface. Finally, *physically-based lighting models* [COO 82] use the physical nature of light and its reflection on the material surface. Further advanced lighting models are described in [HEX 91].

Lighting not only depends on the nature of the material, but also on the surface microstructure. If the microstructure is anisotropic (directional polishing, fabric arrays,...), the lighting is quite likely to be anisotropic as well.

Some of these advanced lighting models should be considered for the rendering of fabrics, as discussed in Part 6.2.1.

The nature of the light sources should also be taken into account. The simplest lighting models consider infinite directional lights, defined by a nominal intensity and lighting direction. Point light sources are defined by a point in the scene, and their relative intensity decreases proportionally by the square of the distance to the surface. For spotlight sources, the intensity also depends on the orientation of the light source. Finally, volumetric light sources "blur" lighting effects through extended light position ranges and produce soft shadows.

B. Global Illumination Methods

Standard lighting models consider the direct lighting from a set of light sources. Additionally, an ambient lighting defines lighting on the surface parts under the shadows. Such model is however quite unsatisfactory, as this ambient lighting is a very rough approximation of reality.

In fact, ambient lighting results from the light produced by the surrounding objects. Modeling this is difficult however, because of the interdependency of lighting between the objects.

Global illumination methods simulate this interdependency between lit surfaces. Among them, *radiosity* is the most accurate, [GOR 84] [NIS 85] [CEN 93]. Basically, all the scene surfaces are discretized into small patches. For each patch, *visibility coefficients* are computed with respect to all other patches, representing the amount of light received by the patch when another patch emits a unit amount of light. This defines a square matrix where the elements are the patches. The visibility coefficients are also modulated by the lighting model, which relates the re-emitted light to the received light, depending on the patch material and light orientation. This matrix is used to build a linear system where the unknowns are the lighting of all the patches and the constants the light sources.

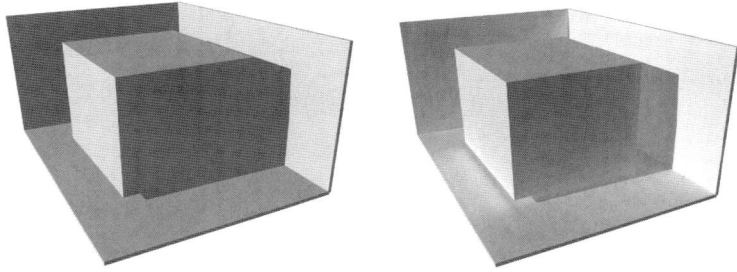

Fig. 6.5. A scene without, and with radiosity lighting.

The major developments in this method aim to increase its performance. The size and the complexity of the system is directly related to the number of patches in consideration. This is usually not sparse and thus is difficult to solve. Most optimization techniques involve adaptive subdivision of the surface, usually related to the expected lighting gradients in the scene. Incremental techniques are available for reducing the computation when the object or light sources move. There are also iterative methods for progressive resolution of the system that increase the efficiency by neglecting selected lighting contributions.

The main advantage of radiosity techniques is the realism of the lighting. It is particularly noticeable where indirect lighting is important, such as indoor scenes. Furthermore, the lighting is not view-dependant and does not need to be recomputed as the camera moves. However, the major disadvantages are the high computation and memory requirements which make this technique unsuitable for real-time animations.

C. Smooth Shading Models for Polygonal Meshes

Once the apparent colors of each objects in the scene have been computed, they can be drawn on the screen.

Objects are usually defined or rendered as polygonal meshes of flat surfaces. If these are based on curved surfaces, the main visual artifact resulting from the discretization are color discontinuities along the polygon edges because of different surface orientations. Smooth shading aims at restoring the smooth appearance of the surface through interpolation. Among the most common interpolation techniques are:

- *Gouraud shading*, which computes the color of each mesh vertex based on orientation approximations at these points. The colors are then linearly interpolated on the polygon surfaces [GOU 71].

- *Phong shading*, which interpolates the orientation approximations on the vertex points linearly on the polygon surface. The color is computed from the interpolated orientation [PHO 75].

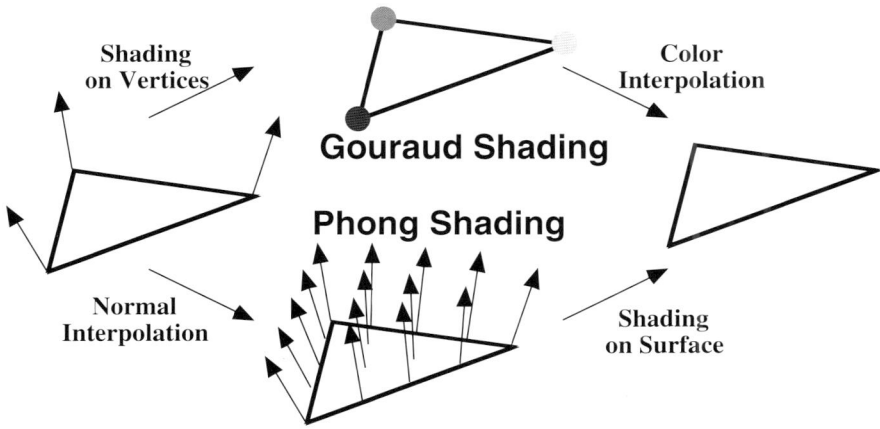

Fig. 6.6. Gouraud and Phong shading processes.

While Gouraud shading is the simplest shading method available, Phong shading gives better results in terms of apparent curvature, particularly when specular lighting and effects are considered on rough meshes. More advanced, smooth shading methods, for better approximations of the interpolated surface orientation exist.

Fig. 6.7. A rough sphere model with no smoothing, Gouraud, and Phong shading.

6.1.1.3 Texture Mapping

A geometrical model defines the shape and the material of the object. The discretization of the geometrical model implies the concomitant discretization of all these properties. For instance, the geometry of polygonal meshes contains shape information whereas the polygons include information on the material. The lighter the resolution of the geometrical model, the more refined its description needs to be.

To overcome the complexity limitations of the geometrical model, the properties may instead be mapped directly on to the surface using a structure containing additional information describing the local coordinates of the surface. Such mappings usually involve value maps as two dimensional arrays and local coordinates as additional information in the geometrical structure. The value of some property at one point of the surface is its value in the array corresponding to local coordinates of that position on the surface. In this way, both geometric and material details of the surface can be added from an image or texture created through some independent procedure, without increasing the surface resolution of the geometrical model.

Different kinds of properties can be defined through mappings, among them those related to surface appearance and local surface deformation.

A. Color Textures

By defining the mapping array as an image, this image can be drawn on the surface. Different kinds of projections and tiling schemes are available for fitting the image position and scale onto the surface. Complex textures, possibly repetitive, can be simulated in this way.

6.1 Rendering Techniques

Mapping can be used to define not only the base color pattern of a surface, but also any property defined by the lighting model. Furthermore, other properties can be controlled through mapping, such as in the use of a transparency map to simulate a surface containing a complex pattern of holes.

B. Bump Mapping

The geometry of an object is perceived through its apparent contour, and through its surface shading related to the surface orientation. Small geometrical details, which do not significantly change the apparent contour, are visible only through shading.

Bump mapping aims to reproduce small surface deformations by shading. A bump map is defined as a grayscale image that conveys the "surface height" deformation of the mapped surface. The map gradient is then used to modify the surface normal accordingly. The shading of the modified surface normal through the lighting model renders the appearance of volume.

Bump mapping is used for rendering small deformation of the surface, such as embossing or wrinkling. For larger deformations, however, the geometrical perturbation caused by the change of surface height cannot be neglected, and advanced techniques such as *displacement mapping* are required.

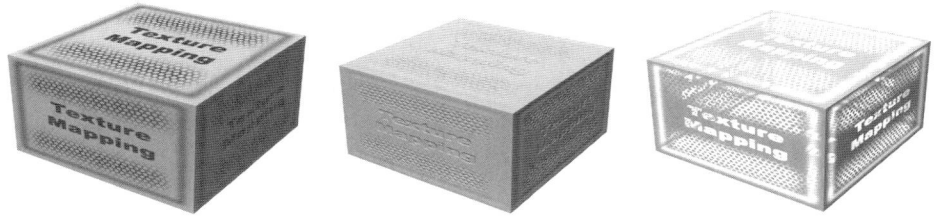

Fig. 6.8. Texture mapping on a box, as diffuse color, as bump map, and as transparency map.

C. Volumetric (Solid) Textures

One problem in texture mapping is the definition of the mapping coordinates. For flat surfaces (possibly deformed), it is easy to find "natural" orthogonal coordinates of the surface. When the object is volumetric, however, it is difficult to find a global mapping on the object that is appropriately scaled all over the object surface. One solution is to use 3D volume mapping, in which the texture is defined as a 3D array and can be mapped onto the actual 3D space. Rather than being "painted" on the surface of the object, the texture is defined in the material volume and appears on the volume surface as the object sculpted out from the volume.

D. Procedural Textures

Procedural textures are defined as analytic functions of texture coordinates rather than as value arrays. The advantages are smaller memory requirement as there is no array to store (this is a great advantage for volumic textures), and scalability without needing interpolation and smoothing. However, accurate designing of complex textures can be difficult.

Fig. 6.9. A brick-textured sphere using a volumic procedural texture. Color, bump, and combined.

6.1.1.4 Antialiasing

The information in computer generated images and animations is discrete both in space and time, which may lead to visible artifacts called *aliasing*.

- *Spatial discretization* is the result of representing the image as pixel arrays.

- *Temporal discretization* in animations is the result of movements being represented by successive frames of still images.

The most obvious artifact is the "stair case" phenomenon that results when the image or animation structure does not follow the discretization grid. The image features seem to "jump" from one pixel to another at discrete positions or times.

The most disturbing effects of aliasing occur when dealing with repetitive images or animations, and the repetition period becomes close to or smaller than the discretization size.

This is particularly true when the image or animation pattern is regular. In these cases, refined grid textures are likely to produce highly visible moiré patterns, and high-speed rotating objects provoke other odd rotation perception.

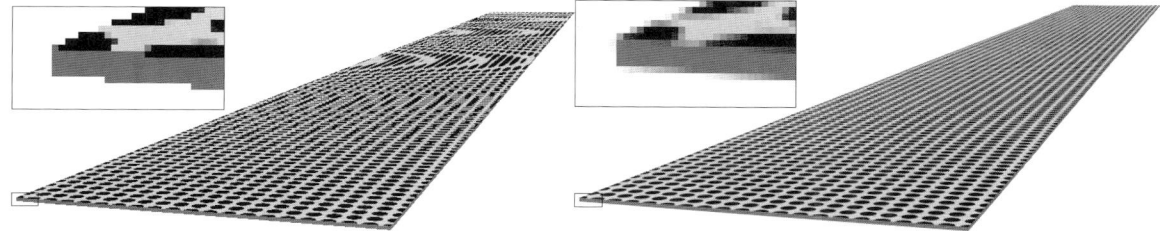

Fig. 6.10. A textured figure, without and with antialiasing.

Suppressing these artifacts often involves blending the pixel colors relative to the expected coverage of the colors within the pixel size or frame duration. When the exact pixel coverage of the objects on the pixels can be computed, this blending is straightforward. However, in most cases, only an approximate evaluation by supersampling within the pixel area and the frame duration, can solve the problem. Advanced techniques use filter patterns to distribute the sample effects accurately and random perturbation (jittering) of the sample positions to prevent the artifacts caused by regular patterns.

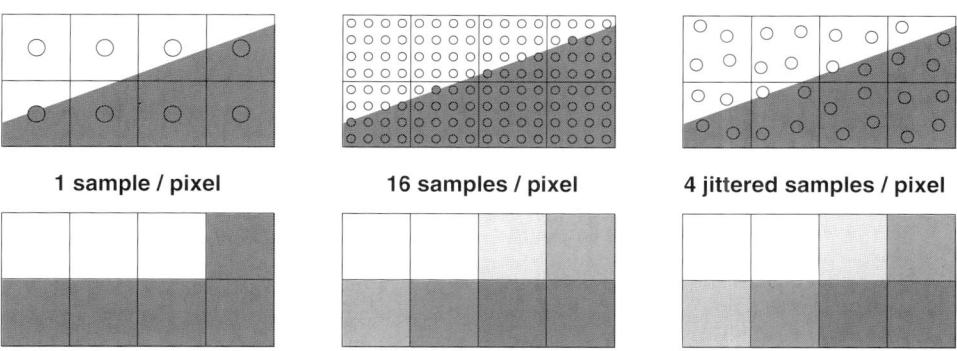

Fig. 6.11. Antialiasing through supersampling with regular and perturbed samples.

6.1.2 Rendering Systems

The implementation of a rendering system requires the assembly of the techniques described in the previous section in an algorithm combining projection methods, lighting models, texture mapping and antialiasing.

There are two approaches to rendering:

- *Painting methods*, which compute the projection of the scene object on the screen and compute the color of the corresponding pixels.

- *Scanline methods*, which compute, for each pixel on the screen, and render the color of the displayed objects.

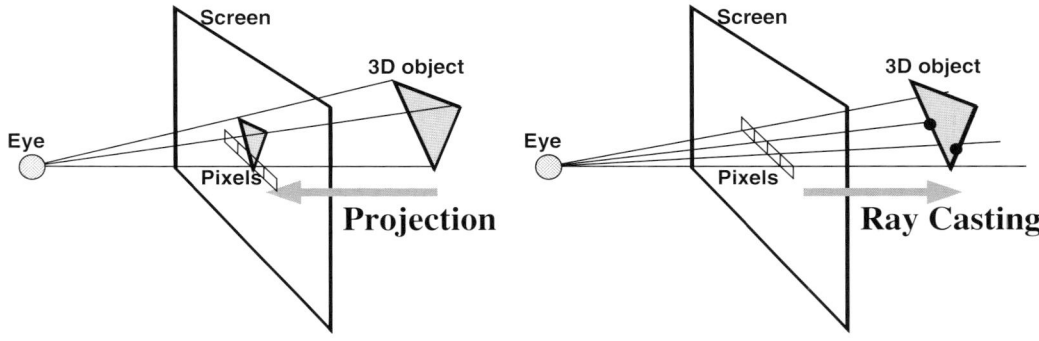

Fig. 6.12. Principle of the painting and scanline methods

While painting methods are simple and fast and thus adaptable for fast, real-time display, only scanline methods allow accurate rendering of complex visual features such as reflection, refraction and lighting. The methods can be implemented by high quality rendering systems where long computations are performed offline.

6.1.2.1 Interactive Display

The most straightforward way to render objects is to draw their components successively on the screen. This kind of painting algorithm is particularly suited for polygonal models, which are composed of flat surfaces. For more complex, curved primitives (Bezier or spline patches, implicit surfaces), rendering usually requires prior polygonalisation of the surface.

A. Wireframe Display

The fastest way of displaying a 3D model is to display the lines defining the object. For polygonal meshes, this corresponds to displaying the mesh edges. Since the number of pixels to be colored is very small, and since the shading models are primitive or non-existent, high speed is possible.

This method is suitable for fast and accurate visualization of highly complex models. As the models are virtually "transparent" and can be seen through, their inner structure is visible. Wireframe display is widely available in all CAD systems.

B. Polygonal Display

Displaying plain polygons can render the object geometry quite accurately.

Hidden surface removal is a non-trivial problem with this kind of rendering. Older systems use complicated, depth-sorting and clipping algorithms to efficiently manage the visibility. Instead, current systems implement a Z-buffer scheme, which is a parallel pixel array containing the "depth" corresponding to each, current pixel as currently drawn. Pixels are overwritten only if the new depth is smaller than the current one. Z-buffering became popular when memory availability could satisfy its requirements and dedicated graphics hardware could manage the process automatically.

Polygonal displays are well suited for Gouraud-shaded smooth surfaces and for texture mapping as well. Most of the current 3D graphic hardwares handle these features, sometimes with additional antialiasing.

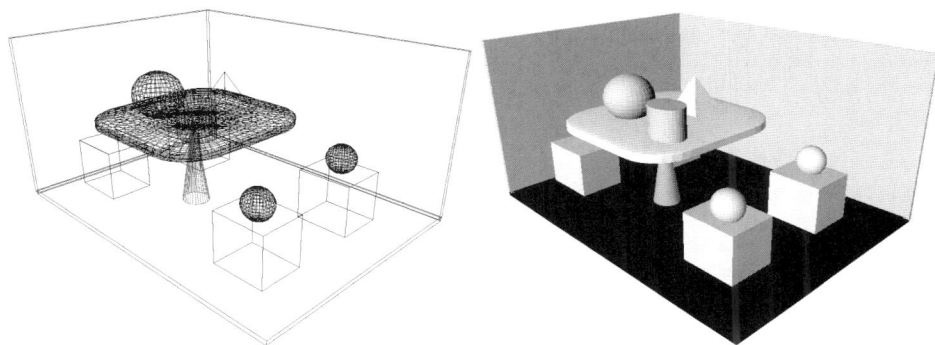

Fig. 6.13. Wireframe rendering and Flat polygonal rendering of a scene.

With the availability of dedicated graphics hardware, this form of rendering has become the standard of real-time display. Most current hardware accommodates the display of several million 3D triangles per second, including shading and texture mapping.

6.1.2.2 High-Quality Rendering

A further step in visual realism of the images is obtained by advanced schemes that accurately compute the color of each pixel according to advanced light propagation models.

A. Scanline Rendering

Instead of "painting" the surfaces successively on the pixels of the screen, scanline methods compute the color of each pixel successively.

Any kind of illumination model can be implemented with scanline techniques, as the lighting and camera directions are precisely known for each rendered pixel. When dealing with polygonal meshes, Phong shading is often used for smooth curvature appearance. Texture and bump mapping are also easy to implement in these methods, as the color and shading of each pixel are computed separately.

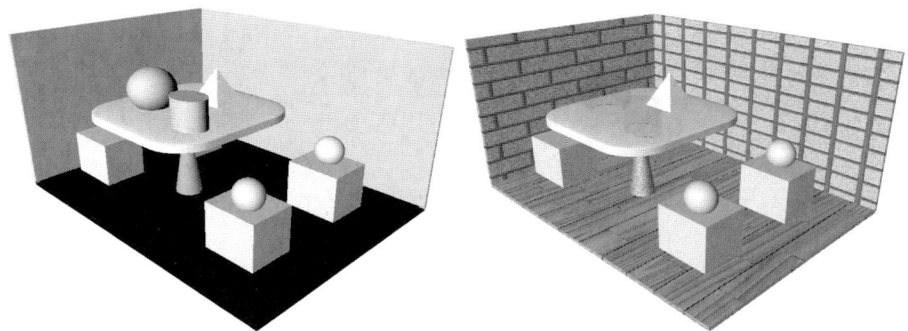

Fig. 6.14. Gouraud shaded polygonal rendering and textured scanline rendering of a scene.

B. Ray Tracing

As a further step toward realism, ray tracing is designed to reproduce additional visual effects, such as reflection, transparent refraction, and shadowing among several objects, and atmospheric effects.

Ray tracing is an extended scanline method that propagates the rays recursively from one object to another through reflection and refraction. Rays can also be altered by environmental interference, producing volumetric effects such as atmospheric mist or haze. Finally, the shadow cast on each rendered surface point is accurately computed by casting "shadow rays" from the point in the direction of the light sources, to see if they are obstructed or altered by other opaque or transparent objects. Advanced ray tracing systems even take into account the indirect lighting due to reflected and refracted light. Details on the ray tracing techniques can be found in [GLA 89].

Fig. 6.15. Raytraced and radiosity raytraced rendering of a scene.

C. Volume Rendering

Rendering methods visualize the object surface described explicitly in the form of polygonal meshes. However, when the object geometry is described in volumetric form (voxel or octree representation), extraction of the surface is not easy, and the accuracy is hard to achieve. In this situation, directly rendering the volume can be a solution.

Volumetric rendering methods visualize the object as a set of volumetric elements with specified transparency properties. Various rendering methods can then be used, which take into account the combined transparencies, such as using ray traversal algorithms similar to ray tracing or superposing of transparent textures. The lighting of solid surfaces is difficult with these methods.

These methods are in medical imaging where the objects are systematically obtained as 3D voxel representations (image stacks).

6.2 Rendering Textiles

Realistic and accurate rendering of fabric materials requires an appropriate combination of the rendering techniques discussed in the previous sections. The specific nature of the textile and its particular thread and fiber structure produce particular lighting effects that have to be considered. Different techniques are available, depending on the scale of the visualization scale to be considered and the visibility of the corresponding fiber structure.

Not much has appeared on special rendering techniques for textiles in the literature. Often, the rendering methods employed are the usual rendering methods using techniques discussed in the previous sections. However, we believe that this area merits further exploration for higher accuracy in cloth or garment rendering.

6.2.1 Anisotropic Lighting of Textiles

The structure of fabric materials is not isotropic. For woven textiles, the fiber directions are usually orthogonal, whereas for knitted fabrics, the directions follow a complex and repetitive pattern. The global reflectance of all the fibers therefore, depends on the light direction and on the position of the observer.

6.2.1.1 Anisotropic Lighting Models

In anisotropic lighting models, the amount of light reflected by the material depends mainly on two parameters:

- The angles of the light source to the material surface (incidence angle measured from the surface normal, and the orientation angle measured from the surface structure direction).
- The angles of the eye point (measured in the same way).

6.2 Rendering Textiles

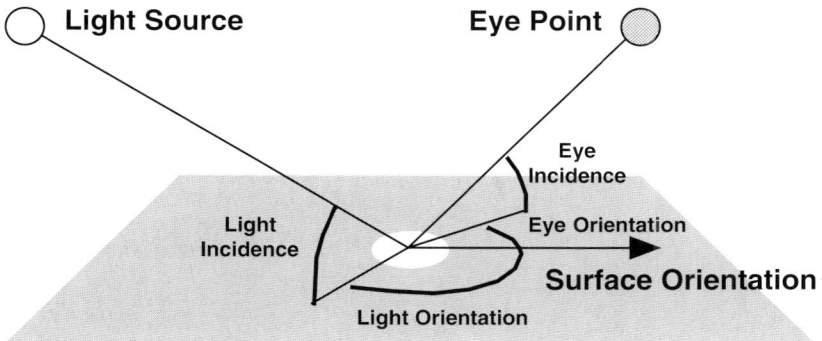

Fig. 6.16. Parameters of an anisotropic lighting model.

For complex models, additional parameters may be taken into account, such as the wavelength of the light and polarization. These parameters are particularly important for physically-based lighting models [COO 82].

While anisotropic models only consider the relative, orientation angle between the light source and the observer, they also take into account the orientation relative to the anisotropic surface structure. The orientation of the threads in the fabric is the main parameter. Additional information on anisotropic lighting models can be found in [POU 90] and [WAR 92].

6.2.1.2 Lighting Models for Fabric Materials

Considering how the threads are arranged in a fabric leads to anisotropic lighting models of fabric materials.

A. Mapping Models
Since the explicit 3D modeling of the thread structure would be cumbersome, it seems natural to use a texture map to define a cell of the fabric. Hence, the whole surface is described as a tiling of the texture cell. Lighting can then be computed using advanced texture and bump map techniques, such as described in [CAB 87]. Accurate lighting on such structures would take into account the masking effects between the bump features occurring for small viewing incidence angle, and self-shadowing of the bump features when the light incidence angle is small [BEC 93].

B. Macroscopic Lighting Models

The thread structure of the fabric is often quite small compared to the size of the garment surface. Hence, for global viewing of the entire garment, the thread structure is not directly apparent. In these cases, it is futile to render the bump map structure as discussed previously. Moreover, rendering such a structure is likely to cause unwanted aliasing artifacts that are difficult to prevent for excessively refined repetitive texture patterns.

The details of thread patterns are not visible by the thread structure alone, but with the lighting produced by the scene. A macroscopic lighting model can be computed as being the average lighting produced by the thread structure on a textile surface region for given lighting and viewing angles.

By using a light source and a camera and testing the apparent luminosity of a fabric sample depending on the light and view angles, such a model can be determined experimentally. A moderate number of sample points suffice for performing the measurement, and interpolation between these points would then model the lighting in all possible configurations.

Another approach would be to simulate this experiment using a 3D sample model of the fabric containing the exact representation of the thread structure with the appropriate fiber material. A grid containing few cells of the repetitive thread structure pattern, would be rendered using a realistic rendering technique such as raytracing, with different light and viewing angles. The luminosity of the resulting image area would be averaged to a single value, which would henceforward serve as a proportionality coefficient for lighting intensity of the angles considered. Such model could accurately take into account, the visibility masking and shadowing between the fibers, as well as transparency light reflection phenomena.

6.2.2 Volumetric Textile Models

The rendering of the precise arrangement of the fibers and threads in the textile is a very accurate way of producing realistic appearances of textiles.

Rather than using an inaccurate texture map of the textile thread structure, a 3D volumetric model could be invoked, on which volumetric rendering techniques could be used. Small scale fibers in the thread could be modeled as a particular density function which would reflect the compound transparency effects from the contributing fibers.

Such model would be particularly efficient for rendering the "softness" of the fabric material for small scale visualization. It would, however, be inappropriate for large-scale visualization of whole garments where the fabric structure is not visible. In such cases, an adequate, macroscopic lighting model should be used.

6.2.3 Rendering Choices for Realistic Garments

The different rendering techniques described in the previous section should be efficiently implemented in an appropriate context for obtaining realistic cloth and garment images. Depending on whether the degree of realism or the display speed for motion perception and interaction is primordial, different implementation schemes are indicated, possibly combined according to level-of-detail considerations.

6.2.3.1 Interactive and Real-Time Simulation Systems

Interactive applications with animated objects should be able to display at the rate of at least five images per second. The only available techniques reaching this frame rate for complex objects are painting methods for displaying polygonal meshes, possibly with texture mapping and smooth shading.

The rendering hardware found in current computers usually able to render several million shaded and textured triangles per second. Shading is computed by a user-defined lighting model and smoothed through Gouraud shading. Color and transparency texture mapping is directly available through the definition of appropriate mapping coordinates. Bump-mapping is, however, not usually available. In addition, 3D-optimized hardware includes the management of projection from 3D world coordinates to 2D screen coordinates and z-buffering for hidden surface removal. Finally, antialiasing improves the rendering quality.

A. Rendering Tools
Access to these capabilities is through dedicated graphics libraries. Among them, *OpenGL* is a popular standard, originally developed for Silicon Graphics systems and now becoming cross-platform. Older systems would use the standard libraries *PHIGS* or *GKS*.

While these libraries only handle the rendering of basic primitives (points, lines, polygons), additional component libraries add the definition of scene objects including structured descriptions of the geometries. The most common description of surface objects are polygonal meshes described by indexed face sets (a list of vertices carrying the geometry, and a list of polygons represented as indices on the vertex list). Additional information is included, such as material and texture with mapping coordinates. The objects are then structured into hierarchies which include geometrical transformations between the nodes. Viewing parameters and light definitions can also be included in the scene hierarchy. Among those libraries, *OpenGL Optimizer* and Silicon Graphic's *Open Inventor* are popular. Other standards focus on the file format, such as the various versions of *VRML* or *3DMF* (Quicktime3D). Additional formats are defined by the various commercial packages available, such as *DXF* (Autocad) or *Obj* (Alias-WaveFront).

B. Implementing Interactive Cloth Software

The major considerations for good interactive cloth software are the quality of the animation, the rendering realism, and the interactive possibilities.

- The *quality of the animation* depends largely on the number of frames that can be redrawn on the display during a unit of time. While correct motion perception starts at 5 frames per second, good animation contains at least 15 frames per second. "Perfect" animation is obtained when the frame rate corresponds to the refresh rate of the display.

- The *realism of the rendering* is achieved when the geometry of the object is correctly perceived to include all its desired features. Current standards for interactive display use antialiased renderings of polygonal surfaces with a Lambertian lighting model and surface curvature smoothing through Gouraud shading. Texture mapping should also be available.

- The *interactive possibilities* are related to how the user can move around the scene and visualize the objects through modification of viewing parameters. Object edition is related to how objects or surface regions are selected, moved and deformed, and what quantitative accuracy is available for these operations.

The geometrical complexity of the cloth objects is the most important consideration, as the rendering time (as well as the computation time of the animation) is directly proportional to the number of polygons to be displayed. The primary effects of rough models are the disturbances in the apparent silhouette of the objects. Well-smoothed shading may be able to reduce the visibility of the discretization inside the object surface. Finally, texture mapping is an important key to realism as the apparent complexity of the object can be greatly increased and hide shading artifacts resulting from rough models.

The implementation of an interactive clothing system should be carried out with an efficient graphics library such as *OpenGL*, which is tightly optimized for the underlying hardware and supports all the rendering options detailed previously. Additional scene representation libraries facilitate the description of complex scenes and can manage object picking and editing. If the display hardware supports it, 3D stereo display can be obtained using switch dual display systems with LCD glasses.

Commercial 3D design and rendering packages are not usually suited for the 3D interactive display of moving cloth objects, as their rendering methods (realistic but slow) are not optimized for supporting animations. Furthermore, the built-in manipulation tools are very general and are not adapted to the particular tasks required for the manipulation of cloth objects. They may however be suited to the accurate design of cloth objects, which requires quantitative placement of the geometrical features.

6.2.3.2 Realistic Rendering of Garments

Realistic rendering requires accurate lighting and propagation models, which are usually implemented through raytracing algorithms. These algorithms feature advanced lighting related to various surface properties, many forms of texture mapping including bump, displacement and reflection mapping, reflective and transparent light propagation with refraction, shadow casting, atmospheric effects, extended light types, and possibly radiosity global illumination.

Raytracing cannot be carried out at interactive rates, and the time required for rendering an image is counted in minutes, at least. Simplified models may however compute preview images in a matter of seconds. Still, this is not enough for a system computing animations in real-time. Animations are therefore computed off-line and stored in animation media (for example in *MPEG* or *AVI* formats).

A. Realistic Textiles

For rendering textile material and garments, advanced texture mappings and complex lighting models are the main features contributing to visual realism. The scale of the rendering is the key to determine the appropriate technique.

- *Small-scale rendering* is required when the fabric structure should be visible in the fabric material. While very enlarged views would require complex 3D models of the thread structure of the fabric as discussed in Part.6.2.2, the usual degree of accuracy only requires approximate modeling of the structure as texture and bump maps, particularly suited for the repetitive patterns often encountered in textiles. Bump mapping is preferred when much detail is required, and it also produces more realistic lighting. Simulating the thread structure through color texture mapping is a less accurate, but easier solution.

- *Large-scale rendering* should be considered when the fabric structure is too small to be visible, which is most often the case when viewing complete garments. Explicit rendering of the structure should also be avoided because of the aliasing generated as the texture becomes comparable to or smaller than the size of the pixel. The textile structure, which only appears as lighting effects caused by the alignment of the fibers, can be rendered using complex anisotropic lighting models as discussed in Part.6.2.1. Texture mapping is then suitable for simulating fabric color patterns, while design features of the cloth are perhaps better handled through bump and transparency mapping.

As rendering time is less critical in off-line computations, realism is often increased by using highly discretized cloth surface geometric representations, sometimes with interpolation methods for smoothing the surface curvature.

B. Producing Realistic Garment Images

Raytracing techniques often require complex algorithms not provided in standard libraries. Several public or shareware contributions exist, but a common solution is to produce realistic images and animations through the use of commercial 3D design and rendering systems, such as *3D Studio, Alias-Wavefront* or *Maya*, each of them including all the necessary tools.

This integration can also be achieved by using a separate mechanical simulation and animation program to compute cloth animation. The successive 3D models in each frame are saved and imported into the rendering software to produce the images. Another solution is to integrate the animation program directly into the rendering software as a plugin, by re-using the software's interface and internal data structures. In either cases, the complex texturing and lighting models which make cloth reflection and glare look so realistic have to be developed and integrated into the rendering software.

7 The MIRACloth Software

The previous chapters have detailed the technical aspects of cloth simulation, garment animation and visualization. A more practical approach is now described for the actual design and simulation of virtual garments.

Virtual clothing is produced through the implementation of a powerful simulation system that integrates the mechanical simulation of cloth objects into virtual body animations, with an interface for design and visualization of garment models.

The practical concepts of garment pattern design are explained in this chapter, followed by a description of MIRACloth, a garment simulation software developed at MIRALab, University of Geneva.

7.1 Introduction

As we have already mentioned, there are several ways of approaching 3D-garment building. However, the most intuitive and natural method derives from traditional cloth and apparel industry.

To illustrate, let us take a real example. The first step is the design of garment patterns. Someone inexperienced in the field might draw the patterns of a pair of trousers as in Fig. 7.1:

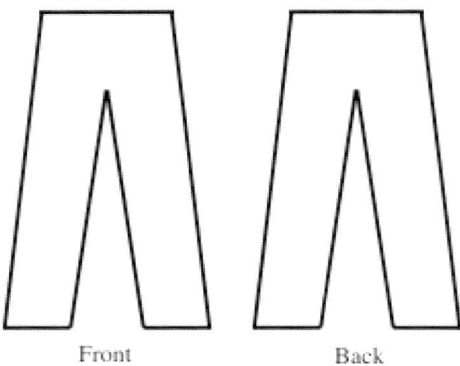

Fig. 7.1. "Naive" and incorrect garment patterns for trousers.

This is of course visually recognizable, but totally wrong in terms of patterns. A garment made from these patterns will fit no-one, because they do not take the body volume into account. There will be no problem with the legs, but they will not fit the pelvis because they make no allowance for the crotch. To see how to obtain a proper shape, we can examine a real pair of trousers. First of all, by looking at the seams, we can pick out four pieces (pockets excepted). If we lay the garment out flat down, then we can extract the exact shape of the pattern:

Fig. 7.2. The shape of trousers.

In fact, the complete set of patterns is as in Fig. 7.3, with seaming information added:

7.1 Introduction

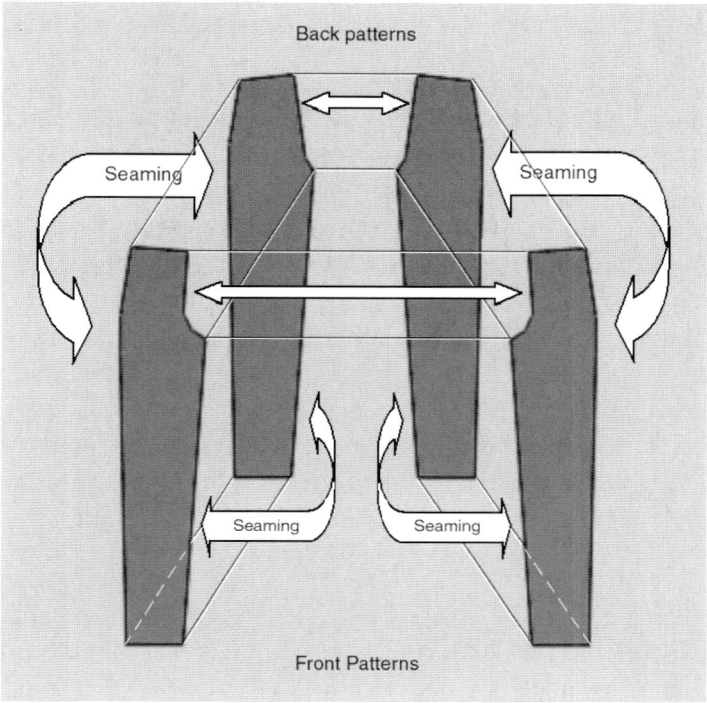

Fig. 7.3. Garment patterns for trousers, and their seam relations.

Some of the current 3D clothing software currently use this methodology, from 2D patterns to 3D assembly. They are discussed in Appendix.

In this chapter however, we will describe MIRACloth, developed at MIRALab, to illustrate the succession of steps on virtual garment creation. This software consists of two units; the first is dedicated to 2D-design and the second to 3D assembly and simulation. While the former is basically a powerful editor, the latter is more than a program specifically designed for building and animating garments. As a simulation system, it is a general framework for animating a whole range of different deformable surfaces and the objects that can be modeled with them, either through mechanical simulation, by using prerecorded sequences or with user interaction.

7.2 Approach

The most intuitive and natural approach for building garments takes its inspiration from the traditional garment industry, where garments are created from two-dimensional patterns and then seamed together. MIRACloth uses this approach. Working with 2D patterns is the simplest way of keeping an accurate, precise and measurable description and representation for a cloth surface. In the traditional garment and fashion design approach, garments are usually described as a collection of cloth surfaces, tailored in fabric material, along with the description of how these patterns should be seamed together to obtain the final garment. Our virtual garment design system reproduces this approach by providing a framework for accurately designing the patterns with the information necessary for their correct seaming and assembly. Subsequently, these are placed on the 3D virtual bodies and animated along with the virtual actor's motion. In the following sections, we provide the different steps and tasks involved in dressing virtual actors constructing and animating garments on them.

7.2.1 Design of Garment Patterns

As mentioned earlier, the system is inspired by what happens in the reality. The garment is made up of 2D patterns of cloth surfaces. In real life these patterns are based on 3D measurements on the customer's body. In the system presented here, these patterns are constructed using an editor which allows specification of the 2D measures. In addition, it contains information on where a pattern should be joined to other patterns. Working in 2D allows better precision and easy manipulation.

This program is basically a polygon editor, which edits a garment as a set of 2D polygons linked together by seaming lines. Designing a garment is done in several steps:

The definition of the garment patterns is done on a grid defined in a window. The operations include inserting, moving or deleting polygon vertices on the current pattern polygon. The current pattern can be selected in a separate window displaying all the patterns of the garment.

Seaming lines are defined on the borders of the garment patterns, referring to the polygon edges which are to be joined during garment construction process.

7.2 Approach

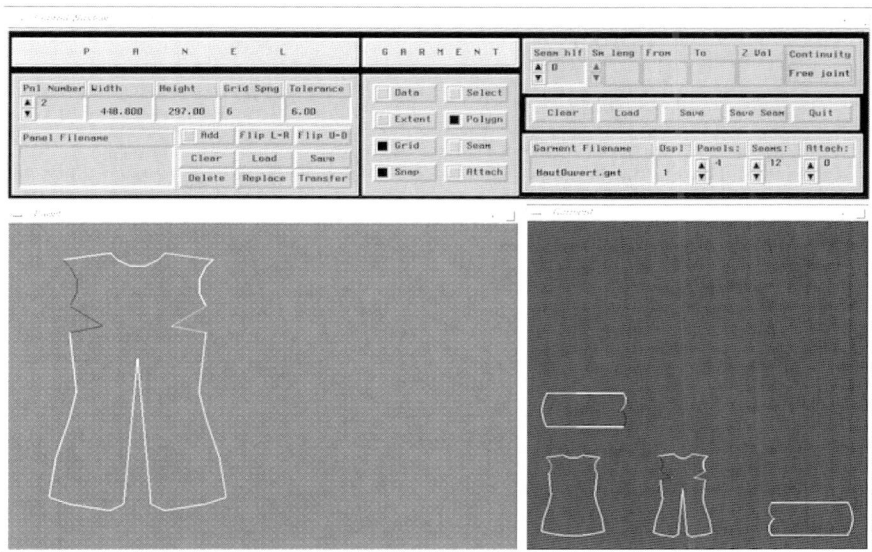

Fig. 7.4. Building garment patterns in the 2D interface.

This software unit was designed to match the capabilities and requirements of the system presented in [CAR 92] and [WER 93]. This system performed mechanical computation using regular grids, and also needed to perform the simulation on each pattern individually, and they were constantly maintained together through seaming forces. In contrast, the current software works on irregular triangular meshes, and seams by merging the pattern mesh, topologies, resulting in a single garment surface that can be easily handled and edited at will. This allows the use of adapted meshes where the discretization varies from place to place in the garment, and is adapted to the kinds of cloth deformations expected at each locations. The patterns can be saved in a simple format into a file, from where they can be re-loaded to be modified or to be used for constructing the 3D garments.

7.2.2 Putting Patterns on Bodies

The patterns constructed in the previous module are discretized into a triangular mesh. The planar patterns are then placed around a 3D virtual body using manipulators. This constitutes an initial rough positioning of the patterns around the body and can be done using mouse interaction or other 3D manipulating devices. The patterns are placed with an offset to the body surface so that when they approach the body, the shape of the body guides the surface of the cloth as a result of the collision response.

Garment patterns are imported from a garment file generated by the 2D-garment pattern design program. They are automatically discretized into a polygonal mesh corresponding roughly to the design grid smoothness modulated by a user-specified discretization parameter, which controls the density of triangles.

Considering that the seam elastics will pull some of the pattern borders together, only a rough approximation of the initial positions is needed. Several factors are considered in finding a suitable position. While being attracted toward each other, seamed pattern edges might encounter the body on their way as they get closer. Passing through the body, the elastics will pull the surfaces sliding along the body so as to minimize the distance between the seamed edges. The starting position should be such that these edges encounter the correct, curved side of the body, in order to slide in the right direction.

The starting gap between the seaming lines should be minimum, in order to speed up the seaming process and also to obtain a more accurate final garment placement. While collision response may automatically solve small initial collision problems, the patterns should not interpenetrate each other, or penetrate the body initially to any large extent.

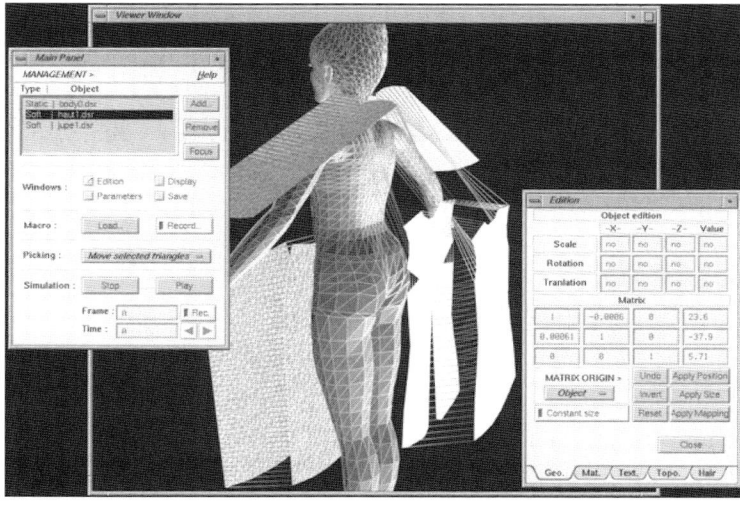

Fig. 7.5. Interactive 3D pattern placement.

7.2 Approach

Pattern placement is usually guided by mouse interaction, using translation, rotation of the individual patterns, as well as scaling to adjust the pattern size to the body. A specific selection mode allows the mouse to pick individual patterns, as well as rotations which can either be free, or constrained to discrete values around the axes in order to ensure constraints such as parallelism of patterns.

It is also possible to move only a selected region of the pattern, mainly to deform it and to give an initial curvature more suitable in some situations (e.g. constructing a cylinder shape from one of the patterns).

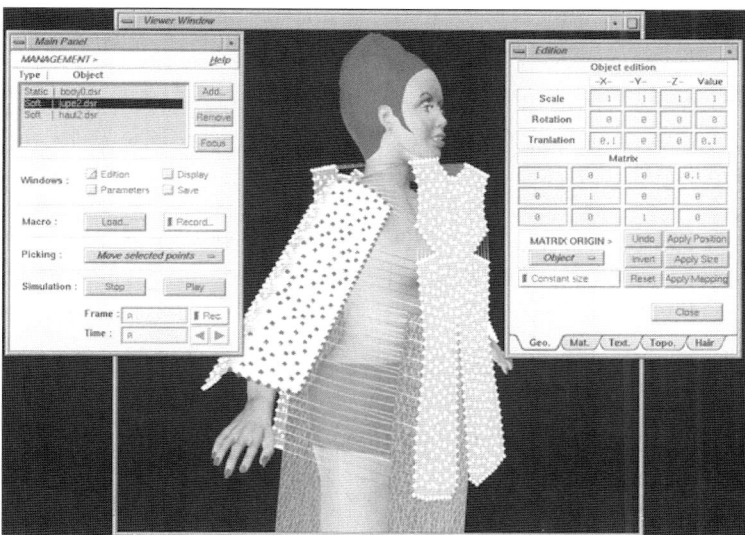

Fig. 7.6. Adjusting patterns.

7.2.3 Seaming and Constructing Garments

Once the 2D patterns have been placed around the body a mechanical simulation is invoked, forcing the patterns to approach each other along the seaming lines. As a result, the patterns are attached and seamed on the borders as specified and attain a shape influenced by the form of the body. Thus, the garment is constructed around the body.

The seaming process relies on a simplified mechanical simulation, where the seam elastics pull the matching pattern borders together. Rather than trying to simulate the exact behavior of fabric, the simplified model optimizes seaming speed using parameters adapted for that purpose, that is to say under no gravity, no friction, etc.

Interactive editing tools are still available during the simulation process, allowing the user to correct the position of patterns that do not reach a good final position on their own.

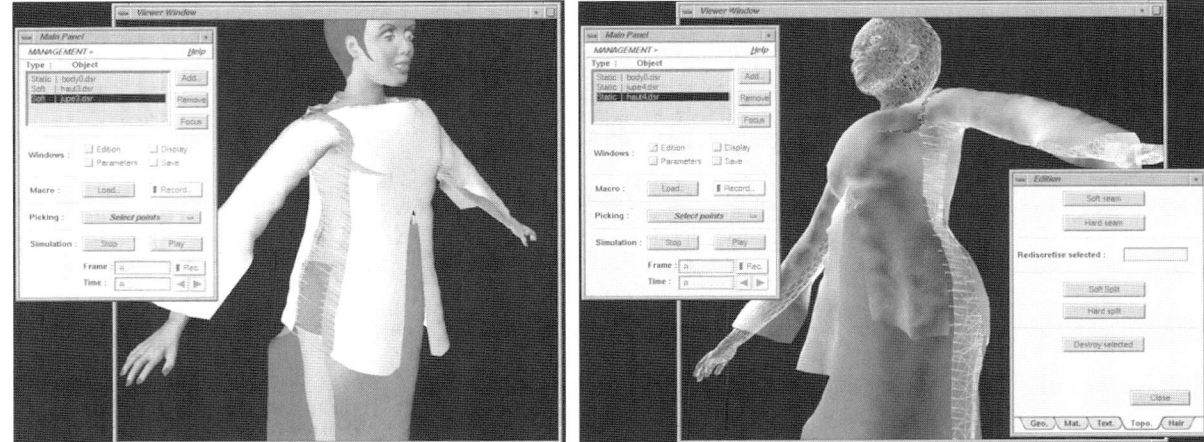

Fig. 7.7. The elastics pull the garment patterns together.

Once the pattern borders are close enough to allow seaming geometrically, the surface seaming can be performed: The elastics are removed and corresponding mesh vertices are merged together and placed at the midpoint of their two positions. A single surface mesh then represents the combined garment pieces.

If the seamed garment pattern borders were at an appreciable distance from each other, the resulting cloth geometry might not be compatible with the actual body shape. However, if the seamed vertices have not penetrated the body too deeply, collision response will generally clear up the problem after a few mechanical computation iterations. These iterations are also necessary to distribute the seaming constraints initially localized along the seaming lines and to allow the cloth to reach a global relaxed configuration.

After this, the mechanical parameters of the actual fabric are set, as well as gravity, in order to put the cloth into actual mechanical conditions. A few more mechanical iterations will then bring the cloth to a resting position that is compatible with the actual mechanical context. These iterations are performed until the cloth stabilizes dynamically.

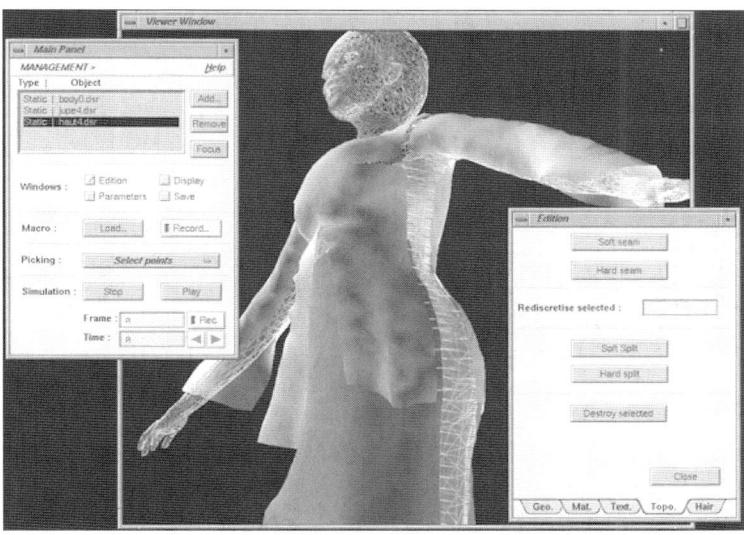

Fig. 7.8. After seaming, texture adjustments can be made on the garments.

The resulting position is a suitable starting point for garment simulations having identical garment fabric properties and initial body position.

7.2.4 Animation of Garments

Animation of a garment here pertains to its movement along with the body of a virtual actor. This is accomplished with collision response and friction with the body surface. At this stage the mechanical parameters are set and tuned with visual feed back. The settings of the parameters may be different from that was used during the process of seaming and constructing garments. The mechanical simulation then gives the animation of the garment on a virtual actor's body.

For the scene objects, as well as for the garments, the animations make use of a keyframe technique, where the motion is defined by a sequence of successive positions. Intermediate positions are then computed through linear interpolation of the mesh vertex positions.

While most animations are handled with the standard PAL video frequency (25 Hz), the framerates of each object may be individually selected, in order to assign individual motion speeds. For instance, a linear displacement of a scene object may be specified by linear interpolation between its initial and final position.

The mechanical parameters are set up to reflect the correct behavior of the simulated fabric material. This step requires a few additional relaxation iterations to let the cloth reach the equilibrium state defined by the parameters. The cloth is then ready for animation.

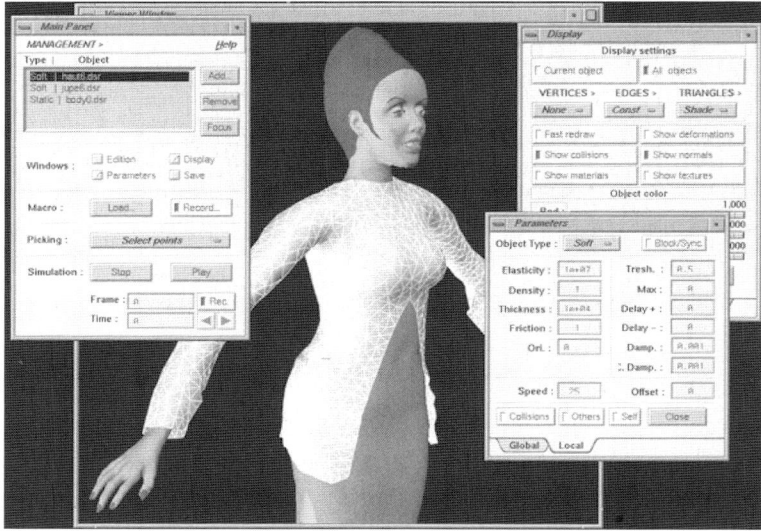

Fig. 7.9. Cloth relaxation and adjustments around the body.

Animation is simply performed by moving the body from a recorded sequence using animation playback. Reacting through collision response and friction, the garments move with the body.

7.2 Approach

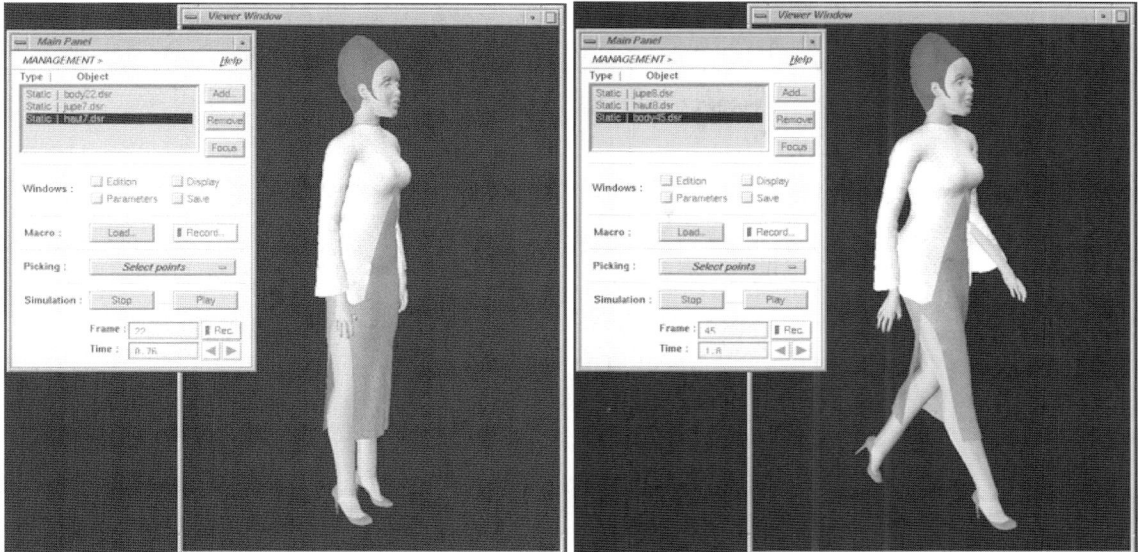

Fig. 7.10. Computing the animation.

It is possible to compute several garments on the same body concurrently. The different garments then react against each other through collision response and friction. Other precomputed garments can be added to the scene, and the mechanical garments will then interact with them, although this interaction will not be complete. (the latter garment won't change the animation of the previously computed one).

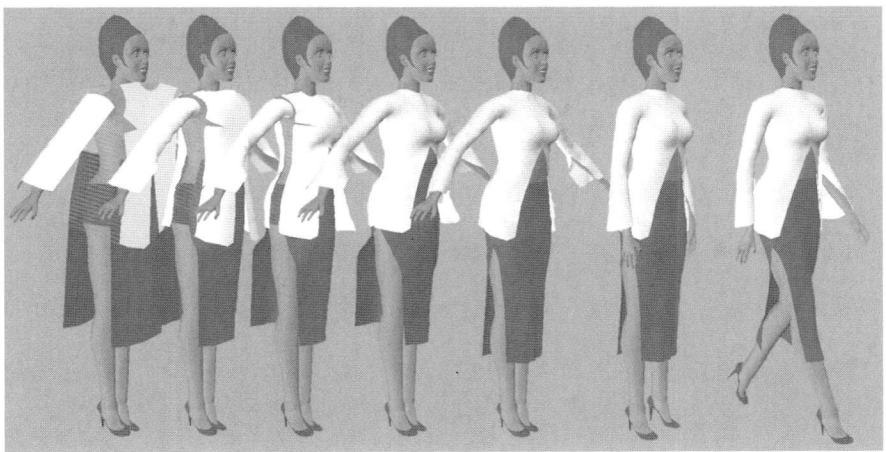

Fig. 7.11. Constructing and animating garments.

7.2.5 Defining the Garment Materials and Textures

The final appearance of the cloth is displayed through its material properties. Surface attributes like material (diffuse color), shininess, and texture, which are primarily rendering parameters, can be defined in the system. Depending on the type of visualization or rendering software being employed, a preview is offered for any configuration of the parameters. A dedicated rendering module for the visualization of cloth may also be included. Materials and textures are handled independently. While materials pertain mainly to the ambient, diffuse and specular colors of the surface, textures refer to image mappings on the surface, based either on the surface texture coordinates, or on its actual geometrical shape, such as for simulating reflection and environment mappings. Some editing tools, for both material and texture, are provided. The cloth can be decorated by assigning materials and textures to regions on the cloth surface. Typically, the user selects a set of triangles and assigns a material name, for which the corresponding properties can be interactively adjusted.

7.2.6 Cutting and Modifications

It is useful to be able to cut a cloth and then re-stitch it to make it fit or adapt to the body shape after removing or adding material. Tools are provided to allow the creation of cutting lines on the cloth surface. These lines may then be seamed together to recreate a continuous surface of different shape. Unwanted material can also be removed from the cloth using cutting.

Using simple garments, several mechanical iterations can be performed in very few seconds, so that immediate visual feedback on the cloth is available during the modifications. Interactive 3D garment editing tools are provided for the user, to modify a cloth by cutting and seaming the cloth material. The possible manipulations include:

- *Removing material*, by discarding selected surface polygons.
- *Cutting the cloth*, by separating polygons along edge lines defined by selected mesh vertices.
- *Adding elastics between mesh vertices*, to maintain cloth together locally.
- *Seaming surface borders together*, along edges lines whose vertices are linked by elastics.

- Rediscretizing the cloth surface mesh locally, by subdividing selected polygons.

- *Moving the cloth surface locally*, by selecting surface vertices or polygons, individually or by selected groups, or deforming a whole object using affine transformations.

- *Deforming the cloth surface*, by modifying the native surface size of selected surface regions through affine transformations.

While these tools are not meant for designing a new garment from scratch, they are nevertheless ideal for editing and enhancing the shape of an existing garment.

7.3 Software Description

The software for 3D simulation, the second unit of the entire system, is not restricted to animating garments, but is in fact a framework for animating a whole range of objects. All the objects are considered in the same way, although the way they are animated can differ: Through mechanical simulation, playback from a file animation, or a static object. However, some of the features and tools are dedicated to the easy manipulation of garments construction and animation. The features and interface of the software for 3D simulation are detailed in the following section.

7.3.1 Program Features

The program was designed to be as general as possible. In particular, there are no dedicated "body" objects, "garment" objects or "scene" objects with preset animation types and parameters. Though slightly less intuitive for a beginner, this approach gives a trained user the full freedom to of creative expression, without the constraints of a standard framework.

7.3.1.1 Animating Objects

3D garments are created and simulated in a framework that manages the animation of a set of objects. Any scene object is basically a polygonal mesh that can be animated using several modes. The different object classes are:

- *Static objects*, that do not move in the scene.

- *Keyframed objects*, that move according to an animation sequence recorded as a succession of keyframe position files.

- *Mechanical objects*, that are animated using mechanical simulation and possibly interact with other objects through collision effects.

- *Moving (rigid) objects*, for which the motion is defined by a linear geometrical transformation along time.

The program allows the user to load objects from files of various description formats and assign to them an animation mode for which the parameters can be controlled at any time. The objects are placed in the 3D scene, possibly edited and animated. The 3D-viewer window always displays the scene at its current state. As the animation is computed, any object motion can be recorded in a keyframe file sequence.

Most of the user interaction is defined using a non-modal scheme, where at any time (whether computation is running or not), the user can open editing or parameter windows and perform actions through them. Any window can be left open and constantly reflects the actual state of the scene.

7.3.1.2 Saving and Loading Animation

An object file contains two kinds of information:

- The *topology* of the object, which is basically the connectivity between its vertices, edges and polygons.

- The *properties* of the object, mainly the vertex positions, the native edge lengths, the mapping coordinates, and other rendering information such as material and texture.

While a single object file contains the topology and all the necessary properties to completely describe the object, an animation sequence is defined by an initial file containing the topology and the initial properties, along with a succession of frame files containing only the properties that have changed since the preceding frame. Typically, frame files contain only the new vertex positions describing the object motion and deformation. If the object topology changes during an animation sequence, a new full object definition file is used as a frame file.

All the frame files define a "keyframe sequence" for successive timesteps. The object properties for any time are computed, if possible, by linear interpolation of the properties of the preceding and succeeding frame files. Interpolation is however, not possible when the next frame contains a topology change. This incremental scheme allows the storage of animation files in a very compact way.

In order to prevent inconsistent files from being mixed in animation, each object has a "magic number" which changes each time its topology is modified. This information is saved in the topology definition file. Property files created with the same object contain the same magic number. An object topology may only have its properties updated by files containing the same magic number.

During playback and simulation, a global time describes the current state of the system. Each object can be saved to animation files with a given frame offset and a given framerate. If an object motion is defined by a file sequence, a user-defined, linear transformation converts the global time into given file frame numbers, with interpolation between successive frames if required.

7.3.2 Interface Description

The interface is composed of a 3D graphics viewer window and an associated main control panel.

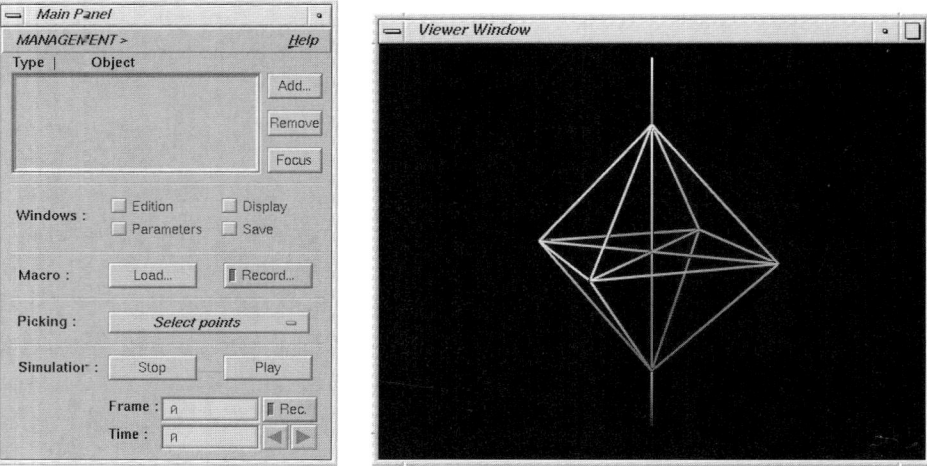

Fig. 7.12. The main panel and the 3D viewer window.

The entire 3D scene, with all the objects, is displayed in the viewer window. To help users, it contains a colored octahedron, representing the X-Y-Z world scene axes that appears during mouse interaction. This octahedron provides immediate visual orientation feedback, as well as visual distance units during eyepoint motion.

At any time during the use of the program, interactive view modification can be performed through mouse interaction in the window. The possibilities include translations and rotations, either free or constrained around major axes. Rotation can optionally be constrained to preserve an arbitrary "vertical" orientation, drawn on the screen octahedron, to correspond to the screen vertical. Additional keyboard controls allow automatic and easy viewing of the alignment snapping to the nearest world X-Y-Z planes or directions. Afterwards, accurate translations or rotations are possible along these axes.

The main panel contains the list of current objects. These can be selected by clicking on their names. Objects can be added and removed using a file browser and the viewing parameters can be set to focus on a particular object (The viewpoint is set to the middle of the object, and the eyepoint is set to an adapted distance to fill the viewer window).

The user can specify selection modes to select groups of vertices or polygons and displacement modes to move vertices or polygons groups or in objects. The user can also block a set of vertices or polygons on simulated objects, and finally add or remove elastics between specified vertices. Keyboard shortcuts also allow quick selection between these modes.

7.3 Software Description

The main panel also contains information about the current simulation time, as well as the current frame number to be recorded. These values can be changed by the user when setting up an animation for playback.

Finally, various alternate panels can be brought to the screen by pressing selectors. Those panels control object editing, mechanical parameters, display parameters and saving options. Their selection can be modified at any time.

Editing panels are used to edit the topology, shape and properties of the object currently selected in the main panel. Geometrical transformations on a selected object, such as translations, rotations and scaling, are available from the geometry subpanel. The material subpanel allows the editing of the different materials defined in a selected object and their application to selected polygons of the objects.

Concerning textures, the texture subpanel allows mapping of a "rgb" image onto a selected object or a set of polygons. For seaming, splitting and destroying polygons, tools are provided in the topology subpanel.

The animation parameters, and particularly the mechanical simulation parameters, are adjusted through the parameters panel. It features two categories: environment (global parameters) and object (local parameters). On one hand, among the global simulation parameters, we will find gravity and wind vectors, space and time wind turbulence, normal and tangent air viscosities and finally collision distance and detection modes. On the other hand, the local parameters include elasticity, surface density, bending rigidity, friction values, Poisson coefficient, as well as viscosity and nonlinear elasticity values, which are the mechanical properties of objects. The object animation type is also defined here (static and immobile, animated by keyframe files, mechanically simulated), as well as its local time scale and offset parameters, and collision detection modes (no collision, collisions with other objects, self-collisions).

At any time, the display can be adapted through a set of tabbed panels containing the display of the current rendering parameters. Display parameters do not affect the definition of the objects nor the simulation computation.

The object display subpanel lets the user control the individual parameters of the selected object, such as vertex-edge-polygon display modes, material or texture activation, surface normal deformation color and collision display and interactive fast redraw display. An object display color may also be specified.

The global subpanel contains the eyepoint and lookpoint positions, as well as the up vector defining the vertical orientation on the screen. User-defined orientation may either be free, or constrained in order to force the up vector to fit the screen vertical. While the former mode is suitable for examining an object, the latter is good for visualizing a scene where the up-down direction has importance. Field-of-view angle and horizontal/vertical scale ratio can also be set.

The lights subpanel is used to define the lighting of a scene. Up to eight lights may be defined by their intensity, color and position, and they may also be toggled on and off. The eyepoint or lookpoint may be applied to a light, making easy and intuitive positioning. The definition of the ambient illumination and the background color are also included.

The stereo subpanel allows the toggling of stereo viewing and the scaling of the apparent distance of the objects relative to the screen plane.

Finally, the software offers the possibility of saving an object to a file, or the current view as a snapshot. Animations can also be recorded frame by frame as the moving scene is being computed. Two panels are provided for this operation: one for the objects, and one for the current view. There are several selectable file formats available for these operations.

7.3.3 V.R. Manipulation Tools

For interactive experimentation, object interaction using 6D tracking devices has been implemented. Currently, selected vertices of a simulated object may be attached to a tracker, and their motion coupled to the tracker's displacement. Several trackers may be used simultaneously to monitor the motion of several objects, or several parts of the same object. In addition, the use of a 3D display (stereo glasses) gives the a perception of depth.

The main drawback of this system is the relative inaccuracy of the spatial tracking technology, which does not allow precise positioning. This problem is aggravated by the inaccuracy of the 3D perception, and the inability to perceive precisely the depth difference between two objects displayed on the screen. The ability to track head movements and update the view accordingly could reduce this problem somewhat.

The major inconvenience of working in a 3D environment remain the lack of quantitative measurement and control of object movement. While working with a mouse provides the support table as a fixed motion referential, controlling a device "in the air" removes any helpful, fixed displacement origin. Furthermore, it is very difficult to visualize and measure distances in the 3D representation, as complex perspective deformations have continually to be taken into account.

For these reasons, the only practical way to design garment panels is as a flat 2D design, with its accurate measurement properties. And mouse control remains a good motion control device for its unequaled accuracy and intuitiveness. While speedier simulation and animation techniques are an important factor in obtaining a fully interactive 3D simulation system, current visualization and interaction tools remain unappealing to people who, despite living in a 3D world, are still used to simple 2D representations of the traditional graphic schemes and design tools.

7.4 MIRACloth at Work

The potent of MIRACloth is the result of the combination of powerful technologies:

- An advanced particle-system based cloth mechanical simulation system provides a simple, yet realistic model for animating cloth described as standard, possibly irregular triangular meshes. It is combined with an accurate Runge-Kutta integration method featuring an optimized adaptive timestep scheme, a scheme optimized for accurate animation of complex garments. Additionally, an implicit midpoint integration method is available for interactive and real-time animation of simple models.

- Collisions are detected through an hierarchical scheme that is optimized for self-collision detection through a surface curvature evaluation algorithm. This algorithm rapidly computes the geometrical collisions between very complex surfaces, without any major performance penalty when dealing with self-collisions.

- Collision response is based on a geometrical correction scheme that includes reaction and friction effects without altering the mechanical simulation process, and provides good performance and stable simulations during the numerous collisions generated by superposed cloth layers. This scheme is extended by the implementation of various constraint and interaction features, such as the "elastics" used for seaming cloth parts together.

- The appearance of garments is enhanced by geometrical interpolation and dynamic wrinkling features, allowing realistic and attractive garments to be animated efficiently despite rough geometrical representations used for fast mechanical computation.

- An interactive 2D and 3D interface implements pattern representation and design of garment models, allowing user interaction and garment editing at any stage of the simulation.

All these technologies contribute to various stages of the design, simulation and animation of pleasing and realistic garment models, and to other applications involving cloth simulation, thanks to the versatility of the implementation.

Several examples illustrate this potential, varying from the simulation of cloth objects in various difficult mechanical contexts to the accurate design of garment models, including the production of computer films and fashion shows.

7.4.1 Versatile Fabric Simulation

While good performance enables the design of complex garments involving the use of several cloth surfaces, model stability, accuracy and robustness are necessary to be able to simulate them in situations unrestricted by specific mechanical or collision contexts. The following simulations illustrate the software's possibilities in situations involving rapid and changing motion and numerous collisions, not encountered in usual garment simulation situations, but which demonstrate the versatility of the system.

7.4.1.1 The Dryer

In order to demonstrate the collision handling with rapidly moving and deforming objects, the dryer test animates a set of cloth and rigid objects in a rotating cylinder.

Simple garments are assembled from their patterns in the middle of the cylinder. They then fall by gravity to the bottom of the rotating cylinder. Friction with the cylinder walls causes the cloth to roll, slide and fall as the cylinder rotates. The cloth also interacts with a number of rigid objects animated in the same way.

7.4 MIRACloth at Work

This test illustrates that collision detection and response in this implementation is robust enough to handle very general motion patterns effectively. At no point did cloth objects interpenetrate or cross each other. The self-collision detection and response also worked as required, preventing the cloth surfaces from interpenetrating in an physically incorrect, but quite irreversible way. The cloth pieces were crumpled by high deformations, but they could be unfolded at any time. This test exhibits the effectiveness of the system in handling complex cloth motion in a very general animation context.

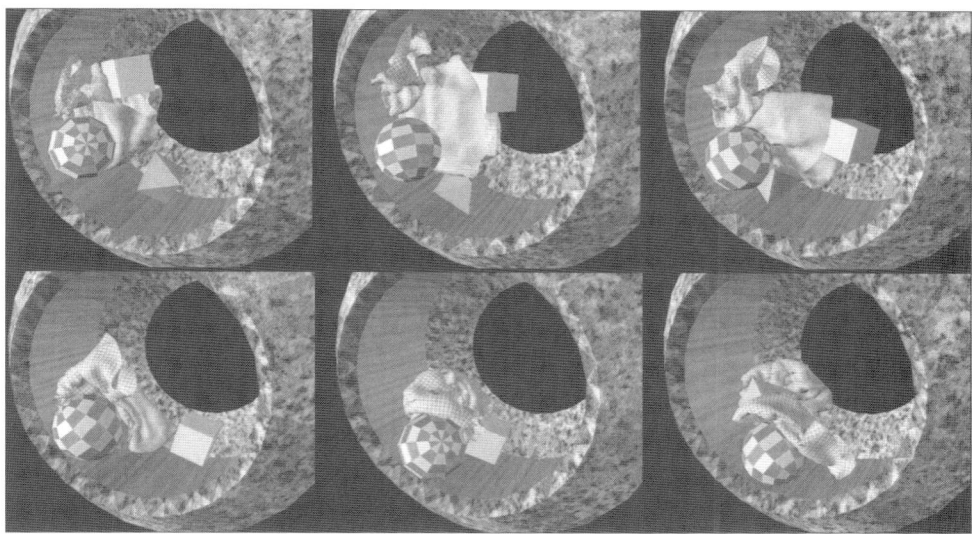

Fig. 7.13. Cloth in the rotating dryer.

7.4.1.2 The Falling Ribbon

A severe self-collision and response demonstration is carried out by letting a very long and flexible ribbon fall on itself.

The ribbon contains 20 000 triangles, forming a globally anisotropic mesh with about ten triangles wide. The ribbon initially hangs vertically above a surface and is then left to fall freely onto the surface. As it falls, the ribbon folds and crumples on the surface and forms loosely folded pile of loops, that soon becomes too heavy and falls over as more cloth material falls. Aerodynamic effects deform the ribbon still in the air from its initial vertical position. While the ribbon falls, the surface slowly tilts so that the ribbon eventually slides off. The loops unfold and disappear as the ribbon is stretched by its falling parts.

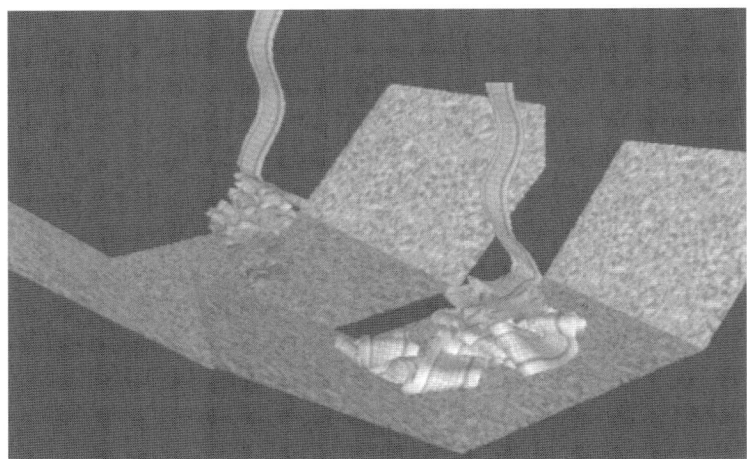

Fig. 7.14. The falling ribbon.

This example exhibits the capacity of the system to handle large numbers of self collisions, as well as the interacting collisions caused by multilayer stacked cloth. Despite the high compression produced by the numerous folds on top of each other, the system was able to maintain the relative surface positions and orientations. The ribbon remains stable as it rests on the surface, despite the highly complex and interacting collisions. Friction is still portrayed correctly, as exemplified when the ribbon slides off the surface. This is an impressive test of the system in handling multilayer cloth, with realistic friction behavior and effective self-collision management.

7.4.1.3 The Crumpling Dress

Another example simulates crumpling surfaces. A dress is assembled in the air and falls onto the ground under its own weight. It crumples as it hits the ground and then remains stable for a while. This demonstrates the ability of the system to handle the high curvature deformations necessary to render cloth crumpling, with the appropriate self-collision detection and response.

7.4 MIRACloth at Work

Fig. 7.15. The crumpling dress.

7.4.2 Computer Films and Fashion Shows

Producing computer animation sequences is the most natural use of a computer cloth simulation system. It is arguably also the easiest, as the accuracy needs only to satisfy visual realism, rather than quantitative mechanical precision. During its development, our system has been used for producing several film sequences. Our productions also contributed to system developments in terms of possibilities and usability.

7.4.2.1 Marilyn at the United Nations

This film portrays Marilyn making a speech at the United Nations assembly. Cloth simulation was used to render a glittering skirt during a four-second walking sequence.

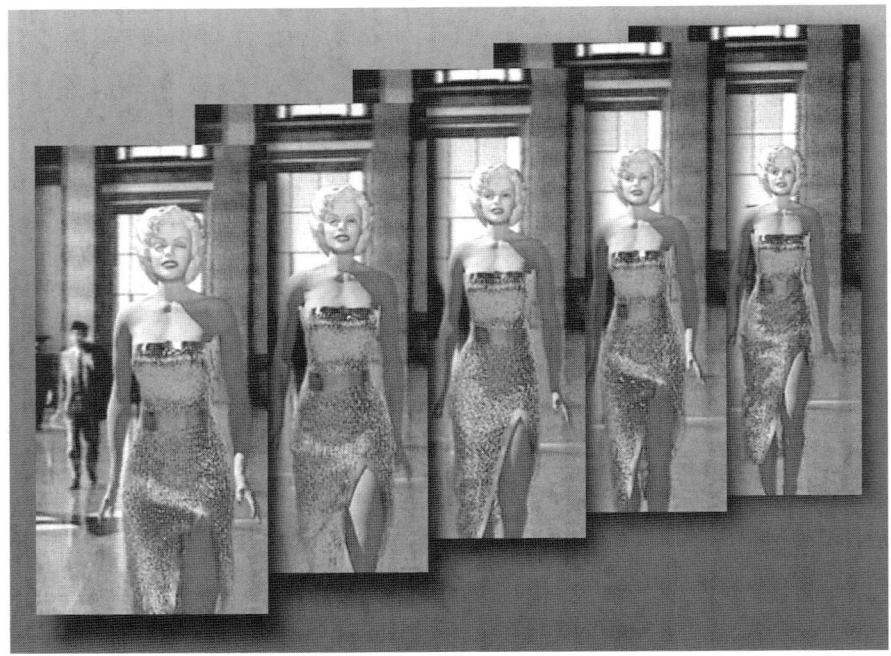

Fig. 7.16. "Marilyn at the United Nations" (see also color section, plate K).

While the tight upper part of the garment was simply generated by a texture mapping of the body, the free-hanging part was computed using mechanical simulation. This high-quality representation is based on more than 3000 triangles. The animation computation was performed in about two hours using Runge-Kutta integration with an accurate mechanical model. The whole simulation process required three hours, including pattern assembly and relaxation around the body.

7.4.2.2 The Virtual Catwalk

Using the system described in this chapter, a fashion show exhibiting several garment worn by different top-models has been created virtually. Some of the garments presented are tight-fitting garments, such as skirts or trousers. Another creation is a wedding dress with a long tail that glides over the ground. A complex decor and high-quality rendering were used.

7.4 MIRACloth at Work

Fig. 7.17. MIRALab's Virtual Catwalk (see also color section, plate R).

The system successfully simulates skirts and trousers clinging to the body using friction only, as well as realistic wrinkles appearing as the wedding dress tail glides over the floor. The same mechanical model was used for all the simulations, demonstrating its versatility for reproducing cloth in various contexts.

7.4.2.3 Kathy

This simpler fashion show sequence exhibits two outfits, one with a skirt and the other with trousers. The mannequin model was generated using measurements taken from a real person.

Each garment part has one to two thousand triangles. Their computation was performed fairly quickly, less than 30 minutes to produce each second of animation using an accurate fabric model. This sequence also illustrates the ability of the model to simulate tight and floating cloth parts concurrently with realistic contact modeling, able to maintain the garment position on the body through friction only.

While computer graphic productions are still the main use of the system, many Computer-Aided Design applications are also available. For instance, the framework has been used in underwear design and testing. Complex models are designed using the system and then simulated on the body.

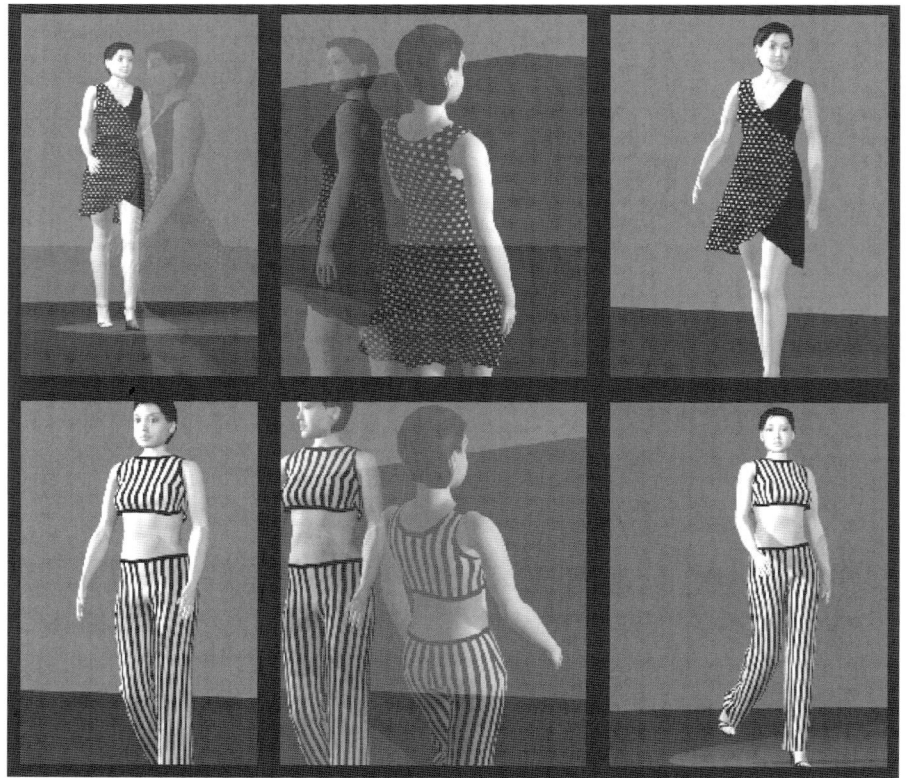

Fig. 7.18: The Virtual Catwalk (see also color section, plate L).

7.4.3 Model Design

In order to demonstrate the capacity of the system to produce virtual garments with considerable realism, a fashion show mixing virtual models with their real counterparts has been produced.

7.4 MIRACloth at Work

Fig. 7.19: Fashion design models, and their virtual counterparts (see also color section, plate M).

This virtual show is presented in parallel with a "real" fashion show. It alternates fully rendered sequences of walking virtual models with simpler sections during which live human models would wear the real garments.

This sequence demonstrates the capacity of the software for producing long and complex scenes using many different garments.

Fig. 7.20: More virtual fashion models (see also color section, plate N).

7.4.4 Garment Prototyping

In this application, the underwear patterns are designed from a model description and then turned into a very refined surface mesh for mechanical simulation. During the fitting, the color gradient along the mesh edge shows the distribution of the deformations on the fabric, which helps to visualize whether the cloth fits well or not, facilitating design improvements. By reducing the friction, the garment quickly reaches its most relaxed position on the body, while turning on the friction back on maintains it realistically as the body is moving.

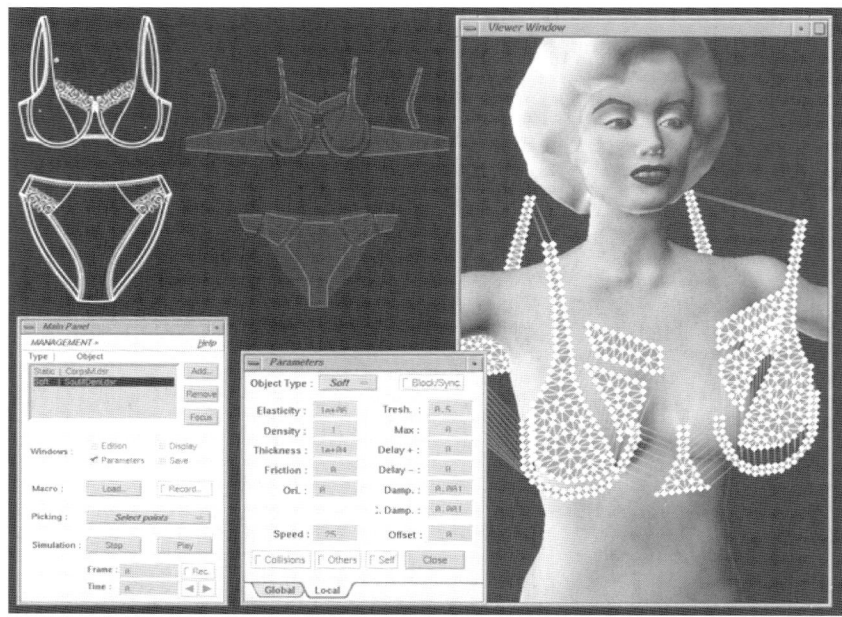

Fig. 7.21: Underwear design.

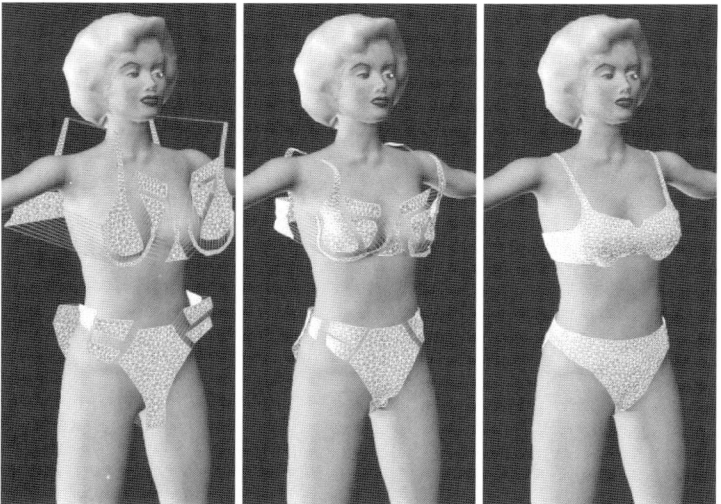

Fig. 7.22: Building underwear

7.4 MIRACloth at Work

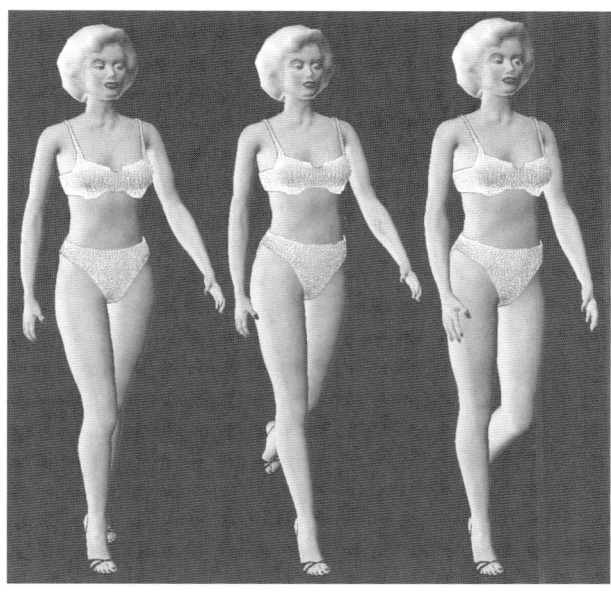

Fig. 7.23: Simulating underwear

These results are only a small preview of the potential of a complete simulation system that combines industry-standard design tools with powerful mechanical computation and virtual-reality techniques for rendering garment models on realistic animated virtual characters.

8 Potential Applications

There is a great potential for cloth simulation in several areas: from computer graphics to industrial CAD and prototyping applications, not to mention design, the entertainment industry and electronic commerce. In particular, cloth simulation can be a real benefit for the garment industry: visualizing a garment without actually making it drastically simplifies the prototyping phase, a task which usually involves significant expenditure on material resources and is time-consuming, requiring manual measuring, cutting, seaming etc. Some of the major applications are as follows.

- Entertainment

The technological explosion over the last few decades has led to the emergence of communication through computer media. This development has stimulated research into the modeling of virtual worlds. These worlds represent the re-creation of whole universes, which may be completely imaginary or, at the other extreme, as realistic as possible. As aesthetically pleasing as they may be, these spaces seem empty and pointless without the presence of virtual inhabitants. Moreover, the increasingly important role of computers and multi-media tools in communication reinforces the need of a virtual population. Indeed, much of human communication is based on non-verbal elements and physical action. Gesture and facial expression are an integral part of speech activity. The body has a social function: it allows for the recognition of the individual and is the platform for gestural communication. The introduction of digital clones provides a way of integrating these elements into virtual worlds and enabling interaction and exchange at many levels. The creation of imaginary characters may of course be pleasing, diverting and artistic, but creating human clones as realistically as possible presents a particularly interesting challenge in that it raises many rather specific types of problem. One of these, by no means the least, is how to dress virtual people. Aside from the face and the overall shape of the body, the first impression of an individual has to do with how she or he is dressed. From a modeling point of view, then, more realistic clothes are essential for more realism in synthetic actors.

In computer animation and entertainment industry, the demand for more realistic virtual actors increases the need for more convenient tools which are faster, easier and better at designing clothes on virtual actors. Many tools have been developed in this effect and have moved from research labs to the animation studios. Some of these tools are presented in the Appendix -B.

- CAD/CAM

Modeling tools of clothing can allow fashion designers to experiment easily with a variety of fabrics and patterns on a 3D dynamic virtual mannequin before the actual garment is manufactured. Once the design is complete, it can be sent to a computer-controlled fabrication machine for weaving the cloth and cutting out the appropriate patterns. Potential buyers may even try the virtual garment before actually ordering it, using an augmented reality system. In this way, customized clothing can be designed and made in an automatic fashion.

- Textile Engineering

Textile modeling requirements for industrial applications are quite different from requirements for entertainment and apparel design applications. In the composites domain, cloth is not allowed to freely drape over another object. Instead, it is forced into a specific predetermined shape. Textile engineers focus on correctness and accuracy about the properties and behavior of cloth as material: Young's modulus, bending modulus, Poisson's ratio, stress-strain curves, load-extension relationship, etc. Attention is also given to the micromechanical relationships of a single thread crossing. This gives a detailed understanding of the low level behavior of cloth, which is helpful for verifying the validity of any textile model.

Study and analysis of cloth's dynamic properties and predicting its motion in reaction to applied forces are critical in solving the control problem in the context of computer aided manufacturing.

- E-Commerce

With the internet explosion and web based browsers, concepts like Electronic Commerce (E-commerce) are becoming popular. In this context, cloth and garment modeling offer a variety of opportunities for a typical business -to –customer, interactive E-Commerce. One can imagine setting up a made to made-to-order corner where an individual can supply the personal body measurements, and a garment is designed with the options supplied about the material, color, texture, etc., from a multimedia catalogue. The constructed garment may be tried on a 3D virtual body which may be representative of the individual.

Bibliography

[ABB 51] : N.J. Abbott, *The Measurement of Stiffness in Textile Fabrics*, Textile Research Journal, Textile Research Institute (TRI/Princeton), 21, pp 435-555, 1951.

[AJA 95] : J.O. Ajayi, H.M. Elder, *Resolution of Stick-Slip Friction Traces of Fabrics*, Journal of the Textile Institute, The Textile Institute, 86 (4), pp 600-609, 1995.

[AMI 86] : J. Amirbayat, J.W.S. Hearle, *The Complex Buckling of Flexible Sheet Material*, Int. Journal of Mechanical Science, Elsevier, 28(6), pp 339-358, 1986.

[AMI 89] : J. Amirbayat, J.W.S. Hearle, *The Anatomy of Buckling of Textile Fabrics*, Journal of the Textile Institute, The Textile Institute, 80, pp 51-69, 1989.

[AMI 91] : J. Amirbayat, S. Bowman, *The Buckling of Flexible Sheets under Tension*, Journal of the Textile Institute, The Textile Institute, 82(1), pp 61-77, 1991.

[ANA 91] : R.D. Anandjiwala, G.A.V. Leaf, *Large-Scale Extension and Recovery of Plain Woven Fabrics*, Textile Research Journal, Textile Research Institute (TRI/Princeton), 61(11-12), pp 619-634;743-755, 1991.

[ANS 84] : S.Ansaldi, L.D. Floriani, B. Falcidieno, *Edge-Face Representation of Solid Objects*, Proceedings of the Workshop on Computer Vision, IEEE, pp 164-169, 1984.

[ANS 85] : S.Ansaldi, L.D. Floriani, B. Falcidieno, *Geometric Modeling of Solid Objects Using a Face Adjacency Graph Representation*, Computer Graphics (SIGGRAPH'95 proceedings), Addison-Wesley, 19(3), pp 131-139, 1985.

[ANT 87] : H. Anton, *Introduction to Numerical Methods of Linear Algebra*, Elementary Linear Algebra, J. Wiley & Sons, pp 371-419, 1987.

[AON 90] : M. Aono, *A Wrinkle Propagation Model for Cloth*, Computer Graphics International Proc., Springer-Verlag, 1990.

[AON 94] : M. Aono, D.E. Breen, M.J. Wosny, *Fitting a Woven Cloth Model to a Curved Surface* Computer-Aided Design, Elsevier, 26(4), pp 278-292, 1990.

[ASC 96] : J. Ascough, H.E. Bez, A.M. Bicis, *A Simple Beam Element, Large Displacement Model for the Finite Element Simulation of Cloth Drape*, Journal of the Textile Institute, The Textile Institute, 87(1), pp 152-165, 1996.

[BAI 95] : S. Bais-Singh, B.C. Goswami, *Theoretical Determination of the Mechanical Response of Spund-Bonded Nonwovens*, Journal of the Textile Institute, The Textile Institute, 86 (2), pp 271-288, 1995.

[BAJ 92] : C.L. Bajaj, I. Ihm, *Smoothing Polyhedra using Implicit Algebraic Splines*, Computer Graphics (SIGGRAPH'92 proceedings), Addison-Wesley, 26(2), pp 79-88, 1996.

[BAN 95] : S. Bandi, D. Thalmann, *An Adaptative Spacial Subdivision of the Object Space for Fasc Collision Detection of Animated Rigid Bodies*, Computer Graphics Forum (Eurographics'95 proceedings), Blackwell Publishers, 14(3), pp 259-270, 1995.

[BAR 89] : D. Baraff, *Analytic Methods for Dynamic Simulation of Non-Penetrating Rigid Bodies*, Computer Graphics (SIGGRAPH'89 proceedings), Addison-Wesley, 23(3), pp 223-232, 1989.

[BAR 90] : D. Baraff, *Curved Surfaces and Coherence for Non-Penetrating Rigid Body Simulation*, Computer Graphics (SIGGRAPH'90 proceedings), Addison-Wesley, 24(4), pp 19-28, 1990.

[BAR 92] : D. Baraff, A. Witkin, *Dynamic Simulation of Non-Penetrating Flexible Bodies*, Computer Graphics (SIGGRAPH'92 proceedings), Addison-Wesley, 26(2), pp 303-308, 1992.

[BAR 94] : D. Baraff, A. Witkin, *Global Methods for Simulating Flexible Bodies*, Computer Animation Proc., Springer-Verlag, pp 1-12, 1994.

[BAR 96] : D. Baraff, A. Witkin, *Linear Time Dynamics Using Lagrange Multipliers*, Computer Graphics (SIGGRAPH'96 proceedings), Addison-Wesley, pp 137-146, 1996.

[BAR 98] : D. Baraff, A. Witkin, *Large Steps in Cloth Simulation*, Computer Graphics (SIGGRAPH'98 proceedings), Addison-Wesley, 32, pp 106-117, 1998.

[BAU 74] : B.G. Baumgart, *Geometric Modeling for Computer Vision*, Computer Science Dept. of Stanford Univ., 1974.

[BEC 93] : B.G. Becker, N.L. Max, *Smooth Transitions Between Bump Rendering Algorithms*, Computer Graphics (SIGGRAPH'93 proceedings), Addison-Wesley, 27, pp 183-190, 1993.

[BEH 61] : B. Behre, *Mechanical Properties of Textile Fabrics*, Textile Research Journal, Textile Research Institute (TRI/Princeton), 31(2), pp 87-122, 1961.

[BLI 77] : J.F. Blinn, *Models of Light Reflection for Computer Synthetized Pictures*, Computer Graphics (SIGGRAPH'77 proceedings), Addison-Wesley, pp 192-198, 1977.

[BLI 78] : J.F. Blinn, *Simulation of Wrinkled Surfaces*, Computer Graphics (SIGGRAPH'78 proceedings), Addison-Wesley, 12, pp 286-292, 1978.

[BOU 91] : W. Bouma, G. Vanecek, *Collision Detection and Analysis in a Physical based Simulation*, Eurographics Workshop on Animation and Simulation, pp 191-203, 1991.

[BRA 93] : I.C. Braid, *Boundary Modeling*, Fundamental Developments of Computer-Aided Geometric Modeling, Academic Press, pp 165-183, 1993.

[BRE 92] : D.E. Breen, D.H. House, P.H. Getto, *A Physically-Based Particle Model of Woven Cloth*, The Visual Computer, Springer Verlag, 8(5-6), pp 264-277, 1992.

[BRE 94] : D.E. Breen, D.H. House, M.J. Wozny, *A Particle-Based Model for Simulating the Draping Behavior of Woven Cloth*, Textile Research Journal, Textile Research Institute (TRI/Princeton), 64(11), pp 663-685, 1994.

[BRE 94]: D.E. Breen, D.H. House, M.J. Wozny, *Predicting the Drape of Woven Cloth Using Interacting Particles*, Computer Graphics (SIGGRAPH'94 proceedings), Addison-Wesley, pp 365-372, July 1994.

[BRE 97]: D.E. Breen, *Cost Minimization for Animated Geometric Models in Computer Graphics*, The Journal of Visualization and Comp. Graphics 8(4), pp 201-220, 1997.

[BRQ 96]: G. Barequet, B. Chazelle, L.J. Guibas, J.S.B. Mitchell, A. Tal, *BOXTREE: A Hierarchical Representation for Surfaces in 3D*, Computer Graphics Forum, Blackwell Publishers, 15(3), pp 387-396, 1996.

[BRU 85]: P. Brunet, I. Navazo, Geometric Modeling Using Exact Octree Representation of Polyhedral Objects, Eurographics'85 proceedings, 1985.

[BRU 90]: P. Brunet, I. Navazo, *Solid Representation and Operations Using Extended Octrees*, ACM Transactions on Graphics, 9(2), pp 170-197, 1990.

[BRZ 88]: R. Barzel, A. Barr, *A Modeling System Based on Dynamic Constraints*, Computer Graphics (SIGGRAPH'88 Proceedings), Addison-Wesley, pp.179-187, 1988.

[BRZ 92]: R. Barzel, Physically-Based Modeling for Computer Graphics, Academic Press, 1992.

[CAB 87]: B. Cabral, N. Max, R. Springmeyer, *Bidirectional Reflection Functions from Surface Bump Maps*, Computer Graphics (SIGGRAPH'87 proceedings), Addison-Wesley, 21, pp 273-281,1987.

[CAL 83]: C. R. Calladine, *Theory of Shell Structures*, Cambridge University Press, 1983.

[CAM 97]: S. Cameron, *Enhancing GJK: Computing Minimum and Penetration Distances Between Convex Polyhedron*, IEEE International Conference on Robotics and Automation,1997.

[CAN 86]: J.F. Canny, *Collision Detection for Moving Polyhedra*, IEEE transactions on Pattern Analysis and Machine Intelligence, 8(2), pp 200-209,1986.

[CAN 91]: J.F. Canny, D. Manocha, *A new approach for Surface Intersection*, International journal of Computational Geometry and Applications, World Scientific, 1(4), pp 491-516, 1991.

[CAP 97]: T.K. Capin, I.S. Pandzic, H. Noser, N. Magnenat-Thalmann, D. Thalmann, *Virtual Human Representation and Communication in VLNET Networked Virtual Environments*, IEEE Computer Graphics and Applications, Special Issue on Multimedia Highways, 1997.

[CAR 92]: M. Carignan, Y. Yang, N. Magnenat-Thalmann, D. Thalmann, *Dressing Animated Synthetic Actors with Complex Deformable Clothes*, Computer Graphics (SIGGRAPH'92 proceedings), Addison-Wesley, 26(2), pp 99-104, 1992.

[CEN 93]: M.F. Cohen, R. Wallace, *Radiosity and Realistic Image Synthesis*, Academic Press, 1993.

[CHA 88]: K.C. Chan, S.T. Tan, *Hierarchical Structure to Winged-Edge Structure: A Conversion Algorithm*, The Visual Computer, Springer Verlag, 4(3), pp 133-141, 1988.

[CHE 95]: B. Chen, M. Govindaraj, *A Physically-Based Model for Fabric Drape using Flexible Shell Theory*, Textile Research Journal, Textile Research Institute (TRI/Princeton), 65(6), pp 324-330, 1995.

[CHE 96]: B. Chen, M. Govindaraj, *A Parametric Study of Fabric Drape*, Textile Research Journal, Textile Research Institute (TRI/Princeton), 66(1), pp 17-24, 1996.

[CHN 88]: H.H. Chen, T.S. Huang, *A Survey of Construction and Manipulation of Octrees*, Computer Vision, Graphics and Image Processing, Academic Press, 43(2), pp 409-431, 1988.

[CHU 60]: C.C. Chu, M.M. Platt, W.J. Hamburger, *Investigation of the Factors Affecting the Drapeability of Fabrics*, Textile Research Journal, Textile Research Institute (TRI/Princeton), 30, pp 66-67, 1960.

[CLA 90]: T.G. Clapp, H. Peng, *Buckling of Woven Fabrics*, Textile Research Journal, Textile Research Institute (TRI/Princeton), 60, pp 228-234 & 285-292, 1990.

[COH 95] : J.D. Cohen, M.C. Lin, D. Manocha, M.K. Ponamgi, *I-COLLIDE: An Interactive and Exact Collision Detection System for Large-Scale Environments*, Symp. of Interactive 3D Graphics proc., ACM SIGGRAPH, Addison-Wesley, pp 189-196, 1995.

[COK 89] : R.D. Cook, D.S. Malkus, M.E. Plesha, *Concepts and Applications of Finite Element Analysis*, Third edition, John Wiley & Sons, 1989.

[COL 91] : J.R. Collier, B.J. Collier, G. O'Toole, S.M. Sargand, *Drape Prediction by means of Finite-Element Analysis*, Journal of the Textile Institute, The Textile Institute, 82 (1), pp 96-107, 1991.

[COO 82] : R.L. Cook, K.E. Torrance, *A Reflectance Model for Computer Graphics*, ACM Transactions on Graphics, 1(1), pp 7-24, 1982.

[CPR 60] : D.N.E. Cooper, *The Stiffness of Woven Textile*, Journal of the Textile Institute, The Textile Institute, 51, pp 317-335, 1960.

[CRL 85] : I. Carlbom, I. Chakravarty, *A Hierarchical Data Structure for Representing the Spatial Decomposition of 3D Objects*, IEEE Computer Graphics and Applications, 5, pp 24-31, 1985.

[CRL 87] : I. Carlbom, *An Algorithm for Geometric Set Operations Using Cellular Subdivision Techniques*, IEEE Computer Graphics and Applications, 7(5), pp 44-55, 1987.

[CUL 86] : R.K. Culley, K.G. Kempf, *A Collision Detection Algorithm Based on Velocity and Distance Bounds*, IEEE Int. Conference on Robotics and Automatons proceedings, pp 1064-1069, 1986.

[CUS 68] : G.E. Cusick, *The Measurement of Fabric Drape*, Journal of the Textile Institute, The Textile Institute, 59(6), pp 253-260, 1968.

[DAH 61] : B. Dahlberg, J. Lindberg, *Mechanical Properties of Textile Fabrics*, Textile Research Journal, Textile Research Institute (TRI/Princeton), 31, pp 94-99 & 99-122, 1961.

[DEN 76] : E. F. Denby, *The Deformation of Fabrics during Wrinkling - A Theoretical Approach*, Textile Research Journal, Landcaster PA., Textile Research Institute (TRI/Princeton), 46, pp 667-670, 1976.

[DER 98] : T. DeRose, M. Kass, T. Truong, *Subdivision Surfaces in Character Animation*, Computer Graphics (SIGGRAPH'98 proceedings), Addison-Wesley, 32, pp 148-157, 1998.

[DES 99] : M. Desbrun, P.Schröder, A. Barr, *Interactive Animation of Structured Deformable Objects*, Proceedings of Graphics Interface, Morgan Kaufmann Publishers, 1999.

[DHA 93] : S.G. Dhande, P.V.M. Rao, S. Tavakkoli, C.L. Moore, *Geometric Modeling of Draped Fabric Surfaces*, IFIP Trans. Graphics Design and Visualisation, North Holland, pp 349-356, 1993.

[DIA 98] : J.M.S. Dias, M.N. Gamito, J.M. Rebordao, *Modeling Cloth Buckling and Drape*, Eurographics'98 Short Presentations, ss 2.1, 1998.

[DUF 92] : T. Duff, *Interval Arithmetic and Recursive Subdivision for Implicit Functions and Constructive Solid Geometry*, Computer Graphics (SIGGRAPH'92 proceedings), Addison-Wesley, 26(2), pp 131-138, 1992.

[DWO 93] : P. Dworkin, D. Zelter, *A New Model for Efficient Dynamic Simulation*, Eurographics Workshop on Animation and Simulation, pp 135-147, 1993.

[EBE 96] : B. Eberhardt, A. Weber, W. Strasser, *A Fast, Flexible, Particle-System Model for Cloth Draping*, Computer Graphics in Textiles and Apparel (IEEE Computer Graphics and Applications), pp 52-59, Sept. 1996.

[EIS 96] : J.W. Eischen, S. Deng, T.G. Clapp, *Finite-Element Modeling and Control of Flexible Fabric Parts*, Computer Graphics in Textiles and Apparel (IEEE Computer Graphics and Applications), pp 71-80, Sept. 1996.

[FEY 63] : R.P. Feymann, R.B. Leighton, M. Sands, *The Feymann Lectures on Physics*, Addison-Wesley, 1963.

[FLO 88] : L.D Floriani, B. Falcidieno, *A Hierarchical Boundary Model for Solid Objects*, ACM Transactions on Graphics, 7(1), pp 42-60, 1988.

[FLO 95] : L.D Floriani, E. Puppo, *Hierarchical Triangulation for Multiresolution Surface Description Geometric Design*, ACM Transactions on Graphics, 14(4), pp 363-411, 1995.

[FOL 93] : J. Foley, A. VanDam, S. Feiner, J. Hughes, *Computer Graphics: Principles and Practice*, Second edition, Addison Wesley, 1993.

[FUD 97] : I. Fudos, C. Hoffmann, *A Graph-Constructive Approach for Solving Geometric Constraints*, ACM Transactions on Graphics, pp 179-216, 1997.

[FUJ 83] : K. Fujimura, H. Toriya, K. Yamagushi, T.L. Kunii, *Octree Algorithms for Solid Modeling*, Computer Graphics, Theory and Applications (InterGraphics'83 proceedings), Springer-Verlag, pp 96-110, 1983.

[GAN 91] : L. Gan et al, *A Finite Element Analysis of the Draping of Fabrics*, Proc. of the 6th Int. Conf. on Finite Element Methods, Australia, UAH (University of Alabama in Huntsville) Press, pp 402-414, 1991.

[GAN 95] : L. Gan et al, *A Study of Fabric Deformation using Non-Linear Finite Elements*, Textile Research Journal, Textile Research Institute (TRI/Princeton), 65(11), pp 660-668, 1995.

[GAR 94] : A. Garcia-Alonso, N. Serrano, J. Flaquer, *Solving the Collision Detection Problem*, IEEE Computer Graphics and Applications, pp 36-43, 1994.

[GAY 93] : K.L. Gay, L. Ling, M. Damodaran, *A Quasi-Steady Force Model for Animating Cloth Motion*, IFIP Trans. Graphics Design and Visualisation, North Holland, pp 357-363, 1993.

[GIE 97] : T. Gieng, K.I. Joy, B. Hamann, G. Schussman, I.J. Trotts, *Smooth Hierarchical Surface Triangulations*, Proceedings of Visualization, IEEE, pp 379-386, 1997.

[GIE 98] : T. Gieng, B. Hamann, K.I. Joy, G. Schussman, I.J. Trotts, *Constructing Hierarchies for Triangle Meshes*, IEEE Transactions on Visualization and Computer Graphics, 4(2), pp 145-161, 1998.

[GIL 88] :	E.G. Gilbert, D.W. Johnson, S.S. Keerthi, *A Fast Procedure for Computing the Distance Between Objects in Three Dimensional Space*, IEEE Journal on Robotics and Automation, 4, pp 193-203, 1988.
[GIL 90] :	E.G. Gilbert, C.P. Foo, *Computing the Distance Between General Convex Objects in 3D Space*, IEEE Transactions on Robotics and Automation, 6(1), pp 53-61, 1990.
[GLA 89] :	A.S. Glassner, *An Introduction to Ray Tracing*, Academic Press, 1989.
[GLA 95] :	A.S. Glassner, *Principles of Digital Image Synthesis*, Morgan Kaufmann, 1995.
[GOL 87] :	J. Goldsmith, J. Salmon, *Automatic Creation of Object Hierarchies for Ray Tracing*, IEEE Computer Graphics and Animation, 7(5), pp 14-20, 1987.
[GON 93] :	R.H. Gong, S.K. Mukhopadhyay, *Fabric Objective Measurement: A Comparative Study of Fabric Characteristics*, Journal of the Textile Institute, The Textile Institute, 84(2), pp 192-198, 1993.
[GOR 84] :	C.M. Goral, K.E. Torrance, D.P. Greenberg, B. Battaille, *Modeling Interaction of Light Between Diffuse Surfaces*, Computer Graphics (SIGGRAPH'84 proceedings), Addison-Wesley, pp 213-222, 1994.
[GOS 90] :	T.K. Ghosh S.K. Batra, R.L. Barker, *The Bending Behavior of Plain Woven Fabric*, Journal of the Textile Institute, The Textile Institute, 81(3), pp 245-287, 1990.
[GOT 96] :	S. Gottschalk, M.C. Lin, D. Manocha, *OBB-Tree: A Hierarchical Structure for Rapid Interference Detection*, Computer Graphics (SIGGRAPH'96 proceedings), Addison-Wesley, pp 171-180, 1996.
[GOU 71] :	H. Gouraud, *Computer Display of Curved Surfaces*, IEEE Transactions on Computers, 6, pp 623-629, 1971
[GOU 88] :	H. Gould, J. Tobochnik, An introduction to computer simulation methods: Applications to physical systems, Reading Mass., Addison-Wesley, 1988.
[GRA 98] :	S. Gray, *In Virtual Fashion*, IEEE Spectrum, pp 19-25, 1998.

[GRB 94] : H. Grabowsky, Z. Bao, *Graphic and Analytic Collision Control Using Polytree Representations*, ICARCV'94 proceedings, pp 479-483, 1994.

[GRG 82] : I. Gargantini, *Linear Octree for Fast Processing of Three Dimensional Objects*, Computer Graphics and Image Processing, 20, pp 365-374, 1982.

[GRO 66] : P. Grosberg, N.M. Swani, *The Mechanical Properties of Woven Fabrics*, Textile Research Journal, Textile Research Institute (TRI/Princeton), 36, pp 338-345, 1966.

[HAD 99] : S. Hadap, E. Bangerter, P. Volino, N. Magnenat-Thalmann, *Animating Wrinkles on Clothes*, IEEE Visualization'99 conference proceedings, 1999.

[HAL 93] : M. Halstead, M. Kaas, T. DeRose, *Efficient, Fair Interpolation, using Catmull-Clark surfaces*, Computer Graphics (SIGGRAPH'93 proceedings), Addison-Wesley, pp 35-44, 1993.

[HAU 88] : D.R. Haumann, R.E. Parent, *The Behavioral Test-Bed: Obtaining Complex Behavior with Simple Rules*, The Visual Computer, Springer-Verlag, 4(6), pp 332-347, 1988.

[HEC 86] : P.S. Heckbert, *Survey of Texture Mapping*, IEEE Computer Graphics and Applications, 6(11), pp 56-67, 1986.

[HEL 95] : M. Held, J.T. Klosowski, J.S.B. Mitchell, *Evaluation of Collision Detection Methods for Virtual Reality Fly-Throughs*, Proceedings of the 7th Canadian Conference on Computational Geometry, 1995.

[HEX 91] : D.X. He, K.E. Torrance, F.X. Sillion, D.P. Greenberg, *A Comprehensive physical Model for Light Reflection*, Computer Graphics (SIGGRAPH'91 proceedings), Addison-Wesley, 25, pp 175-186, 1991.

[HIN 90] B.K. Hinds, J. McCartney, *Interactive garment design*, The Visual Computer, Springer-Verlag, 6, pp 53-61, 1990.

[HIN 91] B.K. Hinds, J. McCartney, G. Woods, *Pattern Developments for 3D Surfaces*, Computer-Aided Design, Elsevier, 23(8), pp 583-592, 1991.

[HLL 89] : R. Hall, Illumination and Color in Computer Generated Imagery, Springer-Verlag, 1989.

[HNG 95] : H.N. Ng, R.L. Grimsdale, W.G. Allen, *A System for Modeling and Visualization of Cloth Materials*, Computers and Graphics, Pergamon Press / Elsevier Science, 19(3), pp 423-430, 1995.

[HNG 96] : H.N. Ng, R.L. Grimsdale, *Computer Graphics Techniques for Modeling Cloth*, Computer Graphics in Textiles and Apparel (IEEE Computer Graphics and Applications), pp 28-41, 1996.

[HOP 96] : H. Hoppe, *Progressive Meshes*, Computer Graphics (SIGGRAPH'96 proceedings), Addison-Wesley, pp 99-108, 1996.

[HUB 93] : P.M. Hubbard, *Interactive Collision Detection,* IEEE Symp. on Research Frontiers in VR, pp 24-31, 1993.

[HUB 95] : P.M. Hubbard, *Collision Detection for Interactive Graphics Applications*, IEEE Trans. on Visualisation and Computer Graphics, (3), pp 218-230, 1995.

[HUB 96] : P.M. Hubbard, *Approximating Polyhedra with Spheres for Time-Critical Collision Detection*, ACM Trans. on Graphics, 15(3) pp 179-210, 1996.

[HUJ 96] : J. Hu, Y.F. Chan, *Effect of Fabric Mechanical Properties*, Textile Research Journal, Textile Research Institute (TRI/Princeton), 68(1), pp 57-64, 1996.

[HUT 96] : D. Hutchinson, M. Preston, T. Hewitt, *Adaptative Refinement for Mass-Spring Simulations*, Eurographics Workshop on Animation and Simulation, Poitiers, France, pp 31-45, Aug. 1996.

[JOU 96] : A. Joukhadar, A. Wabbi, C. Laugier, *Fast Contact Localisation Between Deformable Polyhedra in Motion*, Computer Animation'96 Proceedings, pp 126-135, 1996.

[KAN 95] : T.J. Kang, W.R. Yu, *Drape Simulation of Woven Fabric Using the Finite-Element Method*, Journal of the Textile Institute, The Textile Institute, 86(4), pp 635-648, 1995.

[KAW 73] : S. Kawabata, M. Niwa, H. Kawai, *The Finite Deformation Theory of Plain-Weave Fabrics*, Journal of the Textile Institute, The Textile Institute, 64(1-2), pp 21-85, 1973.

[KAW 75] : S. Kawabata, *The Standardization and Analysis of Hand Evaluation*, Hand Eval. and Stand. Committee of the Textile Machinery Society of Japan, Osaka, 1975.

[KEM 58] : A. Kemp, *An Extension of Peirce's Cloth Geometry to the Treatment of Non-Circular Threads*, Journal of the Textile Institute, The Textile Institute, 49, pp 44-48, 1958.

[KIL 63] : W.F. Kilby, *Planar Stress-Strain Relationships in Woven Fabrics*, Journal of the Textile Institute, The Textile Institute, 3, pp 75-90, 1963.

[KLO 97] : J.T. Klosowski, M. Held, J.S.B. Mitchell, *Efficient Collision Detection Using Bounding Volume Hierarchies of k-dops*, IEEE transactions on Visualization and Computer Graphics,4(1), 1997.

[KNO 79] : A.L. Knoll, *Modified Equations for the Energy Analysis of Plain Weave, Including Yarn Extension*, Journal of the Textile Institute, The Textile Institute, 70(8), pp 355-358, 1979.

[KUN 90] T.L. Kunii, H.Gotoda, *Singularity Theoretical Modeling and Animation of Garment Wrinkle Formation Process*, The Visual Computer, Springer Verlag, 6(6), pp 326.336, 1990.

[KUN 90] T.L. Kunii, H.Gotoda, *Modeling and Animation of Garment Wrinkle Formation processes*, Computer Animation'90 proceedings, Springer-Verlag, pp 131-146, 1990.

[KUN 98] T.L. Kunii, T. Wachi, *Topological Dress Making as Fashion Media Modeling*, MultiMedia Modeling'98 proceedings, IEEE, IEEE Computer Society, pp 148-152, 1998.

[KUR 93] : S. Kuriyama, *Surface Generation from an Irregular Network of Parametric Curves*, Modeling in Computer Graphics, IFIP Series on Computer Graphics, Springer-Verlag, pp 256-274, 1993.

[KUR 97] : S. Kuriyama, K. Tachibana, *Polyhedral Surface Modeling with a Diffusion System*, Computer Graphics Forum (Eurographics'97 proceedings), Blackwell Publishers, 16(3), pp 39-46, 1994.

[LAF 91] : B. Lafleur, N. Magnenat-Thalmann, D. Thalmann, *Cloth Animation with Self-Collision Detection*, IFIP conference on Modeling in Computer Graphics proceedings, Springer-Verlag, pp 179-197, 1991.

[LEA 85] : G.A.V. Leaf, R.D. Anandjiwala, *A Generalized Model of Plain Woven Fabric*, Textile Research Journal, Textile Research Institute (TRI/Princeton), 55, pp 92-99, 1985.

[LIN 91] : M.C. Lin, J.F. Canny, *A Fast Algorithm for Incremental Distance Calculation*, IEEE Int. Conference on Robotics and Automatons proceedings, pp 1008-1015, 1991.

[LIN 92] : M.C. Lin, J.F. Canny, *Efficient Collision Detection for Animation*, Eurographics Workshop on Animation and Simulation, 1992.

[LIN 93] : M.C. Lin, D. Manocha, *Interference Detection between Curved Objects for Computer Animation*, Models and techniques in Computer Animation (Computer Animation'93 proceedings), Springer-Verlag, pp 43-55, 1993.

[LIN 95] : M.C. Lin, D. Manocha, *Fast Interference Detection between Geometric Models*, Springer-Verlag, 11(10), pp 542-561, 1995.

[LIN 98] : M.C. Lin, S. Gottschalk, *Collision Detection Between Geometric Models: A Survey*, Proceedings of IMA Conference on Mathematics and Surfaces, IMA Mathematics of Surfaces Conference Proceedings series, Information Geometers, 1998.

[LIU 96] : J.D. Liu, M.T. Ko, R.C. Chang, *Collision Avoidance in Cloth Animation*, The Visual Computer, Springer-Verlag, 12(5), pp 234-243, 1996.

[LLI 93] : L. Ling, L. Damodaran, R.K.L. Gay, *A Quasi-Steady Force Model for Animating Cloth*, Graphics, Design and Visualization (Int. Conference on Computer Graphics proceedings), pp 181-188, 1993.

[LLI 96] : L. Ling, M. Damodaran, R.K.L. Gay, *Aerodynamic Force Models for Animating Cloth Motion in an Air Flow*, The Visual Computer, Springer-Verlag, 12, pp 84-104, 1996.

[LLO 78] : D.W. Lloyd, W.J. Shanahan, M. Konopasek, *The Folding of Heavy Fabric Sheets*, International Journal of Mechanical Science, Elsevier ,20, pp 521-527, 1978.

[LOD 93] : S. Lodha, *Filling N-sided Holes*, Modeling in Computer Graphics, IFIP Series on Computer Graphics, Springer-Verlag, pp 319-345, 1993.

[LOO 90] : C. Loop, T. DeRose, *Generalized B-Spline Surfaces of Arbitrary Topology*, Computer Graphics (SIGGRAPH'90 proceedings), Addison-Wesley, 24-4, pp 347-356, 1990.

[LOO 94] : C. Loop, *Smooth Spline Surfaces over Irregular Meshes*, Computer Graphics (SIGGRAPH proceedings 1994), Addison-Wesley, pp 303-310, 1994.

[LOV 54] : L. Love, *Graphical Relationships in Cloth Geometry for Plain, Twill and Sateen Weaves*, Textile Research Journal, Textile Research Institute (TRI/Princeton), 24(12), pp 1073-1083, 1954.

[MAN 92] : A.H. Manich, M.D. De Castellar, *Elastic Recovery of Polyester Staple Fiber Rotor Spun Yarn*, Textile Research Journal, Landcaster, Textile Research Institute (TRI/Princeton), 62, pp 196-199, 1992.

[MAX 89] : N. Max, *Smooth Appearance for Polygonal Surfaces*, The Visual Computer., Springer-Verlag, pp 160-173, 1989.

[MEA 82] : D. Meager, *Geometric Modeling using Octree Encoding*, Computer Graphics and Image Processing, Academic Press, 19(2), pp 129-147, 1982.

[MEI 98] : M. Meissner, B. Eberhardt, *The Art of Knitted Fabrics, Realistic & Physically Based Modelling of Knitted Patterns*, Computer Graphics Forum (Eurographics'98 proceedings), Blackwell Publishers, 17(3), pp 355-362, 1998.

[MIR 98] : B. Mirtich, *V-CLIP: Fast and Robust Polyhedral Collision Detection*, ACM Transactions on Graphics, 1998.

[MOO 88] : M. Moore, J. Wilhelms, *Collision Detection and Response for Computer Animation*, Computer Graphics (SIGGRAPH'88 proceedings), Addison-Wesley, 22(4), pp 289-298, 1988.

[MOR 62] : W.E. Morton, J.W.S. Hearle, *Physical properties of textile fibers*, Manchester and London, The textile institute, Butterworths, 1962.

[MNT 88] : M. Mantila, *Introduction to Solid Modeling*, Computer Science Press, Rockville, 1988.

[MRT 85] : M.E. Mortenson, *Geometric Modeling*, Wiley & Sons, 1985.

[NAV 87] : I. Navazo, J. Fontdecaba, P. Brunet, *Extended Octrees: Between CSG trees and Boundary Representations*, Eurographics'87 proceedings, 1987.

[NIS 85] : T. Nishita, E. Nakamae, *A Continuous Tone Representation of 3D Objects Taking Account of Shadows and Interreflections*, Computer Graphics (SIGGRAPH'95 proceedings), pp 23-30, 1995.

[OKA 92] : H. Okabe, H. Imaoka, T. Tomiha, H. Niwaya, *Three Dimensional Apparel System*, Computer Graphics (SIGGRAPH'92 proceedings), Addison-Wesley, 26(2), pp 105-110, 1992

[OLO 64] : B. Olofsson, *A General Model of Fabric as a Geometric Mechanic Structure*, Journal of the Textile Institute, The Textile Institute, 55, pp 541-557, 1964.

[OVE 97] : C.W.A.M. VanOverveld, B. Wyvill, *Phong Normal Interpolation Revisited*, ACM Transactions on Graphics, 16(4), pp 397-419, 1997

[PAL 94] : L.F. Palazzi, D.R. Forsey, *A Multilevel Approach to Surface Response in Dynamically Deformable Models*, Computer Animation'94 proceedings, Springer-Verlag, pp 21-30, 1994.

[PEE 97] : M. Peercy, J. Airey, B. Cabral, *Efficient Bump-Mapping Hardware*, Computer Graphics (SIGGRAPH'97 proceedings), Addison-Wesley, Los Angeles, pp 303-306, 1997.

[PEI 37] : F.T. Peirce, *The Geometry of Cloth Structure*, Journal of the Textile Institute, The Textile Institute, 28, pp 45-97, 1937.

[PHO 75] : B.T. Phong, *Illumination for Computer Generated Pictures*, Communications of the ACM, 6, pp 311-317, 1975

[PLA 88] : J.C. Platt, A.H. Barr, *Constraints Methods for Flexible Models*, Computer Graphics (SIGGRAPH'88 proceedings), Addison-Wesley, 23(3), pp 21-30, 1988.

[PLM 95] : I.J. Palmer, R.L. Grimsdale, *Collision Detection for Animation using Sphere-Trees*, Computer Graphics Forum, Blackwell Publishers, 14, pp 105-116, 1995.

[PON 95] : M.K. Ponamgi, D. Manocha, M.C. Lin, *Incremental Algorithms for Collision Detection between Solid Models*, ACM Symposium on Solid Modeling and Applications, pp 293-304, 1995.

[POU 90] : P. Poulin, A. Fournier, *A Model for Anisotropic Reflection*, Computer Graphics (SIGGRAPH'90 proceedings), Addison-Wesley, 24, pp 273-282, 1990.

[PRE 92] : W.H. Press, W.T. Vetterling, S.A. Teukolsky, B.P. Flannery, *Numerical Recipes in C*, Second edition, Cambridge University Press, 1992.

[PRO 95] : X. Provot, *Deformation Constraints in a Mass-Spring Model to Describe Rigide Cloth Behavior*, Graphics Interface'95 proceedings, Quebec, Canada, pp 147-154, 1995.

[PRM 96] : E. Promayon, P. Baconnier, C. Puech, *Physically-Based Deformations Constrained in Displacements and Volume*, Computer Graphics Forum (Eurographics'96 proceedings), Blackwell Publishers, 15(3), pp 155-164, Aug. 1996.

[QUI 94] : S. Quinlan, *Efficient Distance Computation between Non-Convex Objects*, Int. Conf. on Robotics and Automation proceedings, pp 3324-3329, 1994.

[REE 83] : W.T. Reeves, *Particle Systems – A Technique for Modeling a Class of Fuzzy Objects*, ACM Trans. on Graphics, 2(2), pp 91-108, 1983.

[REQ 80] : A.A.G Requicha, *Representations for Rigid Solids: Theory, Practice, and Systems*, ACM Computing and Surveys, 12, pp 437-464, 1980.

[ROS 74] : D. Rosenthal, *Resistance and Deformation of Solid Media*, N-Y, Pergamon Press, 1974.

[SAB 86] : M. Sabin, *Recursive Subdivision*, The Mathematics of Surfaces, Clarendon Press, Oxford, England, pp 269-282, 1986.

[SAK 91] : Y. Sakagushi, M. Minoh, K. Ikeda, *A Dynamically Deformable Model of Dress*, Trans. Society of Electronics, Information and Communications, pp 25-32, 1991.

[SAM 84] : H. Samet, *The Quadtree and related Hierarchical Data Structures*, ACM Computing Surveys, 16(2), pp 187-260, 1984.

[SHA 85] : M.I. Shamos, F.P. Preparata, *Computational Geometry An Introduction*, Springer-Verlag, N.Y., 1985.

[SHI 91] : M. Shinya, M.C. Forgue, *Interference Detection through Rasterisation*, The journal of Visualisation and Computer Animation, Wiley, 4(2), pp 132-134, 1991.

[SHN 78] : W.J. Shanahan, D.W. Lloyd, J.W.S. Hearle, *Characterizing the Elastic Behavior of the Textile Fabrics in Complex Deformation*, Textile Research Journal, 48, Textile Research Institute (TRI/Princeton), pp 495-505, 1978.

[SIL 94] : F. Sillon, C. Puech, *Radiosity and Global Illumination*, Morgan Kaufmann, 1993.

[SKE 76] : J. Skelton, *The Fundamentals of Fabric Shear*, Textile Research Journal, Textile Research Institute (TRI/Princeton), 46, pp 862-869, 1976.

[SNY 93] : J.M. Snyder, A.R. Woodbury, K. Fleisher, B. Currin, A.H. Barr, *Interval Methods for Multi-Point Collisions between Time-Dependant Curved Surfaces*, Computer Graphics annual series, pp 321-334, 1993.

[SUH 98] : Y.S. Suh, Y. Endou, D. Gotoh, A. Kiyota, H. Okabe, H. Niwaya, I. Shigeru, *Virtual Sewing System for Apparel Design*, Eurographics'98 Short Presentations, ss 2.2, 1998.

[TAI 91] : F. Taillefer, *Mixed Modeling*, Compugraphics'91 proceedings, pp467-478, 1991.

[TER 87] : D. Terzopoulos, J.C. Platt, H. Barr, *Elastically Deformable Models*, Computer Graphics (SIGGRAPH'97 proceedings), Addison-Wesley, 21, pp 205-214, 1987.

[TER 88] : D. Terzopoulos, K. Fleischer, *Modeling Inelastic Deformation: Viscoelasticity, Plasticity, Fracture*, Computer Graphics (SIGGRAPH'88 proceedings), Addison-Wesley, 22, pp 269-278, 1988.

[TER 88] : D. Terzopoulos, K. Fleischer, *Deformable Models*, The Visual Computer, Springer-Verlag, 4(6), pp 306-331, Dec. 1988.

[TIM 82] : S.P. Timoshenko, J.N. Goodier, *Theory of Elasticity*, Third edition, McGraw-Hill Int. Editions.

[THA 91] : N. Magnenat-Thalmann, D. Thalmann, *Complex Models for Visualizing Synthetic Actors*, IEEE Computer Graphics and Applications, 11(5), pp 32-44, 1991.

[THA 96] : P. Volino, N. Magnenat-Thalmann, J. Shen, D. Thalmann, *An Evolving System for Simulating Clothes on Virtual Actors*, Computer Graphics in Textiles and Apparel (IEEE Computer Graphics and Applications), pp 42-51, 1996.

[THI 90] : J.A. Thingvold, E. Cohen, *Physical Modeling with B-Spline Surfaces for Interactive Design and Animation*, Computer Graphics (Interactive 3D Graphics Proceedings), 24(2), pp 129-137, 1990.

[TSO 91] : N. Tsopelas, *Animating the Crumpling Behavior of Garments*, Eurographics Workshop on Animation and Simulation Proc., UK, 11.24, 1991.

[VHE 90] : B. Von Herzen, A.H. Barr, H.R. Zatz, *Geometric Collisions for Time-Dependant Parametric Surfaces*, Computer Graphics (SIGGRAPH'90 proceedings), Addison-Wesley, 24(4), pp 39-48, 1990.

[VLA 95] : L. Van Langenhove, W.R. Wu, *Simulating the Mechanical Properties of a Yarn Based on the Properties and Arrangement of its Fibers*, Textile Research Journal, 67(4-5-6), Textile Research Institute (TRI/Princeton), pp 263-268;406-412, 1995.

[VOL 94] : P. Volino, N. Magnenat-Thalmann, *Efficient Self-Collision Detection on Smoothly Discretised Surface Animation Using Geometrical Shape Regularity*, Computer Graphics Forum (Eurographics'94 proceedings), Blackwell Publishers, 13(3), pp 155-166, 1994.

[VOL 95] : P. Volino, M. Courchesne, N. Magnenat-Thalmann, *Versatile and Efficient Techniques for Simulating Cloth and Other Deformable Objects*, Computer Graphics (SIGGRAPH'95 proceedings), Addison-Wesley, pp 137-144, 1995.

[VOL 97] : P. Volino, N. Magnenat-Thalmann, *Developing Simulation Techniques for an Interactive Clothing System*, Virtual Systems and Multimedia (VSMM'97 proceedings), Geneva, Switzerland, pp 109-118, 1997.

[VOL 97] : P. Volino, N. Magnenat-Thalmann, *Interactive Cloth Simulation: Problems and Solutions*, JWS'97 proceedings, 1997.

[VOL 98] : P. Volino, N. Magnenat-Thalmann, *The State-of-Art in Virtual Clothing*, ISCIS'98 proceedings, 1998.

[VOL 98] : P. Volino, N. Magnenat-Thalmann, *The SPHERIGON: A Simple Polygon Patch for Smoothing Quickly your Polygonal Meshes*, Computer Animation'98 proceedings, 1998.

[VOL 99] : P. Volino, N. Magnenat-Thalmann, *Fast Geometrical Wrinkles on Animated Surfaces*, WSCG'99 proceedings, 1999.

[WAR 92] : G.J. Ward, *Measuring and Modeling Anisotropic Reflection*, Computer Graphics (SIGGRAPH'92 proceedings), Addison-Wesley, 26, pp 265-272, 1992.

[WEB 92] : R.C. Webb, M.A. Gigante, *Using Dynamic Bounding Volume Hierarchies to improve Efficiency of Rigid Body Simulations*, Communicating with Virtual Worlds, (CGI'92 proceedings), pp 825-841, 1992.

[WEB 93] : R.C. Webb, M.A. Gigante, *Distributed, Multi-Person, Physically-Based Interaction in Virtual Worlds*, Visual Computing (CGI'93 proceedings), pp 41-48, 1993.

[WEI 86] : J. Weil, *The Synthesis of Cloth Objects*, Computer Graphics (SIGGRAPH'86 proceedings), Addison-Wesley, 24, pp 243-252, 1986.

[WER 93] : H.M. Werner, N. Magnenat-Thalmann, D. Thalmann, *User Interface for Fashion Design*, Graphics, Design and Visualization (ICCG'93 proceedings), pp 165-172, 1993.

[WLR 85] : K.J. Weiler, *Edge-Based Data Structures for Solid Modeling in Curved Surface Environments*, IEEE Computer Graphics and Applications, 5(1), pp 21-40, 1985.

[WLR 86] : K.J. Weiler, *Topological Structures for Geometric Modeling*, Rensselaer Polytechnic Institute, 1986.

[WIT 90] : A. Witkin, W. Welch, *Fast Animation and Control of Non-Rigid Structures*, Computer Graphics (SIGGRAPH'90 proceedings), Addison-Wesley, 24, pp 243-252, 1990.

[WUY 97] : Y. Wu, P. Kalra, N. Magnenat-Thalmann, *Physically-based Wrinkle Simulation & Skin Rendering*, Computer Animation'97 proceedings, Geneva, Switzerland, pp 69-79, 1997.

[YAM 84] : K. Yamaguchi, T.L. Kunii, K. Fujimura, *Octree Related Data Structures and Algorithms*, IEEE Computer Graphics and Applications, pp 53-59, 1984.

[YAM 85] : F. Yamaguchi, *An Unified Approach to Interference Problems using a Triangle Processor*, Computer Graphics (SIGGRAPH'85 proceedings), Addison-Wesley, 19, pp 141-149, 1985.

[YAM 86] : F. Yamaguchi, T. Tatemichi, R. Ebisawa, *Applications of the 4*4 Determinant Method and the Triangle Processor to Various Interference Problems*, Advanced Computer Graphics (Tokyo Computer Graphics'86 proceedings), pp 335-347, 1986.

[YAN 91] : Y. Yang, N.Magnenat-Thalmann, *Techniques for Cloth Animation*, New trends in Animation and Visualisation, John Wiley & Sons Ltd, pp 243-256, 1991.

[YAN 93] : Y. Yang, N.Magnenat-Thalmann, *An Improved Algorithm for Collision Detection in Cloth Animation with Human Body*, Computer Graphics and Applications (Pacific Graphics'93 proceedings), 1, pp 237-251, 1993.

[YAS 92] ; Takami Yasuda, Shigeki Yokoi and Jun-ichiro Toriwaki, *A Shading Model for Cloth Objects*, IEEE Computer Graphics & Applications, 12 (6), pp 15-24, November 1992.

[YIC 96] : K.L. Yick, *Comparison of Mechanical Properties of Shirting Materials Measured on the KES-F and FAST Instruments*, Textile Research Journal, Textile Research Institute (TRI/Princeton), 66(10), pp 622-633, 1996.

[ZYD 93] : M. Zyda, D. Pratt, W. Osborne, J. Monahan, *Real-Time Collision Detection and Response*, The journal of visualisation and Computer Animation, Wiley, 4(1), pp 13-24, 1993.

[ZOR 96] : D. Zorin, P. Schröder, W. Sweldens, *Interpolating Subdivision for Meshes with Arbitrary Topology*, Computer Graphics (SIGGRAPH'95 proceedings), Addison-Wesley, pp 189-192, 1996